Information Society Working for Inclusiveness

Sarolta Németh

Information Society Working for Inclusiveness

Scales, Actors and Peripheral Regions

VDM Verlag Dr. Müller

Impressum/Imprint (nur für Deutschland/ only for Germany)
Bibliografische Information der Deutschen Nationalbibliothek: Die Deutsche Nationalbibliothek
verzeichnet diese Publikation in der Deutschen Nationalbibliografie; detaillierte bibliografische
Daten sind im Internet über http://dnb.d-nb.de abrufbar.
Alle in diesem Buch genannten Marken und Produktnamen unterliegen warenzeichen-, marken-
oder patentrechtlichem Schutz bzw. sind Warenzeichen oder eingetragene Warenzeichen der
jeweiligen Inhaber. Die Wiedergabe von Marken, Produktnamen, Gebrauchsnamen,
Handelsnamen, Warenbezeichnungen u.s.w. in diesem Werk berechtigt auch ohne besondere
Kennzeichnung nicht zu der Annahme, dass solche Namen im Sinne der Warenzeichen- und
Markenschutzgesetzgebung als frei zu betrachten wären und daher von jedermann benutzt
werden dürften.

Coverbild: www.purestockx.com

Verlag: VDM Verlag Dr. Müller Aktiengesellschaft & Co. KG
Dudweiler Landstr. 99, 66123 Saarbrücken, Deutschland
Telefon +49 681 9100-698, Telefax +49 681 9100-988, Email: info@vdm-verlag.de
Zugl.: Joensuu, University of Joensuu, Diss., 2008

Herstellung in Deutschland:
Schaltungsdienst Lange o.H.G., Berlin
Books on Demand GmbH, Norderstedt
Reha GmbH, Saarbrücken
Amazon Distribution GmbH, Leipzig
ISBN: 978-3-639-11310-5

Imprint (only for USA, GB)
Bibliographic information published by the Deutsche Nationalbibliothek: The Deutsche
Nationalbibliothek lists this publication in the Deutsche Nationalbibliografie; detailed
bibliographic data are available in the Internet at http://dnb.d-nb.de.
Any brand names and product names mentioned in this book are subject to trademark, brand or
patent protection and are trademarks or registered trademarks of their respective holders. The use
of brand names, product names, common names, trade names, product descriptions etc. even
without a particular marking in this works is in no way to be construed to mean that such names
may be regarded as unrestricted in respect of trademark and brand protection legislation and
could thus be used by anyone.

Cover image: www.purestockx.com

Publisher:
VDM Verlag Dr. Müller Aktiengesellschaft & Co. KG
Dudweiler Landstr. 99, 66123 Saarbrücken, Germany
Phone +49 681 9100-698, Fax +49 681 9100-988, Email: info@vdm-publishing.com
Joensuu, University of Joensuu, Diss., 2008

Printed in the U.S.A.
Printed in the U.K. by (see last page)
ISBN: 978-3-639-11310-5

Sarolta Németh

Information Society Working for Inclusiveness:

Scales, Actors and Peripheral Regions

Doctoral Dissertation defended at the Faculty of Social Sciences and Regional
Studies, University of Joensuu, Finland on 4th April, 2008

TABLE OF CONTENTS

Abstract

The aim of this doctoral dissertation is to find the answer to the broad question: *How can the benefits of information and communication technologies (ICTs) and the so-called, information society (I.S.) be extended to rural-peripheral regions and communities?* To achieve this, some insight is provided into the more recent developments of the I.S. as an evolving theoretical conception as well as a political vision; and it is showed how much these perceptions are in line with, and how much they have been projected onto, the actual socio-economic processes on three spatial and political scales.

Information Society means much more than the growth in ICTs. The socio-territorial inclusiveness of the advantages they offer is a central issue in this work; however, these benefits are seen as coming from the mutual and complicated interactions between society and these technologies. The broad definition of *access* used in this work also reflects a non-techno-centric view. Besides, the main approach in this research is a social geographical one; and *I.S. is observed from the position of rural-peripheral regions in particular.*

The key concepts of *access* and *(socio-technological) networks* are used as analytical tools in investigating how the problem of inclusiveness is seen, monitored and influenced on various *spatial and political scales* by different *actors*: 'top-down' by global forums and the European Union, as well as in two selected countries (Finland and Hungary); and bottom-up by local communities in rural-peripheral regions.

The findings from both the theoretical and empirical investigations indicate that without systematic (policy) intervention, disparities in access in the I.S. and the traditional spatial inequalities in socio-economic developments mutually reinforce each other. So far, this has caused rural-peripheral regions to lag persistently behind economic centres and urban areas. The case studies also indicate that there exists (yet, not a clear-cut) division of responsibilities between the various spatial scales in terms of improving access and inclusiveness.

The Finnish and Hungarian national developments (I.S. realities and visions, institutions, strategies and programmes) are given a more detailed insight in the dissertation. The Nordic example is often referred to as the welfare model of a highly developed I.S., while Hungary, as one of the transition countries loaded with problematic legacies, is still looking for its own special way to achieve similar success and recognition. It is found that although, the respective I.S. models of Finland and Hungary differ in many ways, both their spatial patterns in access, and their policy objectives are rather similar and in tune with the broader international guidelines and processes. Despite the differences in for instance, their historical developments, social structures and behaviours, some of the fundamentals of the Finnish welfare model (e.g. inter-institutional networking, on-line public services targeting citizens and businesses) could be successfully transplanted into the Hungarian I.S. strategy as long as enough caution is paid to necessary adjustments. Likewise, interesting local developments and creative civil action in Hungary can potentially be a rich resource for learning to any country where ICTs need to be better matched with the needs of rural society and economically disadvantaged peripheries.

In fact, in the spirit of mutual learning, the dissertation culminates in a short account of cooperation between Finnish and Hungarian local actors across national borders, *who try to rely both on their respective national institutions and their shared European framework in realising their joint community intranet.* This example brings top-down and bottom-up initiatives together, highlights the obstacles emerging from cultural and technological differences, underlines the importance of the human (mental) factors in access, and emphasizes the (under-utilised) potentials of innovative 'cross-border' (horizontal) networking.

A major conclusion is that cooperation between various actors in a network configuration is a key condition for bridging the digital divides across countries and regions, as well as for peripheries to developing their livelihood. Therefore, I.S. should be, and most recently, has been understood more and more as a *communication society*, the welfare of which is based on connectedness, horizontal cooperation, interactivity and learning between spatial-administrative levels, organisations and people. Connectedness and learning however, are only supported, and not *de facto*, granted by the new ICTs.

Acknowledgements

I have been frequently told that writing a dissertation is a *process*, and a long one. My work has been such, a journey directed by a lot of critical and constructive, inevitable or coincidental influences on the way. I first encountered the concept of 'information society' (I.S.) in 1999 as a seminar paper assignment during my geography undergraduate studies at the Eötvös Loránd University, Budapest. The idea then was hardly known there, and I had to rely mostly on international literature and dial-up Internet connections... In course of the almost ten years that has passed since, the world as I know it, has gone through dramatic changes due to various objective and subjective reasons. The technologies, the definitions and the expectations have changed, and are changing increasingly fast. Hungary, my country of origin as well as the field for some of my case studies has gone through significant transformation, too. Besides, as a result of my personal move not only across time but also, in geographical space, I have got richer in perspectives and in experience of these changes. My life in the capital of Hungary and then, my move to Eastern Finland about seven years ago, have put me in a very special position: as a "metropolitan girl" from Central Europe (but also, a former Eastern Bloc country undergoing a problematic transition process) relocated to a small provincial town "in the middle of the taiga" (but also, to one of the most advanced information societies in the world), I have had the constant opportunity to contrast, conflict, and compare realities, to draw analogies, parallels, and to constantly redefine, reposition, question, and reconnect ideas and observations. It has been an especially rewarding experience to me both as an individual and as a geographer to shift my angle from urban to rural, from south to north, from one sort of periphery to another and from one kind of centre to another; to distance myself from the familiar and then, approach it again from a different direction.

Nevertheless, beyond the shifts and changes, there are things which have been and will be constant. Among these never-changing things I need to mention first of all, my gratitude and respect towards my professors and teachers both at my old and new *alma maters*, the Institute of Geography, Eötvös Loránd University in Budapest, and the Department of Geography, University of Joensuu. I want to express here my gratitude to the late professor György Perczel, who gave me the opportunity to start doctoral studies in Budapest in 2000, and to professors József Nemes-Nagy and Mária Rédei whose professional influence, friendly help and trust in my abilities have encouraged and inspired me throughout the years. I am interminably indebted to my supervisor professor Markku Tykkyläinen at the Department of Geography in Joensuu who invited me in 2001 to continue and finish my doctoral work in Finland under his expert supervision. I would like to thank him for his constructive criticism, all the practical advice and his patience with which he assisted my work from the planning stage to completion. I owe special thanks to professor Heikki Eskelinen for his continuous guidance, his invaluable comments, and his encouragement for my work, as well as for offering me the opportunity to work in an ESPON research project related to my own investigations. I would also like to thank the official pre-examiners of this work, professor Andrew Gillespie, Newcastle University and professor Ulf Wiberg, Umeå University, whose reviews helped me fine-tune this dissertation.

From the Department of Geography, I am grateful also to professor and head of department Jarmo Kortelainen and assistant professor Paul Fryer for all the support and friendly help they have given me in my daily work and struggles; and Kaarina Huotilainen and Timo Pakarinen for their almost telepathic abilities to understand and solve promptly all my problems related to administration, official forms and stubborn computers. I very much appreciate the help and friendship I have received from my fellow PhD candidates, some of whom have graduated already, showing me a good and instructive example: Dr Minna Piipponen, Evgenia Prokhorova, Dr Jaana Nevalainen, Dr Kenneth Kamwi Matengu, Mattias Spies, Katja Polojärvi, Kati Pitkänen, Timo Kumpula and Jussi Semi. Thank you, guys, also for the cheerful moments! I would like to express my gratitude especially to Minna for her constant support and for her kind tolerance of my spontaneous lectures and mood changes about my work which she had to endure sharing the office with me for three years...

Furthermore, I wish to thank Dr Jukka Oksa and his colleagues from the Karelian Institute in Joensuu for the consultations, their advice and the possibilities to exchange ideas with their expertise about local I.S. developments. I also owe many thanks to Dr László Z. Karvalics and his colleagues at the BME-UNESCO Information Society Research Institute (ITTK), Budapest for the thought-provoking discussions and counsel they have provided me both during a few personal meetings and within their *Palesztra* network on-line. I am grateful for the advice and insights I gained from the discussions with professor Jørgen Ole Bærenholdt, University of Roskilde, professor Walter Leimbgruber, University of Fribourg, and Harley Johansen, University of Idaho. I would like to express my appreciation of the openness, help and enthusiasm from the local I.S.-developers whose work I have been studying: Ilpo Koskikallio and his colleagues from Nurmes in Finland, and the telecottagers from Hungary –

Mátyás Gáspár and his colleagues especially in Szeged and the village of Mártély. It has been a great pleasure and an interesting learning experience for me to get involved a bit in their work and objectives.

I owe many thanks to the Hungarian Scholarship Committee (MÖB), the Faculty of Social Sciences and Regional Studies, Joensuu and the Graduate School of Geography in Finland for providing funds during different phases of my research. Without their financial support, it would not have been possible for me to carry out research in both Finland and Hungary, to participate in interesting conferences and courses further abroad, and to complete my doctoral studies in Joensuu.

Last but not least, this dissertation would not exist without my care and respect for my home and the values I have been brought up with – which all I owe to my Beloved Parents. The emotional and moral support, the trust and the unceasing care from them and my whole family have been protecting me from a distance of over 2000 km, and gave me much strength and inspiration during the critical times, as well as doubled my enjoyment of my success in work. My little sister, Ági has been giving me a lot of encouragement, too; what is more, she assisted my work with constructive comments, a critical eye and good humour, which support I hope one day I can return her. Finally, I would like to thank all my relatives as well as my friends beyond the university, in Joensuu, Hungary and elsewhere, who have been there for me, giving me a sense of security and much encouragement during my work.

List of Figures

IX

List of Tables

1 INTRODUCTION

1.1 Research questions

This dissertation takes a *multi-scalar spatial approach* in understanding the phenomenon that is most frequently referred to as *'the Information Society'* (I.S.). Its focus is the *social and territorial inclusiveness* of the emerging I.S. The research carried out (2002-2007) for the studies included in this book was concerned principally with the situation in rural-peripheral regions, and aimed to respond to the following broad question:

How can the benefits of information and communication technologies (ICTs) and the so-called, information society (I.S.) be extended to rural-peripheral regions and communities?

In order to find the answer, more concrete research questions have to be specified, which are also relevant to the selected set of targets of empirical analysis. Nevertheless, breaking up this general enquiry into deliberate and geographically relevant sub-questions requires an analytical approach.

This initial question contains at least three preliminary assumptions, which all bring up a complexity of concerns and further questions. The first such assumption is that ICTs mean benefits to society, they are 'good', and the same positive significance is attached usually to the concepts of information, and especially, knowledge. Their goodness however, is not intrinsic, they are social products, and their implementation and their relevance to society is where their benefits can manifest. Rural-peripheral

regions are usually distinguished as special social contexts; therefore it is important to understand what particular ways these technologies may be introduced to them. Information Society as a development concept must have a special implication to the populations and the economies of these regions. What are the mechanisms that bring about (or restrict) the benefits of ICTs, how do these mechanisms work in the rural-peripheral context? Understanding fully the relationship between society and the ICTs is crucial to successfully decrease the extent and occurrence of digital divides.

Another claim is, however, that information society is not inclusive of everyone, e.g. there are rural-peripheral communities and regions even in the developed world which are excluded from its advantages. (From among several competing terminologies, I.S. is the phrase chosen in this book, but definitely not in a techno-centric way but in its broadest socio-cultural interpretation.) This is relatively easy to see the point of, with the exception of one problem: to really see what is included and what is excluded, one needs to have a clear idea, delineation of the 'thing'. However, it is common knowledge, that neither societies nor technologies are static – so then, what is the baseline, the fixed point for inclusion/exclusion or for comparisons? How can the I.S. be defined and measured, and who is to give that definition and measurement? Certainly, there is no lack of definitions in policy documents across the world, but quite the reverse, there is an almost infinite number of them. Probably for a good reason, they contain as many commonalities as much they differ in their foci on I.S. What is expected from I.S. by the different stake-holders, potential actors? 'Information Society' is not only a moving target, but a political-social construct, and therefore very subjective and flexible.

Finally, it is also suggested that there should be ways to help the situation in rural peripheries. Who should be responsible? Is that the national government, is it the IT companies? Or is it the local communities directly affected? Whose interest(s) are involved in this problem? Also, relating back to the problems of definition and inclusiveness, what is the spatial-administrative scale (level) on which the impartiality of the I.S. can be / should be attained.

For the reasons mentioned above, the first part of this dissertation is devoted to providing conceptual clarification of different meanings behind key terminology, and giving an insight into the more recent developments of the I.S. as an evolving theoretical conception as well as a political vision. Only after this, it becomes possible to see *who* has potentially the power and means to act, and *where*; as well as to establish *what* can be done, and *by what means*, in order to extend the advantages of I.S. to rural-peripheral regions.

Beyond these, it is important to note that the rural context also, is an abstraction: though rural-peripheral regions have certain distinctive common features, they are all embedded in their own national backgrounds, individual cultural settings, economic circumstances and path-dependences (hence is also, the problematic delineation for policy what can be considered 'rural'). Consequently, the second, empirical section of this dissertation contains comparisons across European countries, and in more detail, describes the situation in rural regions from two selected states, Finland and Hungary. These two national contexts are dissimilar enough for to prove the existence of analogies, general truths, but are also similar enough to justify that certain cultural, economic, historical, etc. features are especially responsible for the emergence of different I.S. development pathways or even, 'models'.

Figure 1. Key concepts and their linkages

There are three more or less distinct aspects present in every part of this work:

One is related to the complexities of access – on the interaction surface between ICTs and society. The second is related to networks, and the problem of governance and co-ordination. Thirdly, the empirical chapters show what extent the described theoretical perceptions and political visions are in line with, and how much they have been projected onto, the actual socio-economic processes on three different spatial, political-administrative scales. These three aspects are underlying the concrete Research Questions (see below) and are defined and applied as analytical tools in the empirical studies. All three have a relevance to policies and practices aiming at a spatially-socially inclusive I.S., yet the first one concentrates more on the *objects* of policy (*what to influence?*), the latter two are focussing more on the actors, their inter-relationships and responsibilities (*who and how should influence things?*)

So quite a few fundamental concepts arise that can be understood in divergent ways. In Chapter 2 they are clarified for the purposes of the current work, and explained also in the context of recognized social theories. Figure 1 above summarises them within a theoretical framework.

Based on the arguments above, the initial and general enquiry is broken up into concrete Research Questions (RQs) which identify the actual objects for investigation in the empirical studies. Set already into specific geographical contexts, the RQs in this dissertation are the following:

RQ 1: What are the factors behind the differentiation in access, the emergence of digital divides concerning the rural peripheries of developed countries?

RQ 2: What are the suitable points of intervention to help resolve digital divides? What are the different actors' roles and responsibilities at a) the international or European, b) the national and c) the regional / local levels in order to achieve a spatially more inclusive I.S.?

RQ 3: Is the diffusion of ICTs or the emergence of an I.S. making horizontal interactions and flows more powerful, and thus administration and decision making more transparent and democratic?

RQ4: What can Hungary learn from the achievements of the 'Finnish model'?

These four research questions indicate the chain of arguments and explanations towards answering the broad question, starting from elementary processes leading to more complex issues such as the potential transfers of I.S. practices and models.

1.2 The case studies in the dissertation

The case studies in the empirical section represent different geographical scales (political-administrative levels) and various sets of actors, and are themselves composite in terms of perspective and methods.

From Chapter 3 to Chapter 5, the concrete geographical scope of the empirical investigation zooms in from the international and European processes, perceptions and actions to the developments in selected rural regions and communities in Finland, and in Hungary, via descriptions of the respective national strategies and observable sub-national tendencies. Similar issues are investigated on all these different scales. There is a vertical-hierarchical connection between them based on inclusiveness in terms of territory and (to different extents,) policy-making. Besides, these scales emerge also as actors in the same 'horizontal' socio-political network. Considering this duality of positions, the interrelations of these scales and actors are a most interesting field for investigation.

In Chapter 3, I describe how international organisations have approached the problem of equality in the I.S., and especially, what the European Union has been trying to do for an inclusive I.S. I describe the main interests and motivation behind these efforts, and what methods international actors can rely on; and especially, what tools the EU can employ to achieve an advanced and fair 'e-Europe'. It becomes obvious from these investigations that the international scale, and political-administrative level has strong limitations in competence, yet it does have a very specific and irreplaceable function in providing guidelines, forums, networks for innovation, and some co-ordination and control of processes.

In Chapter 4, I give accounts of the relevant national developments and policy development in Finland and Hungary, and their respective approaches to, and positions within, their European context. The Nordic example is often referred to as the welfare model of a highly developed I.S., while Hungary, as one of the transition countries loaded with problematic legacies, is still looking for its own special way to achieve similar success and recognition. An interesting consideration may be at the end, the possibility for mutual learning despite the differences in for instance, their historical developments, social structures and behaviours. Chapter 4 also provides the background information for the respective regional and local initiatives in these two countries, which are the subject of the next chapter.

Finally, in Chapter 5, I describe the general trends in sub-national inequalities in these two countries, and regarding certain aspects of access; and I continue shifting attention towards the smaller but even the more crucial players: the local and regional initiatives which by trying to match the expectations and opportunities coming from their national and European backgrounds, have managed to achieve a lot in terms of e-inclusiveness in their rural societies.

The last case study (5.4) lets us zoom out again partially as it gives an account of the encounter of the two national cultures in the form of cooperation in planning a joint development project by rural - local actors from a Hungarian village and a set of Finnish rural communities, much within the European context.

This relatively short account is particular for its special approach and methodology, and has a distinctive and important role in the dissertation. It is the outcome of action research: the cooperation between local actors across considerable physical and cultural distances was triggered

4

by my personal involvement first as a researcher, a mediator, a voluntary interpreter, then as advisor and assistant. Besides, this 'story' is a kind of a connecting point of many threads woven in previous theoretical and empirical chapters: the co-operating partners themselves rely heavily on ICTs and (local, international) networks in order to achieve local rural- development; they act across geographical, and administrative-political borders; and they are challenged and inhibited by not only technological and economic asymmetries, but cultural differences, too. Furthermore, their work has been embedded in and greatly influenced by, the European and their respective national frameworks, interests and actions.

This way, this experience rounds up all the empirical investigations pointing at possible interconnections and interactions between the many spatial-political scales dealt with in the dissertation, and showing how intricate connection there is between the means and the ends, the tools and the purposes, of developing the I.S. Although it is definitely

Every case study on these three spatial and political-administrative levels contributes to the explanation of more than one of the RQs, and they all represent some solutions or problems related to access and networks. I start each empirical chapter by posing three sub-questions to be answered in their own separate summary sections.[1] However, the fullest comprehension of the problem comes from cross-analogies,

changing and repeated patterns, and concrete linkages between the cases, which are discussed mainly in the final conclusions and synthesis (Chapter 6), i.e. in answer to the four Research Questions.

2 CONCEPTUAL FRAMEWORK AND METHODOLOGY

In search of an *a priori* or *theoretical* answer to the general opening question, the meanings of well-known, yet ambiguous and 'fuzzy' concepts will be examined, as well as some hypothetical linkages between them. Figure 1 above provides a framework of these ideas; the conceptual arena within which dissertation operates.

The first section of this chapter (2.1) provides some insight into the many ways of interpreting and dealing with (e.g. measuring) *information, knowledge,* and *technology*. These fundamental concepts are crucial to the understanding of some current processes related to technological development and influencing the (spatial) organisation of society and economy. The variety of perceptions on information, knowledge and technology explains also the divergence between the conceptualisations of the set of ongoing social and economic phenomena that may be encapsulated in the term *information society*. I.S. is discussed in 2.2, first as part of the political rhetoric and as an object of planning, then based on what scholars from a variety of scientific disciplines consider important in this issue; and I also emphasize the essentiality of the

---

[1] See more details on the structure and empirical chapters in 2.5 'Research design and methodology'.

5

interaction and overlaps between these two fields.

In 2.3, I proceed by inserting the fundamental concepts into the context of human geography, giving brief accounts on some of the spatial concerns arising from the previously mentioned interactions between the human intellect, the features and needs of society, and innovative technology. The notions of *access* and *network* are introduced and defined in 2.3 for the purpose of employing them as central analytical tools later on, in the empirical sections of this book. Besides, these two concepts are built up from the three fundamentals discussed in 1.1 and have strong relevance to both political and academic debates about the I.S. 'Access' and 'network' help to see information, knowledge and technology in spatial terms and to set the 'I.S. phenomenon' into a geographical context: digital divides are manifest also spatially; and the territorial heterogeneity of social and technological networks, as well as the inequalities in the many dimensions of access are useful aspects for studying and influencing *regional development*. I highlight the possible conceptual connections between regionalisation and networks drawing on ideas such as those proposed by the actor-network and social capital theories.

As such, the concepts of *access* and *network* help bridging over 'the cognitive gap' between the broader theoretical starting points (2.1-2) and the observed social and spatial phenomena and patterns (Chapters 3-5). Furthermore, they also function as cornerstones in formulating the precise research questions; and, in search for the answers to these enquiries, they link together the different case studies by providing the common main aspects of empirical-analytical investigation.

Finally, regional development (and policies), 'regionness', bonding-bridging networks and digital divides operate and manifest in diverse *scales* and involve many different *actors*. It is important to identify these because of the multiscalarity of the investigations presented in this work: ultimately, I.S. is a result of the interactions and intersections of horizontal and vertical, individual to global processes, conflicts and forms of cooperation.

2.1 The fundamental concepts: information, knowledge and technology

"Where is the Life we have lost in living? Where is the wisdom we have lost in knowledge? Where is the knowledge we have lost in information?"

T.S. Eliot (1888-1965): The Rock, 1934

In popular media, political proclamations, and in academic papers dealing with the on-going transformative or revolutionary processes, *information*, *knowledge*, and *technology* are frequently used terms. They usually indicate something positive such as opportunities, competitiveness, growth, and development; yet they are most often (dis)credited with rather unclear and imprecise meanings. These words have taken up some abstract, symbolic air; akin to the ways 'cyber' (cyberspace, cyber terrorism), 'digital' (digital age, digital gap, digital rights), 'e-' (as in e-government, e-commerce, e-health), and 'virtual' (virtual community, virtual university), etc. have entered our reality, or at

6

least have become the essentials of 'cyber hype'. After all, *information society* (I.S.) is part of the political rhetoric and media fashion, which may make its integrity questionable when used, for instance, in academic writing.

Why have information, knowledge, and technology become the objects of such remarkable attention? Where is their significance, their positive value rooted? Having no illusions about the scale and intricacy of such a venture, at least an attempt should be made here to conceptualise these universal ideas. This is necessary because different schools of thought around the I.S. may be traced down to the various approaches taken up towards these different forms of intellectual capital. Also, I wish to call attention to the natural conceptual overlaps as well as the often unconscious and self-inductive, but sometimes intentional simplification of their meanings for certain purposes. The latter may lead to exaggerated fears and expectations, misunderstanding and misplaced strategies, failing projects in the fields of policies and application.

2.1.1 Conceptualising information

There is vast literature on the definitions and distinctions of *information* and *knowledge*, and besides philosophers, epistemologists, and linguists, mathematicians and informaticians, as well as experts in education, psychology, sociology and other social sciences, or knowledge-managers like librarians, have been for long interested in the topic.

Starting with **information**, cybernetics deserves a mention, which provides one of the foundations of information theory. Cybernetics was introduced by nature scientist Wiener[2] (1948), who defines information as *probability*, and claims that its simplest form is a choice between two equally probable simple alternatives (0 or 1 in the binary scale), and thus "*the number of choices made and the consequent amount of information is infinite*" (Sveiby, 1994/98). Besides pointing out the quantifiability, measurability of information, Wiener also launched the tradition of thinking about information as something organised into a system, connected to decisions, feedback mechanisms in communication and control (Farkas, 2002:73). These two conceptualisations of information – as quantifiable objects, i.e. facts, and as a process, that is, communication - are innate to the thinking of system theory, informatics and computer science.

---

[2] Norbert Wiener (1894-1964) born in the U.S.A., was primarily a mathematician. Besides mathematics and cybernetics, he published works also on mathematical physics and philosophical issues. His work "*Cybernetics or Control and Communication in the Animal and the Machine*" (1948) was based on findings about the role of bioelectric signals (Sveiby 1994/98). He was greatly influenced by Leibniz, and he used the Greek word 'kubernetike' (steersman of a ship) to describe "the theory of regulation and of signal transmission applied to technical devices, living beings and even societies" (ISSS).

The mathematician Shannon[3] defines information as a purely quantitative measure of communicative exchanges. As claimed by the information theory rooted in Shannon's definition, it is indifferent whether it is a fact, a judgement, a lie or just nonsense that is communicated: according to him, everything transmitted over a telephone line is information.[4] He attributes the word 'information' not only with a technical meaning but also, a measure (binary digits, or in short, bits). For instance, the physicist Bekenstein however, does not share this point of view. He claims that information has many levels of *meaning*, various *relations to 'truth'*, and several forms and purposes, based on which he distinguishes between a simple sensory input, a message, a pattern, or an influence (2003:58).

There have been a few social scientists bold enough to enter the perilous field of information theory. Anthropologist Bateson[5] maintains for example that "the elementary unit of information – is a *difference which makes a difference*" (Bateson, 1072:453, his italics). This is in harmony with the etymological-semantic origins of the term 'information': it is derived from the Latin verb *informare* meaning 'give form to' (Oxford English Dictionary). Therefore information is the form that is given to some 'mass' to distinguish it from the rest, and also, it is the 'system' that Wiener argues for (as opposed to Shannon's 'chaos').

By contrast, there are enthusiasts, who consider 'information' already as the alpha and omega of basically everything. The following citation from an IT magazine declares this passionately:

Information is an activity. Information is a life form. Information is a relationship. Information is a verb not a noun, it is something that happens in the field of interaction between minds or objects or other pieces of information. Information is an action which occupies time rather than a state of being which occupies physical space. (*Wired*, March 1994)

One can discover some confusion even in the definition provided by the prestigious Oxford English Dictionary, where

---

[3] Claude Shannon (1916-2001), a mathematician in the U.S., had a degree in electric engineering as well, and worked for the Bell Laboratories for almost three decades. His paper titled "*A mathematical theory of communication*" initiated the subject of information theory, and the idea (which was then yet new) to transmit pictures, words, sounds by sending a stream of 1/ 0 -s via a wire, also originates from his new, linear schematic model of a communications system (Bell Labs Computing and Mathematical Sciences Research Division).

[4] It is interesting to observe that in this case, two mathematicians, and at the *same* time, defined information in two *opposite* ways: Wiener described it as the order, the system in things; while Shannon regarded it as entropy, as chaos. It is interesting to see, nevertheless, that for some other authors who attempt to define 'information', having a truthful, valuable meaning is a basic requirement. Shannon's critiques suggest that his model should rather be called "signal transmission theory" instead of "information theory" (Sveiby, 1994/98).

[5] Gregory Bateson (1904-1980) was born in Britain, and moved to the United States later. He was involved in many different areas of study: he moved through zoology, psychology, anthropology and ethnology. He was not only a contemporary but also a colleague of Wiener and Shannon, and several other thinkers of *cybernetics*. His best known writings are included in his books, *Steps to an Ecology of Mind*, 1973, and *Mind and Nature*, 1980 (Associazione Oikos).

information is linked both to knowledge and communication.

Information is *"Knowledge communicated concerning some particular fact, subject or event; that of which one is apprised or told; intelligence, news."* (Oxford English Dictionary)

So 'information' can refer to both facts in themselves, and the transmission of them. Yet the term 'knowledge' included in the quote above, gives reason for some alert: are information and knowledge in any way equal to or directly, identical with, each other? Some on-line encyclopaedias, such as *wordiq.com* in fact, deliberately warn the reader about the richness of these concepts and the fact that these notions are closely related, but not identical, and that they are often misused, even confused:

Information is a term with many meanings depending on context, but is as a rule closely related to such concepts as *meaning, knowledge, instruction, communication, representation,* and *mental stimulus.* (...) Although many people speak of the advent of the "information age," the "information society," and *information technologies,* and even though information science and *computer science* are often in the spotlight, the word "information" is often used without careful consideration of the various meanings it has come to acquire. (*Word IQ* defining 'information')

Society has always been organised around information, since it is a key resource for decision-making. People make millions of simple and complicated choices every day of their lives based on the information they receive directly or indirectly. Companies invest in obtaining information about

demand, competitors, innovation and the regulatory environment; so do political decision-makers act and communities organise themselves: relying on the pieces of information they gather through different channels. Of course, these actors themselves supply and disseminate information, too. Information management is a crucial task to all, ranging from national scientific networks and regional information systems to local organisations and individual citizens. Being cut from information permanently usually leads to serious malfunction. Information, though not in itself, can mean a competitive advantage. Yet this depends not only on its quality (its shape, its credibility, validity, relevance, confidentiality or publicity, its timing and speed of delivery, etc.) but on the ability of the decision-maker to process and use it adequately in certain situations. Dispatching, receiving, interpreting and utilising information by unprivileged groups and communities in the rural/peripheral regions is even the more important concerning the risks of their further falling behind the rest of society in socio-economic development.

2.1.2 Conceptualising knowledge

There has recently been an explosion of information, yet this does not necessarily mean an increase in knowledge (Dénes, 2000). Information may be a crucial resource, yet it can contain much noise and disorganisation; it is "its value of utility which matters, not its quantity" (Farkas 2002:53; translated by S.N.). The most common stance is that as structure contains more information than chaos, by 'engineering' information (i.e. by 'adding value' to, by selecting, construing and updating it) it can be turned into knowledge (Sveiby, 1994/98). It seems, put in a simple way, that while some kind of (not necessarily direct and inter-personal) communication is usually a prerequisite for information, knowledge is not an indispensable, but only a potential 'outcome' of information.

Bell[6] defines knowledge as *"a set of organised statements of facts and ideas, presenting a reasoned judgement or an experimental result, which is transmitted to others through some communication medium in some systematic form"* (Bell, 1974:175). The keywords here are *'organised'*, *'reasoned'*, *'communicated'*, and *'systematic'*, distinguishing knowledge from news and entertainment. Bell claims that his definition concentrates more on *what* is known.

Machlup's[7] is a broader, more comprehensive approach; and a subjective interpretation. "(A)ccording to the meaning which the knower attaches to the known, that is *who* knows and *why* and *what for*" (Machlup, 1962:21), there are five types: practical (professional), intellectual (i.e. fulfilling one's intellectual curiosity), small-

talk and pastime, spiritual / religious, and unwanted knowledge.[8]

According to Polanyi[9], knowledge is action oriented, a *dynamic process* itself. This means that knowledge or the process of knowing is synonymous with 'learning'. Also, Polanyi and several other thinkers on the subject argue that there are 'tacit' (underlying, implicit, unreflected, or informal) and 'focal' (explicit, codified) levels of knowledge. In the course of the cognitive processes, we use implicit / tacit knowledge as a tool to gather more (explicit) knowledge, some of which will be incorporated into the former. Human beings are constantly switching between these two levels, and hence our basic ability "to blend the old and well-known with the new and unforeseen", without which we could not live in the world (Sveiby, 1997). Another important thesis of Polanyi's is that knowledge is *public* as well as to a high degree, *personal*. Knowledge contains very personal emotions, so-called *passions* (e.g. of

---

[6] Daniel Bell is known for his theory of the post-industrial society (1974), and proposes economic and occupational definitions of the information age.

[7] His work to identify the 'information industries' links Fritz Machlup (1902-1983), an Austrian-born economist closest to the economic conceptualisation of the I.S. phenomenon; see more below (p. 33).

[8] Bell argues that definitions by Machlup and others are neither wrong nor right: they are "boundaries of usage". For the purposes of social policy, however, i.e. to determine the allotment of societal resources, he feels the need to propose a restricted, utilitarian definition that of knowledge "objectively known", or "intellectual property" (Bell 1974:175). By the latter he means certified, socially recognised publications, which are value-judged by the market, by administrative or political decision-makers or by peers, commissioned by the communication and educational media, etc. This narrow definition is required for 'measuring' knowledge, too.

[9] Michael Polanyi (1891-1976) born in Hungary, started his career by gaining doctoral degrees both in medicine and physics in Budapest and Karlsruhe. After emigration to Britain, he shifted to social science and philosophy. His most famous work is *Personal Knowledge* (1958).

discovery), and it is socially communicated, expressed. "Socially conveyed knowledge blends with the experience of reality of the individual" (Sveiby, 1997).

Knowledge is a term increasingly dominant in discourses of development, especially through its being essential in innovation processes (e.g. Calestous and Yee-Cheong, 2005).

What Andersson (1989) suggests as a hierarchy of knowing deserves some consideration, too. The order he proposes is based on how rules are followed. The lowest level of knowing is *skill*: it means following rules which can be controlled by the subject itself. On the next stage, rules are established by a social context outside the individual (a professional institution, or a tradition), and pursuing them results in obtaining know-how. *Know-how* is 'procedural knowledge', and it involves problem solving. The highest level of knowing is *competence* or *expertise*, which is in fact, know-how complemented with the ability of reflection: being able (and entitled) to not only submit but change or influence the rules themselves. Expertise is "a relation between individual actors and a social system of rules" (Sveiby, 1997). All three levels contain elements of both tacit and focal knowledge as two, complementary dimensions of the same knowledge.

Thrift points out that "social knowing" or the constant practices of creating the stocks of knowledge (Thrift 1996: 97) are embedded in time and space. The actors' capacity to use and generate knowledge is limited by these contexts, i.e. by their biographically distinctive experience. Besides, the availability of

empirical knowledge[10] has always been to some extent, spatially uneven, regardless of the current technology. The distribution of knowledge in society depends on the various aspects of social structuration (gender, age, race, class, state and region) and their different combinations; and "is associated with institutional nodes like home, school, university or office which form a set of points that selectively channel the life-paths of actors according to their membership of a particular social group" (Thrift, 1996: 114). Even knowledge that is only indirectly linked with practical needs, but which tries to "unify a number of bodies of knowledge into one whole, as knowledge about knowledge" (Thrift, 1996: 105; i.e. "natural philosophy") evolves through a long period of time and depends on the availability and type of the stocks of knowledge it builds from. In this sense, or 'timespace-geographically' (May and Thrift, 2003), the accumulated knowledge stocks in a specific location or region may therefore be understood simply as 'culture'.

To put it briefly, knowing and learning are subjective, relational, space and time dependent. Yet, "the fact that knowledge is physically available does not mean that it has to be acted upon nor that it is unquestioned or undisputed" (Thrift, 1996: 97). It does not mean either, that it is interpreted and used as relevant to the given context. Knowledge definitely has 'a geography', and therefore must play an

---

[10] Thrift describes empirical knowledge as the kind of knowledge that can be distanciated in time and space from the experiences, e.g. in codified, printed, digitalised form (Thrift 1996: 103).

imperative role in regional development, which is discussed in 2.3.

2.1.3 Measuring, selecting and managing information / knowledge

In view of the above, let us now consider the following statements, the likes of which are rather common in mass media articles and political speeches, and which also have made their ways into academic accounts:

The amount of knowledge in the world has doubled in the past 10 years and is doubling every 18 months according to the American Society of Training and Documentation ... (Gonzalez, 2004 – the author is Enterprise Information System Training/Computing Administration Manager)

This is the "Information Age". Half of what we know today, we did not know fifteen years ago. The amount of knowledge has doubled in the last fifteen years and is said to be doubling again every eighteen months. (Wetmore, 'Productivity Institute, Time Management Seminars' CT USA, on 'Speed reading')

Explosion of the information - There are projections that enunciate that the total amount of humanity knowledge doubled from 1750-1900, and that this one doubled again from 1900-1950, and from 1960-1965 (...) According to the projections for the 2020, the knowledge can be doubled every 73 days. (Appleberry, 1992; in a university speech titled "Changes in our future..." – quote taken from Morgan.)

Most of these statements are based on *measurements* of such as the volume of scientific articles (which method in fact, Bell suggested, too)[11], or expenditures on R&D, etc., so they are based on the assumption that the input in the production or the sheer quantity, of symbols directly equals the 'amount of knowledge'. There is no need after having mustered up the above theses and definitions to explain why these claims are at least, suspicious.

To be fair, not all popular accounts refer to knowledge as to something quantifiable and compare volumes of human knowledge across time confusing not only information, but the dimension of data flow with knowledge. *The missing links between data (through information) towards knowledge, and then, to know-how and expertise constitutes the active and creative mind of the individual persons and their*

---

[11] Bell relies on the calculations by a university librarian, F. Rider, and D. Price's more generalised findings: "In recent years we have become accustomed to the statement that the 'amount' of knowledge is increasing at an exponential rate (...) in the early part of the eighteenth century, the Yale library possessed somewhere around 1,000 volumes.. had continued ... to double every sixteen years... " , ""it seems beyond reasonable doubt that the literature in any normal, growing field of science increases exponentially, with a doubling time in an interval ranging from about ten to about fifteen years'" (1974:177; 180 quote from Price, 1961). Bell discusses the idea of the limit of growth, a saturation point in a theoretical S-curve. However, the S-curve model is only applicable to close systems, fixed environments. To Bell's credit, however, it is important to note that he recognised the difference between (the utilitarian, objective) 'gross' and (the socially complicated, subjective) 'net' measures of scientific knowledge: "To plan for social policy on the basis of such plotted curves would be highly misleading. To deal with such questions, we have to turn to less 'exact' but sociologically more meaningful observations on the patterns of the development of knowledge" (Sveiby, 1974:185).

social contexts (rules, traditions, networks). An implication to the significance of the Mind and also, the role of technology as a tool, is made in the following extract of a news report:

Worldwide information production has increased by 30 percent each year between 1999 and 2002, according to the team led by professors Peter Lyman and Hal Varian of the School of Information Management and Systems. (...) "Remember, it's not knowledge, just data," cautioned Lyman. "It takes thoughtful people using smart technologies to figure out how to make sense of all this information." (Maclay, 2003; UC Berkeley News.)

As soon as one leaves the level of 'bits' and data becomes at least a symbol, with a meaning that makes sense to at least one human being, a cacophony of ideas is set off. We face all the problems and conceptual ambiguities mentioned above. The progress from data to knowledge and wisdom is far not simple or linear.

Consequently, the further we get from data and facts, the least measurable these entities turn out to be - as they become more and more socially sensitive and shaped. Measuring the amount of existing knowledge possessed by a society, or in a field of science, or weighing the knowledge an individual has, is of course, nonsense. How much has been forgotten, how much do we actually preserve in our minds? What is useful and relevant knowledge (and to whom, and when...)? What knowledge is more useful and important than other knowledge? How can an outsider know the 'amount' of knowledge an individual holds? Even the person him- or herself does not know. Then

there is a problem occurring at the point of communication (or 'publication'): what, and how well do I communicate (publish) in a particular situation? How does the receiver understand and integrate the meaning of my communication? What is the real importance, the weight of a scientific article? (The citation index?) These are just few of the questions that point at the inaccuracy of attempts at measuring the growth in the quantity and 'flows' of information, skills, know-how, and knowledge.

Furthermore, there are authors concerned with such phenomena as 'information overload' and 'information anxiety'. The former is a term introduced by Alvin Toffler as early as in 1969. After three decades everyone in the developed world understands through their own experience what this concept means, and how it feels. Sveiby (1997) makes an important observation concerning the un-fixed nature of information, which has been accentuated by the latest technological developments: "digitised information in networks like Internet has no 'final cut' ... (a)s in oral tradition, it is copied and added in a continuous process". This phenomenon increases our sensation of the information overload.

Closely related to this is 'information anxiety', which means "the black hole between data and knowledge", i.e. the frustration that is triggered by the constantly widening gap between what we comprehend and what we think we need to, or should understand; which in fact limits people to being only seekers of, and not allowing time for them to reflect upon, knowledge (Wurman, 1989; Breivik, 1997).

A trend towards 'relative ignorance' has been noticed lately (Charter), which is triggered by the recent technological development: ICTs have increased our individual technological capacity to process, exchange, etc. information, while our mental capabilities to deal with it are constant. Even with technology to help the individual (i.e., even with our "social capacity", that is the combination of all individual capacities and ICTs), "the amount of knowledge that each of us hold as individuals is becoming a smaller proportion of the total amount of knowledge held by society"[12] The result is that we are becoming relatively more ignorant compared to the total knowledge that society produces and embraces.

The capacity to critically detect what makes sense and what is valuable in a definite situation – at a certain time and in a peculiar place, to a given person or group of people, for a certain purpose – helps elevate the pressure of the information overload. This ability (or as Hemingway put it once in a rather colourful and straightforward way, the "crap detector"; Jeffs – Smith, 1999: 26-27) is partly a learnt skill: one obtains it through formal and informal education, via practice, and in the course of social interaction. The tools are diverse, yet some sort of communication is always involved in the process. In addition, the given social context, *determined by both place and time*, defines the value, the relevance of information and knowledge.

So, neither information nor knowledge can be observed and interpreted in themselves, quantified and weighed in an absolute way, isolated from their human, social (geographical) contexts, detached from time and space. In the courses of complicated processes, ranging from those occurring within the individual mind (the microcosm, the unique identity, life-history of and the consequent perception and understanding by, the individual), to the inter-personal interactions guided and driven by rules, traditions, institutions, and requirements defined by a community or society (and culture), pieces of information and knowledge are being constantly re-valuated and contested. The blurriness of the conceptual borderline between information and knowledge, and the disturbing issues of measurability, 'information overload', 'relative ignorance' and 'information anxiety', are all rooted in *human* and *social* contextuality. The involvement of the individual and collective minds is both the origin and the resolution of the same problem.

To sum up the above, I see information as a collection or shape of facts and events that condition our choices. Information is communicated and via the intervention of intelligence, overview and interpretation it may become knowledge. Skills are practical knowledge that develop through application (experience), and can be further transformed into special know-how in a particular environment through internal trial and error as much as through external (social) criticism and suggestions. Finally, our wisdom is being enriched over time while knowledge is overviewed in reflection to, and contested with, that of others and of earlier times. Obviously, this is not a linear

---

[12] Note here again, the quantitative approach to knowledge and the confusion of the concepts 'information' and 'knowledge'.

process, and the factors of *time, spatial and social interactions, review, communication, and learning* are increasingly significant along the intricate paths from facts to wisdom.

2.1.4 Technology: ICT realities

> "The problem with communication ... is the illusion that it has been accomplished."
> George Bernard Shaw (1856-1950)

> "The more elaborate our means of communication, the less we communicate."
> Joseph Priestly
> (English Chemist and Clergyman, 1733-1804)

It may not be surprising having understood the reflections above, that the term *'technology'* has several levels in meaning, too. First, according to the Czech philosopher, Richta, it covers "the *material entities* created by the application of mental and physical effort to nature in order to achieve some value" (1963; my italics). As such, it can be a simple tool or a complicated machine. One may include here manuals and instructions on how to use these tools, too. Second, there is an interpretation as *technique*, meaning the current state of our knowledge how to combine resources to make the desired products, how to solve problems and fulfil needs. So, technology, in this meaning, is some sort of knowledge. Third, it may be perceived as a *cultural force*; e.g. in these terms was the invention of writing a technological one (Borgmann, 2006).

How do these different meanings of 'technology' relate to ICTs – information and communication, or network technologies? Firstly, in concrete, materialised form, ICTs include an endless record of visible and tangible machinery, equipments starting with telephones, radio and television sets, computers and their all related input / output peripheries and extensions (modems, memory cards, digital cameras, and so on); big servers, the physical network infrastructures; mobile phones and related objects like transmitter stations, etc. This is an ever growing list particularly because of their convergence with the broadcasting media as well as other breakthrough (e.g. bio-, nano-, etc.) technologies which blurs the borders between categories, and multiplies solutions.

Secondly, none of these 'smart gadgets' would function properly, or could be joined into a single network without the 'techniques' of digitalisation, shared protocols, languages etc., not to mention the skills and knowledge about how to use and combine them, that is owned, developed and exercised by people. The various types of network technologies through which the World Wide Web and on-line services in general may be accessed belong here as they are constructed of a great diversity of material components and are the results of converging techniques, too.

A great number of competing network solutions (infrastructures, techniques and services) for narrow and broadband data transmission have emerged through innovations driven by the needs of society. The oldest technologies that have been used are analogue telephone lines combined with modems, and ISDN. They are commonly defined as *narrowband* connections, and are often considered outdated if not a sign of disadvantage[13]. Certainly, they provide for only slow data transmission, and a dial-up mode of connection (the latter usually means pay-per-minute); as opposed to the much faster broadband technologies, some of which involve flat-rate pricing allowing unlimited usage. This difference matters a lot concerning consumer behaviour – meaning how much, when and for what Internet is used.

There is a multitude of rival and complementary technologies that can deliver *broadband services*, and each of them has its limits in terms of coverage (or range, from less than 1 to several thousands of kilometres), data-speed (i.e. bandwidth capacities between a couple of Mbps to several Gbps), costs and reliability. Broadband solutions are commonly grouped into *fixed-line* and *wireless technologies*.

The *fixed broadband* solutions can be based on existing infrastructures (xDSL, cable modem, powerlines), as well as networks that have to be constructed from scratch (fibre lines). xDSL systems utilise the twisted copper pair that traditionally facilitates voice services. The hybrid fibre-coax cable-TV networks provide the basis for cable modem connections, and powerline-broadband utilises the power lines feeding into the subscriber's home for transmitting signals. Optical fibre networks have the highest capacity, but they need a lot of investment as they are separate from existing infrastructures. They may carry signals directly to the subscriber or to a node (in the street, in the block) where they are combined with other broadband solutions that make the ultimate links to individual households.

Wireless broadband technologies include for example: data transmission via microwave (which have approx. 5 km reach but low data rates); Wi-fi (that is usually a highly local system providing radio connections to the end users), Direct Broadcast Satellite (with two-way, high-speed capabilities and large coverage but a delay in transmission), and 3G mobile networks (yet, with lower data-speeds).[14]

It is important to note here that the network technologies described above cannot be put in any from-poorest-to-best order: their assessment is along at least four *dimensions* (coverage, costs, reliability and speed), and each has its weaknesses and strengths. The *contexts* where they are applied matter a lot: the peculiar geographical setting (e.g. the topography, settlement patterns), potentially supportive existing infrastructure, and various aspects of social-economic demand. The importance lies in the way ICTs *match* these

---

[13] However, ISDN (Integrated Services Digital Network) was a great breakthrough in the early-nineties because it can make simultaneous data transfer and voice services possible along the same telephone subscription line. It is true though, that its original 'baseband' version does not exceed the capacities of the analogue line solution (both can support data transfer rates of 64 Kbps). There has been a development towards a B-ISDN (1.5 Mbps), yet it could not become wide-spread due to the emergence of more economical, reliable and efficient solutions, such as cable TV and xDSL. This is an example of competing cycles of diffusion and adoption (see below, in this same section.)

---

[14] 3G: traditional GSM technology up-graded with an overlay of GPRS; also called: UMTS – Universal Mobile Telecommunications Services. The exact technical information in this section is extracted from Corning Inc. 2005.

circumstances and requirements the best; and therefore, it is difficult to compare infrastructure across the spatial-social diversity based on absolute technological attributes (e.g. measuring digital divides merely in terms of bandwidths; see more on this in 2.3.2). Frequently, the solution in place is some sort of unique combination of several technologies (permitted by techniques of convergence). Yet, there is a technocratic and commercial tendency pressing for the most state-of-the-art ICTs (in this case, usually meaning the greatest bandwidth), and can easily lead decision-making astray.

The relationality of these network solutions is also evident in their competing *cycles of diffusion and adoption*. The emergence of a new technology (product, service; e.g. ADSL) that promises to fulfil a specific societal function (e.g. digital network for communication) at a higher quality or / and at lower costs than old solutions (e.g. ISDN) take over the latter, and disrupts their S-curves of adaptation.[15] However, there can be many uncertainties involved that shape these curves and the timing of the disruption is often planned and calculated by the investors to maximise profit.

---

[15] The diffusion or life cycle of an innovation, a technological trajectory can be represented graphically by a logistic or so called 'S-curve' of cumulative adoption: it is made up of an initial phase of innovators and early adopters, a dynamic rise or 'takeoff' period, and a stabilizing phase of late adopters. It plots the percentage of adopters on the vertical axis with time on the horizontal one. Its original concept coined by the French sociologist Tarde (1903) was furthered by American sociologist and communications researcher, Rogers in his work titled 'Diffusion of innovations' (1962).

Although the emphasis in the above discussion is on internet-technologies, it is important to note that the more traditional info-communication tools and techniques such as different kinds of printed and broadcasting media still play important roles in the society today. However, they are increasingly getting digitalised and available on the net via, and *converging* with, the new ICTs, following and generating social demand. In fact, this way they become themselves part of the *on-line content*. (Consider for instance, Skype, as an example for services between on-line to land-line telephones; e-books and e-journals; local/national radio stations and TV channels globally receivable via the Internet: are they 'technologies' or content?) People, having previous knowledge and experience of the traditional media forms may use more and more frequently their digital 'equivalents', realising at the same time both the relative shortcomings and the new potentials of digital ICTs.

So finally, recognising the mutuality and the interactions between society and technology (and recalling the quotation from above), one is led to the cultural interpretation of technology in general, and of ICTs, in particular. This cultural approach is unavoidable when studying regional inequalities in the I.S.

2.2 Understanding Information Society

The concepts of information, knowledge, technology, have been frequently applied to signify current changes in society, and used in the context of the rise of an

Information Society. It causes me some sense of discomfort when I have to use this term, though: there are as many connotations and definitions attached to it as many times it occurs in academic, political or more popular texts and speeches. On the other hand, it is just a term, a fashionable symbol; the debate should not be focused on how a set of phenomena should be called but more on the nature of the processes that have emerged in the world, in our lives and society, and the reason why they could set off the production of such terms. Neither do I endeavour here to provide a clear-cut definition. Information society is a blurry but easy to remember catchword which, like a ping-pong ball, bounces back and forth between political rhetoric and academic language; yet during this game it is constantly criticised, contested and re-conceptualised. With no intention to replicate earlier accounts (e.g. Beniger, 1991; Pintér, 2004; Farkas 2002; Karvalics, 2002; Webster, 2002), I give a brief summary of the intellectual challenges and solutions concerning this problem in order to explain why it is the cultural conceptualisation of the I.S. that I reckon the most relevant approach for the purposes of this work.

2.2.1 Information society: a border concept and political rhetoric

Politics or governments are interested in a 'social problem' only if they perceive in it some kind of a 'political problem', if they see it as a challenge, a potential source of crisis, a threat to national security, or a chance to lose their position in global competition (Farkas, 2002:32-33).

This is definitely true for the I.S. as a social problem, and therefore it is a highly political issue, too, starting already with its definition.[16]

In fact, the term 'information society' was coined for political purposes by the Japanese sociologist, Yoneji Masuda (1905-1995). He was the leading character of the "*Japan Computer Usage Development Institute*" in the 1970s, a project initiated by the Ministry of Industry and Foreign Trade. JACUDI was in charge of drafting a far-reaching plan for the country titled "The Plan for Information Society – A national goal toward the year 2000", the English version of which was published in 1980 with the title "*The Information Society as Post-industrial Society.*" The original work incorporated status reports on the Japanese efforts as well as Masuda's views, anticipations and recommendations concerning the societal effects of the complex technological systems he then saw unfolding. (Montagnini, 2003.)

Throughout the past few decades, there have been other examples of scholars working for their governments writing reports about or recommendations for, the elaboration of technological programmes or a national I.S.: Brzezinski (security advisor under Carter's presidency and chief expert of globalisation – 1969), Bell (chief theorist on the post-industrial society – 1973), Sola Poll (theorist of the 'free flow of information' – 1983), Reich (the inventor of the 'National Information Infrastructure') in the United States; Nora and Minc (with their report on the information society for the president –

---

[16] See concrete examples below in Chapter 3 (UN, EU), and especially in sections 4.2.2 (Finland), and 4.3.4 (Hungary).

1978) in France; and Lyotard (the author of the report about knowledge in the I.S. for the government of Quebec – 1979) in Canada; all drafted their visions instructed by some governmental department. (Montagnini, 2003.)[17] In most of these cases, the terminology lived on both in the political language and academic debates, corroborated by mutual reference.

Yet, the issue of the I.S. is a sensitive and a much 'hyped' one. Consequently, definitions are rarely neutral, for they always show *who is defining* the object and *for what purpose*. There is an extremely high number of stakeholders. Economic and consequently political interests are enormous in technology for the reason that the ICT industries comprise the most competitive and profitable sector of the 'new economy'. These technologies, converging and adapting to fit more and more purposes, have infused virtually all social and economic activities. Their significance in the overall transformation gets a special, as well as an exaggerated accent because direct / indirect financial interests in technological innovation, investments in ICT infrastructure and network services influence critical decisions.

Besides, ICTs and the printed and broadcasted media (along with their on-line forms) are closely connected, the latter being not only dominant users, but stakeholders, advertisers of the former. Definitions of the present era and society are of great significance not only for social theory, but in 'practice', since policy needs to draw on abstract concepts and symbols, too. Yet, definitions are frequently (ab)used by political and corporate propaganda, and obscured by the 'independent' media.

On the other hand, some grand expressions are loosely defined or inaccurate for a just reason: they are so-called "boundary concepts", i.e. due to their fuzziness, they are "able to reorganize debates between different disciplines, discourses or fields of life", and "facilitate interdisciplinary dialogue" (Miettinen, 2002:18). They may stay imprecise for their entire life span, and "continue to play an important heuristic role in the construction of new knowledge", and the *dynamics of scientific ideologies* (*ibid.* 20).[18] This must be the way also how I.S. is getting anchored in everyday thinking and is transformed into an object of planning.

---

[17] The relevant works: Bell: The Coming of Post-Industrial Society. A Venture in Social Forecasting (1973); Brzezinski: Between Two Ages. America's Role in the Technotronic Era (1969); Lyotard: The Postmodern Condition (1979); Nora – Minc: L'informatisation de la société, Paris, La documentation française, 1978; Reich: The Work of Nations. Preparing Ourselves for 21st Century Capitalism (1991); Sola Pool: Technologies of freedom (1983).

---

[18] Miettinen (2002) gives a through account on this problem concerning the term "national innovation system", (which is a boundary metaphor) relying on various other authors. An interesting point is that scientific ideology makes claims "under the pressure of pragmatic needs" which "go beyond what has actually been proved by research" (*ibid.* 20). Policy exerts pragmatic pressure on science: tentative boundary concepts that otherwise encourage a rich interdisciplinary debate in academic circles, are simplified for policy, and extended beyond what is scientifically proved. Then science again, tries to clarify the concept taking a critical stance to political rhetoric.

The 'information age' (or by whichever term we might call the phenomenon) has had a relatively long history as a subject of academic thinking, along which a diversity of approaches and explanations have emerged, all trying to get a grip on the main features, some *criteria suitable to identify, and even measure 'what is new'*[19]. Although the various definitions of the I.S. are not mutually exclusive, and most of their thinkers are difficult to position explicitly into a single school, they do vary considerably according to their emphases.

Adopting more or less the categories proposed by Webster (2002), we can distinguish between:

- ... technological,

- economic-occupational,

- and spatial-cultural

conceptualisations of the transformations under way (see Table1 below). The scholars representing the various perspectives come from a rather wide range of disciplines (nature sciences, informatics, sociology, philosophy, economics, and social geography). Although all agree to the point that 'information' has a special relevance in the present world, they are divergent in their understanding and explanation of "what form this information took, why it was central to our present systems, and how it was affecting

---

[19] Criteria and measures are looked for partly because of the pragmatic pressure by policy. See also 2.2.3.

social, economic and political relationships" (Webster, 2002:2). Table 1 lists *some* of the strands of thinking (and the years and titles of major publications) on the topic, loosely categorised into a 'school of approach' to I.S. from the technocratic points of view to more holistic stances. A few of the main characteristics and tendencies (i.e. 'inputs') that these theorists start off from or centre their arguments around are also given, as well as the 'systems' or general phenomena (era, society, economy) within which they examine these processes.

The different interpretations indicate some succession or evolution in thinking. In general, the earliest theories were determined and focussed either technologically or economically; while lately, an increased interest has emerged in the social, spatial, political-cultural and even, psychological implications (i.e. both the broad-scale *reasons* and *consequences*) of the emergence of the new technologies. The recognition of the various strands of change as more complex in themselves, as well as being mutually interrelated, is an observable tendency, too.

The reason for this might be in fact very simple: ICTs and network technologies have relatively recently diffused enough for to set off certain more visible and already examinable social processes. Specifically, we may talk about a continuous *learning* of the I.S. through social experience and expectations: technology and society are both in a constant flux, and the I.S. itself, unfolds only gradually. Nonetheless, this learning is not completely linear, some older accents and ideas have been recurrent, re-adopted by

Table 1. Theoretical perspectives on the I.S.

	'Input' - main features observed	'Output' -- consequence	Proponents (relevant works)
Technological	Technological innovations First phase (1960s): micro-electronics, miniaturisation, robotics Second phase (1990s-): digital revolution, space & biotech. , artificial intelligence and nanotech. (and the convergence of all the above) Moore's Law, Digital Revolution, and the expansion of the Internet.	Techno-deterministic utopias or dystopias (T.-enthusiasm/optimism or T.–phobia/pessimism) Tidal waves of technological development. Being global, prime, equal, and 'unterritorial'...	*(Futurologists:)* Toffler (1972; 1980), Naisbitt (1984), Pearson (1998; 2005) Negroponte (1996, 1998)
	Speed technologies	Dromological societies, deterritorialisation	Virilio (1977)
...	The volume of technological innovation, the scale of its diffusion in social–economic activities.	The third "tidal wave". 'Creative destruction' (Schumpeter) and Kondratiev's long waves of economic development.	*Neo-Schumpeterian school* Great Britain (Also some political documents: *e.g. Charter on Global Information Society -* G8 Summer 2000 Meeting)
Economic-occupational	'Information public utility' infrastructure.	Informational communism I.S. as post-industrial society	Masuda (1980)
	The weight and growth of primary and secondary 'information industries'; knowledge-production workers.	Information-based economy	Machlup (1960s) Porat (1977)
	The rise of the service sector, the white-collar jobs.	Post-industrial society. Consumerism.	Bell (1973)
	Know-how as raw material New labour force: 'thinking smart', inventive, developing and exploiting networks. A global super-class.	Weightless society, new capitalism; 'living on thin air'. Inequality as an acute feature of modern societies.	Leadbeater (1999, 2000)

	"Symbolic analysts" Restructuring, globalisation, fluidity of capital and production, vertical disintegration of corporations.	A new post-Fordism. Space of flows.	Reich (1991) Castells (1998/2000)
Cultural-spatial	Network logic, flexibility. A new and powerful elite. A split between the Net and the Self.	Informational capitalism and its black holes. Network society. Digital divide. ... Fourth World.	Castells (1998/2000)
	Death of the sign, more and more information and less and less meaning.	A post-modern world dominated by signs, hyper-reality, an age of spectacle.	Baudrillard (1983)
	Information flows, spatial logic of electronic information networks, capital 'travelling light'. Flexibility, short-term mentality, uncertainty vs. security.	The devaluation of space in certain spheres of life. Liquid modernity.	Bauman (2001)
	Abundant information, scarcity of time and attention/reflection. New principles in the legitimation of knowledge in society. Search for anomalies and paradoxes.	'Performativity' and 'paralogy' as legitimating principles in the postmodern condition. Little narratives as opposed to meta-narratives.	Lyotard (1984)
	The explosion of symbols, rising virtuality.	Economies of signs and space, consumer capitalism. Media-laden society.	Lash and Urry (1994) Urry (2002) Webster (2002)
	Economic globalization, fast information flows through ICT networks, accelerated pace of consumption. Increasing differentiation, pluralism along with homogenization and unification.	Time-space compression. Disruptive spatiality and the postmodern condition.	Harvey (1989)

| The changes in the Habermasian *public sphere* – media, Internet, citizen participation. Individualization of social inequality. | Cyberdemocracy, electronic democracy. Radicalised modernity Reflexive modernisation and surveillance. Late modernity. Risk society. | Poster (1995), Friedland (1996) Giddens (1990) Beck (1986), Graham (2001) Webster (2002) |
| The fluidity of interaction, sharing competence; new mass-behaviours, social rituals; stress from interaction overload... | Interaction Society. | Wiberg (2004) |

more recent theories (see the years of publication in Table 1, for instance).

First, the proponents of the *technological perception* all believe that technologies or ICTs themselves embody and have given rise to the 'information age', and some also claim that these technologies (their volume, diffusion) and their 'produce' (information transmitted) can be thus suitable measures for gauging I.S. development. This later attempt at measuring the scale of change through the volume of ICT diffusion was natural in the 60s and 70s when there was a tendency towards a positivist or quantitative approach in all fields of science (partly for the reason of the availability of supporting technology itself, i.e. data processing tools). Yet it is important to note that this stand, at least to some extent, has been kept up by policy makers ever since for practical reasons. Digital divides[20] are often measured merely in terms of the amounts of PCs, hosts and servers, or cellular subscriptions compared to the number of population or households.

There are several problems with the technological standpoint. Based on Webster's argumentation (2002), I consider

the following as the most important.[21] First, the *'information'* prefix in the I.S. term suggests *more than just technology* as the main attribute of the society and its transformation (unless one defines information as bits, for instance – or technology as information). Second, probably the most striking and critical ambiguity regarding the technological conceptualisation is related to the issues of *measurement*, and consequently, the basic delineation of the I.S. None of the advocates of this approach have succeeded in featuring ICTs accurately enough to make them useful as reliable measures, i.e. it has not been clearly stated *which* technology and *to what extent* is required to qualify an I.S. (see the arguments in e.g. 1.1.1 and 1.1.3). Considering the diversity of ICTs, their dynamic evolution and creative convergence, the selection of indicators requires careful consideration, and even more caution is needed when interpreting patterns of inequalities based on them.

It might not be of any serious consequence that the difficulty of measurement is simply ignored by popular futurists ("the new technologies are

---

[20] See in 2.3.2.

[21] Selected from Webster, 2002.

announced, and it is unproblematically presumed that this announcement in and of itself heralds the information society"; Webster, 2002: 11), yet this attitude is also taken up without much contemplation by scholars, and politicians. *Those, who use ICTs as major indices of an I.S. often uncritically presume that they are sufficient to mark a new society.* Thirdly, and related to the above, *technological determinism* is at the core of the ICT-based definition of the new society, the flaw of which is well-known and understood: technology cannot be separated from society as an external force (invented by whom and why?), i.e. having an impact on people making *them* adjust to it.

Second, the *economic conceptual-lisation* of the information era is interested in the economic weight of 'informational activities', while the *occupational approach* focuses on the changes in the employment structure. They differ from the technology-oriented approach in terms of their emphasis, since it is on the transformative impact of *information* itself rather than that of the related technologies. This is explained by the emergence and increasing weight of 'informational jobs' such as those of a designer, a deal-maker, an image-creator, a musician, a biotechnologist, a genetic engineer, and a 'niche-finder' (Webster, 2002: 14) – all occupied with some ways of manipulating information. Both the economic and the occupational theories require the separation of certain activities within the economy which, on the basis of some criteria, could be regarded as 'informational' as opposed to 'non-informational' elements of the economy.

Also, according to the established categories, both approaches employ statistical methods to measure and delineate the I.S.: they argue that I.S. is achieved when and where the majority of jobs is found in information work; or when and where the information sector dominates the (national) economy. Yet, there are considerable difficulties in the attempt to define, for statistical purposes, exactly who does information work and who does not (Kasvio, 2001). It is important to note that Castells (1996), also considers the transformations within the social-occupational structure significant in his 'new paradigm', related to which he talks about the emergence of a new and powerful intellectual elite, if not a distinctly new 'class', and the expansion of information-rich occupations. However, he criticizes the classical theory of 'post-industrialism' as he highlights some of the reasons why the traditional handling of this matter is questionable. Primarily, he is judicious of the *simplistic way of describing the re-structuration processes* as a shift from agriculture to industry, and then to services, and argues that the specific nature inherent to the new technologies themselves, gives rise to rather *diverse and complicated developments* in occupational structures. Furthermore, Castells points out that there is *no homogeneity* within the set of activities labelled as 'services', meaning that not all the jobs in this sector are 'informational' to the same extent. Also, the primary and secondary sectors contain some 'informational' labour. Though category-forming and statistical methods may be indicative of certain trends, any more in-depth analysis necessitates a socially more comprehensive scrutiny, and "the unit of analysis ... will necessarily have to change" (Castells, 2000: 247).

Finally, the advocates of the *cultural and spatial conceptualisations* (see Table 1) respond to the technological and economic-occupational approaches by proposing their very post-modern positions. Through their own elaborate efforts of understanding the world, they prove that the mission of constructing a concise, compact and universally accepted theory is in fact, *impossible*[22]. And so they leave little doubt as to the crudeness and simplicity of the technocratic or economic-occupational interpretations. Moreover, they question the meanings and conditions of technology, knowledge, and even, of development.

The thinkers of late or post-modernity raise more troubling questions than provide answers. Most of them reach down to fundamental social-philosophical disciplines such as phenomenological, ontological, epistemological and ethical debates[23]. In general, these theories, though they have ICTs somewhere 'in mind', look much more deeply into the diversity of social and economic processes and their *interactions* than the previous conceptualisations. They rather qualify than categorise or gauge changes. They draw from a broader set of disciplines ranging from sociology, geography, economics, politics, psychology, information science, philosophy, linguistics and semiotics, and all sorts of media related domains – and they are the most enthusiastic about exploring the 'confluence' of all these fields. They surely look for the anomalies and the paradoxes more eagerly than for positive truths. They explore a system of transformations where clear-cut and easy-to-generalise, linear causalities are rarely found.

Also, they are all concerned with either or both the modification of *time / space relations, and culture*. These two issues, in fact are inseparable. *Culture* is indivisible from the relations society has with *time* and *space*, as they are the principle 'material' dimensions of human existence. Culture is the "set of distinctive spiritual, material, intellectual and emotional features of society or a social group ... [their] lifestyles, ways of living together, value systems, traditions and beliefs" (UNESCO; World IQ). While time / space relations and our awareness of them, as well as our perceptions of our lives and 'positions' within these fundamental dimensions are being transformed, our relations to the elements of culture contained in the definition above, are being modified. Surely, this argument retains its validity when reversed: (social) space and time are constructed through social existence and creativity; which in fact, is embodied by culture. Consequently, the spatial and cultural approaches to the information age are connected at several points, the spatial

---

[22] This is often articulated in critical reviews written even about great 'syntheses' such as the one provided by Manuel Castells in his distinguished trilogy, "The Information Age: Economy, Society and Culture" (1996, 1997, 1998); e.g. reviewed by van Dijk, 1999, and Z. Karvalics, 2002:20-23.

[23] Ontology is the study of 'being' (*what is*; existence, reality). Phenomenology is the study of our experience. Epistemology studies how we know. Ethics studies what is right and what is wrong — how we should act.

and cultural 'symptoms' belong to the same 'syndrome' of the informational age.

The technological approach to information age draws a more-or-less straight arrow from technology to society. The economic and occupational arguments take the technology – information / knowledge linkage as fixed and given, and then go on to connect the latter to social-economic development in a similar fashion. In contrast, the cultural-spatial analysts do not take anything for granted, one-directional or even, linear. When it comes to defining the role of technology, they take up the perspective of *the social shaping of technology*[24]. Simplified it may seem, yet it is true: "technology *is* society." "Technology does not determine society: it embodies it. But nor does society determine technological innovation: it uses it" (Castells, 1996/2000:5). Or we can consider the problem to be similar to the popular 'chicken and the egg' question.

It is not surprising considering their focus (i.e. the "absence of criteria we might use to measure the growth in signification"; Webster 2002: 57-58) that the spatial-cultural approaches try to quantify or define a new society *the least* among the conceptual endeavours presented. Therefore it is probably "the most easily

acknowledged" (*ibid*: 18), the least debatable yet also, the least 'pragmatic'. This is not coincidental: maybe there is *really* no way to rate the advance of social transformation like that, to *measure* I.S. in order to define it. The cultural shift is 'in the air', everyone is aware of it; still it has no clear borders. Advocates of this perception of the I.S. "rarely attempt to gauge this development in quantitative terms, but rather start from the 'obviousness' of our living in a sea of signs" (*ibid*: 19.)

2.2.3 The problem of defining an era

Men can do nothing without the make-believe of a beginning.
George Eliot (1819 - 1880),
from "Daniel Deronda"

It is obvious from the above that a great diversity of phenomena is related in some way or another to ICTs and the 'informational revolution'. Yet, may we regard these conditions as signs of a revolution, the birth of something radically and distinctly *new*, or rather as the momentary outcomes, part of a continuous evolution?

We seem to have an inclination for adapting grand concepts, labels that we can attach to societies, countries, or an era: doing this in order to make sense of what is happening to our world. However, it entails several difficulties: "it involves trying to identify the major contours of extraordinarily complex and changeable circumstances" (Webster 2002: 1; also Dessewffy, 2004). When having the opportunity to look at the subject (e.g. a

---

[24] The theory of Social Shaping of Technology (e.g. MacKenzie and Wajcman 1985, William and Edge 1996) rejects the view of 'the social construction of technology' that technology does not shape human action; and it does not accept either, the technological deterministic assertion that technology follows its own developmental path independent from any human impacts. SST incorporates, however, the other main elements of these two theories: technology influences society, *and* society shapes technology.

social system, period) either from a greater distance in time (in their continuities) or from a comparative perspective (contrasting their contemporarily existing forms), we face the constant need to redefine, or at least refine and further qualify, the generalising terminology with attributes like 'emerging', 'developing', 'advanced', or 'liberal', 'authoritarian' or affixes such as 'pre-' and 'post-', etc. Indeed, it is true: "(w)e always name eras and movements 'post-' or 'neo-' when we don't know what to call them" (Naisbitt, 1984). This also suggests probably that people always feel that they live in the time of 'parenthesis', of transition; in an uncertain time *between* eras.

Defining society, economy or the times we are living in is by far not an easy task, especially if one claims that they bear the distinct marks of 'unprecedented' or 'revolutionary' changes. First, one needs much circumspection as to the *continuities* and *discontinuities* of social and economic development over time. What makes *the difference, and what is the level of dissimilarity*, the degree of novelty that is sufficient for distinguishing a 'new era' or 'new society'? Where is the line between two epochs, or two concepts? "When does one date a social change …?" (Bell, 1974: 174). How shall we *name* the current or emerging era at all? In the present work I mostly use 'information society' (I.S.) or 'information era' for the most recent 1-2 decades, yet not indicating that I consider this the most suitable or exclusively correct. As Martin says, it seems that 'information' has "become so important today as to merit treatment as a symbol for the very age in which we live" (1988). Even though some

authors prefer to name the new epoch by other terms (e.g. Bell's 'post-industrial' society, Castell's 'network society'), the concept of 'information' is in the centre of their arguments. All the same, *why and how* is information or knowledge *new* and more significant than before? As it is showed above, already their meanings are much contested, therefore, it is not surprising that when they should come to be a measure or criterion of socially, economically, financially, and of course, politically sensitive phenomena, the debate and criticism over their semantic value becomes even richer and more frantic.

Second, I.S. appears to be raised on the foundations of different social, economic, and political systems and diverse cultures. Consequently, there is at least as much variation as many commonalities between 'information societies' existing or taking shape. Theorists, as well as politicians are divided also on the issue whether I.S. is a fact of life already, or it is something we are heading for: are the ongoing changes already part of the phenomenon, or just leading societies towards, transforming them into, an I.S.? So, *where and when* is there an 'information society'?

Thirdly, we should be aware of the fact that it is rather *difficult to remain objective* regarding this question. It is relatively easy to consider a recent period to be the most eventful, the fastest and most spectacularly changing times, in contrast with the long-gone, 'historic' days: the present (complemented with our anxiety about its implications to the future) can appear to be more significant and eventful than the, (normally...) unchangeable past. Our perception of the time-factor is influenced by history books, too: they shorten the flow of events; select what the authors consider important, while omitting other incidents. The past thus being shortened for our perception, we expect the present time to flow equally fast, and hence is our impatience and anticipation concerning our current period. Also, it might well be that these days we (or at least, a great number of people) simply get more information on current happenings in the whole world than ever before. Could it be possible that some people overestimate the significance of the recent changes influenced by personal involvement or / and pressurized by the media? *Whose* information society are we discussing about?

Nevertheless, information, knowledge, technology and society get their meanings only in terms of space and time, and hence are very important objects for both a social geographical enquiry and regional development policy to consider. Therefore, I am inclined to agree much with the cultural interpretation of the I.S. and propose that soft variables should also be considered when assessing causality regarding the rate of and spatial inequalities in, the development of the I.S. Having established this, the following section picks up the thread of theoretical argumentation started in 1.1 to proceed by discussing some spatial manifestations of the conceptual fundamentals, and their concerns for regional policy in the current information era.

2.3 Knowledge & technology in social-economic geography

2.3.1 Time-space and technology

The sense of a shrinking world has intensified and become more pervasive in the past 150 years with industrialisation, the development of transportation and ICTs at least, in the industrialised regions. This 'shrinking' is connected to three main processes. One is the conquest of the 'friction of distance' or the feeling that "places are 'moving towards one another'" (Allen and Hamnett, 1995:17), i.e. *time-space convergence*. Another phenomenon is the way formerly isolated places getting in contact with each other (*time-space distanciation*; Giddens, 1990). Finally, and as a result of these two, we can experience the acceleration of the pace of life (*time-space compression*), "so ... that the world sometimes seems to collapse inwards upon us" (Harvey, 1989:240).

Yet, these are not simply an outcome of the new technologies: it would mean taking up the stance of technological determinism, "ignoring the social processes in which technology is embedded" (Stein, 2001). Neither can it be claimed that compression is taking place evenly, everywhere and for everyone. Therefore, the prediction of some authors concerning the demise or the end of geography (Toffler, 1972 and O'Brien, 1991 respectively) should not be taken seriously.

Besides, having understood the basic 'realities' of ICTs and the main lines of their innovative evolution (see 2.1.4) one should also be aware of the existence of

28

technological *myths.*[25] No doubt, theoretically, digital networks have the capacity of bridging over distances in a very short time (if not instantaneously), and make global economic activities possible from a single location. There is a popular motto saying that ICTs make it possible for people to reach 'anyone – anywhere – anytime'. Based on this, ICTs have been thought of as a kind of panacea to the problems of spatial inequalities, rural depopulation and urban congestion. However, solutions such as distance learning, e-work, and telemedicine/-conferencing can only potentially and partially help to carry out certain functions from great distances.[26]

ICTs are supposed to be time-savers, too, and it is assumed that flexibility in terms of working time and location will give people more free-time, change their daily routines, leisure choices, and the lives of families. Furthermore, ICTs are expected to help equal opportunity, as allegedly, these networks can distribute certain resources evenly. Yet again, these claims are most probably valid in case of certain cultures and social groups only – provided the existence of other important conditions.

It is important to note that, the significance of physical proximity and personal interaction has remained or even has grown along with the ICT developments.[27] This is valid considering all types of social communication: between companies, their employers and employees, teachers and their students, not to mention the field of healthcare, civil associations, clubs, families, and friends (e.g. Storper and Venables, 2004; Wellman et. al., 2002; DiPiro, 2002). The explanation is but a natural one: "human beings and other social animals have a nervous system that links emotion to vocal and facial expressions, as well as other physiological reactions" (C.A.P.), which are important for forming bonds, establishing confidence.

Negative myths have also been common: some fear estrangement from reality, or the homogenisation of culture across the world, and the dilutive impact of the global web on local values and identities. Yet, can we seriously believe that ICTs mean the end of geography? Not, as long as it is human beings using and creating these technologies.

---

[25] The ideas mentioned do not represent the whole set of positive and negative expectations attached to ICTs, and are included here only to indicate the weight of attitudes and convictions in the formation of the technology–society relationship. Naturally, these are not only myths but possible and on-going phenomena; the relevant cause-effect relations however, need to be examined critically.

[26] See e.g. work decentralisation – electronic cottages (Toffler); as well as a critical account on the teleworking utopia by Lyon (1988). Telework has for long been thought to become dominant in certain sectors so much that it would have an influence on settlement patterns (encouraging, for example, counter- or desurbanisation, or solving the problems of over-agglomeration) – yet it has not diffused pervasively but selectively in terms of regions and sectors, and mostly in part-time employment. (McQuaid et. al., 2003.)

[27] Consider these comments, for instance: "Face-to-face is particularly important in environments where information is imperfect, rapidly changing, and not easily codified, key features of many creative activities" (Storper and Venables, 2004:351). "Technology can be effective for transmitting information but cannot directly influence a career as well as personal interaction" (DiPiro, 2002).

To sum up the above, there has to be a distinction made between realities and myths concerning the world-shrinking powers of technology according to the following aspects: *what* technology is used for the communication between *what kinds of people, where* and *for what purposes.* ICTs in certain situations, for a certain period of time are truly distance-bridging technologies and to a given extent, have the capacity to make physical / geographical distance and location irrelevant. Yet, all these factors which are important for considering this problem are defined spatially and culturally: at the end of the day, there is geography.

2.3.2 The many sides of access

It is suggested by the assertions above that information is more than data, and knowledge is more than a collection of information (and both are also non-static as they denote the processes of 'communication' and 'learning' respectively). Also, it is understood from the cultural-spatial arguments on I.S., that although, ICTs bear some peculiarities to the recent processes, *the human factor is of up-most significance.*

A simple economic way to look at this is that people's needs and their matching creativity produces technologies, and ICT applications are delivered and rolled-out following, perceived and real social demand. Consequently, there are some complications: supply of, and demand for ICTs may differ to an extent that some

form of 'digital divide' occurs[28]. Yet to understand this fully, there is a need to define what I mean by demand, by explaining how I understand *access.*

'Access' has been a key word in both developing and benchmarking I.S. As a verb, generally it means the fact of coming to, reach, contact, to have the right to enter; and as a noun, it stands for "a means, place, or way by which a thing may be approached; a passage way to" (Webster's). Accordingly, and placing the term into our context, there are people who *have access* to ICTs, and those who *have not.* Furthermore, there are people who have *better* access to these technologies (or access to 'better' technologies) than some others do. The distinction again, is deeply rooted in the quantitative vs. qualitative approaches to our core concepts (i.e. technology, information, knowledge). Besides, differentiating between these two points bears a considerable significance when thinking further, because the measure and quality of access are leading to other issues such as 'information haves and have-nots', and the different types of digital divides. The meanings of 'access' and 'divides' are as thick as those of information and knowledge or I.S. itself.

For some, access might have a very straightforward connotation with regard to ICTs: the fact of having connection to the

---

[28] The digital divide defined by OECD (2001:5): "the gap between individuals, households, businesses and geographic areas at different socio-economic levels with regard to both their opportunities to access information and communication technologies (ICTs) and to their use of the Internet for a wide variety of activities."

hard infrastructure, Internet (e.g. Z. Karvalics, 2002:74; Farkas, 2002:120 defining "access gaps") at a workplace, school, home, a 'public access point' such as a library, an Internet café, a '*nettikioski*' in North Karelia, or a village telecottage (see Chapter 5); or the instance of owning a valid cellular subscription.

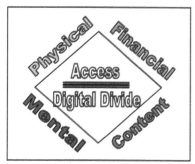

Figure 2. The four interconnected sides of access and the digital divide.

However, quite noticeably, most of these examples are already a combination and coincidence of at least two important occurrences. One is the *potential physical access*; the other is *financial access*. The former is tied more to the supply side, ICT network infrastructure and services provision by telecommunications companies. The latter is related to the income level of potential users and subscribers (i.e. solvent demand in economic terminology). These two are in an intricate relationship. In a free market, private investment into infrastructure and services obviously follow solvent demand. More service providers appear in regions where there is higher demand detected or assumed. More competition push prices down, which may encourage demand

further. Yet, potential physical access does not necessarily lead to new users, while an insufficient level of solvent demand observed or assumed in a region results in the unwillingness on the part of the ICT investor to supply the physical network and services there. The fact that ICTs are developing, and indeed, very fast, complicates this level of access further (e.g. bandwidth makes a difference in the quality of service).

Furthermore, one may distinguish *mental access* as an important step up towards taking a fuller advantage of ICTs as users. Its significance is frequently emphasized: digital literacy, ICT skills, general educational levels and occupational orientation, age, openness, culturally pre-determined attitudes, etc. contribute to how well an individual can 'access' – find, and especially, select, as well as extract, process, use, transmit, etc. – information in a conscious attempt to 'understand', to learn and teach; and ultimately, to improve his or her (or their community's) quality of life. As deficiencies in the skills, abilities, knowledge and attitudes often (but not always!) coincide spatially with lower income levels (and consequently, poor financial accessibility of ICTs), problems may accumulate in certain peripheral regions within and beyond the level of, countries.

Finally, when talking about the usefulness, the real advantages gained from, and the positive impacts of using ICTs, it is necessary to consider the issue of content (Szakadát, 2001). Access to content is the stage where the real worth or utility of exploiting ICTs is realised, where the actual difference (relevant information / knowledge?) they make to our lives may manifest. The availability of rich, relevant and diverse content that consists of reliable, safe, appropriate, user-friendly, interactive, etc. services is one of the most important motivating factors for the potential users of Internet (who may or may not have all the means of physical, financial, and mental access). This side of 'access' again, is very much interconnected with the others. Certain quality or level of technology (physical access) is a prerequisite for some types of content (e.g. higher bandwidths for multimedia, video-conferencing, etc.). Mental access has relevance here, too, as a skilled and motivated user has the potential to shape, to contribute to the content: e.g. to create locally-regionally relevant websites, use the Internet for marketing, paying tax, open forums, or initiate the formation of virtual societies.[29]

Also, the wider the network gets (i.e. the higher the number of people, organisations linked to it) and the richer the content becomes, the greater the necessity and the motivation will be for the non-users to connect; an example for the phenomenon generally referred to as positive network externality, or network effect[30]. Considering the regional development potentials of I.S. developments, this highest level of access, i.e. to content, has probably the most direct consequence to the well-being and sustainable growth of local economies and communities, and also, to the competitiveness and efficiency of national economies.[31]

These four dimensions of access being so much interdependent, *measuring* their levels can be a tricky problem. Physical and financial accesses are relatively easy to gauge by means of indicators of living standard, economic development and the availability and price of network technologies and services (e.g. because about these, quantified information is easier to find); yet even these can present some controversy (see some examples in 3.3.2).

The mental / educational factors and access to content are more difficult to lay hands on. For instance, benchmarking

---

[29] See the variables in Appendix 4: each variable fits more or less into some of these components of 'access'.

[30] The network effect was described by Robert Metcalfe, the founder of Ethernet. A telephone network is a simple example: a single phone is of no use, while with every new phone added to the network, the number of possible connections increases, and it does so exponentially. The larger the telephone network grows, the more valuable it becomes. The same situation occurs with software matching certain operation systems or certain hardware (PCs): the more successful network may eventually dominate the market. See also 2.3.3 below.

[31] Certainly, the above categorisation is not revolutionary or exclusive; it is very much existent in critical thinking. Many authors discuss the same issue using just slightly different terminologies. For instance, Groot and Sharifi (1994) differentiate between accessibility (meaning physical presence of infrastructure), affordability (covering the economic/financial conditions) and availability (relating partly to the feature of content). Viherä (1999) argues that three main factors -- access, competence/skills and motivation – explain the differences in communication capabilities of people, as well as the existence of digital divides. 'Access' in her terminology mean both the physical and financial components, 'competence' is a narrower definition of the 'mental access' I use, and 'motivation' ("the utility gained from communication" – Eskelinen et al., 2003) may include elements of content, the user's culture and financial considerations.

the development of e-government; i.e. on-line public services for citizens and businesses, is a very complex task. These services need to be examined along two main lines: their existence (quantity) and their sophistication (quality). Figure 3 shows a survey framework on on-line availability and sophistication, which was used in a benchmarking exercise ordered by the European Commission.

Furthermore, the actual usage of these services, the real traffic and the feedback by the clients, etc. should be included as well to get a full picture of the development of 'e-government.' Adequate *legislation* to facilitate and secure for instance, on-line transactions and telework are also crucial component of what I

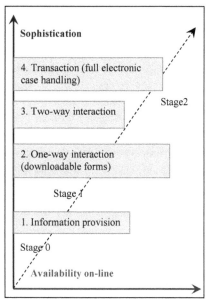

(Based on: Capgemini, 2006: 5: Figure 1; enhanced)

Figure 3. A possible framework for bench-marking e-government

consider access to content. All these aspects require much qualitative research.

As a final point, the different 'sides' of access may be distinguished according to the semantic steps along the line of data–information–knowledge, or in view of the different interpretations of the 'technology' concept. The way they mutually influence and build upon each other can be understood in terms of the various approaches to the I.S.

2.3.3 Networks of people and technology

The important role of communication and cognitive exchanges between the individual and the collective minds were mentioned in the conceptualisation of information and knowledge. *Social networks* provide a significant medium for these interactions. 'Networking' seems to be an inherent feature of ICTs. So the integration of these two (the social and the information and communication technological networks) – become rather straightforward considering also that technology may be defined as creative technique, productive knowledge, and cultural force.

A number of contemporary social theories explore networks, and some of them also relate to technologies and even more concretely, to ICTs. First of all, one should consider some arguments in *Actor-Network Theory* (ANT), which itself, has emerged from science studies[32], and incorporates

[32] ANT was developed in the 1980s by Bruno Latour and Michel Callon, members of the Paris group of Science and Technology Studies, which

33

non-human network elements. In short, an actor-network is a heterogeneous and extremely relational structure of aligned interests, where:

1   the actors' (individuals or groups of people) ability to get others into action and to enrol allies by convincing them to share their visions and goals comprises the power operating (in) the network; these various persuasive courses in fact, create the network.

2   These processes, positions and actions are also controlled, influenced and strengthened by other, also non-human constituents, which are assumed to have some agency capacity as well: material things, mechanical devices, elements of nature, codes, documents, images, and inscribed programs of actions (i.e. the so-called non-human 'actants'[33] in the network);

3   The discourses and representations give purpose, identity and position to

everything and everyone in the network (Ryder, 2004; and Thompson, 2003).

Also, the act of 'networking' and the notion of social capital are inseparable. Since its first definition by sociologist Pierre Bourdieu in the early 1980s (1983/86), most scholars discussing it have agreed that social capital is "capital captured through social relations", and partly re-invested into social interactions and networking to produce profits" (Lin, 2001: 19), It is composed of "those characteristics of social structure or social relations that facilitate collaborative action and, as a result, enhance economic performance" (Johnston et al., 2000: 746; referring to Putnam, 1993). The ways social capital achieves this are: 1) the facilitation of the flow of otherwise not available, but useful information; 2) the influence of social ties on critical decision-making agents; 3) offering "certifications of the individual's social credentials" (his or her social capital, networks); and 4) the reinforcement of identity and recognition, i.e. a sense of belonging and emotional support, as well as public acknowledgement from shared interests (Lin, 2001: 20; italics in original text). Social capital therefore, is both a rich mixture of relational assets such as trust, norms of reciprocity, mutual tolerance, and civic engagement, and the source of producing these resources.[34]

---

explores the ways social, political, and cultural values shape technological innovation and scientific research, as well as how science and technology influence society, politics, and culture (Latour, 1987; Johnston et al, 2000). Originally emerging as a tool for analysing the social nature of scientific experimentation and technological knowledge, ANT spread to cover various other areas: the nature of space, place and time; representational processes; the forms of market exchange; management practices and strategies, the mechanisms and forces of political power; etc. (Thompson, 2003).

[33] Actants can be human actors and non-human elements, but only actors can put actants in circulation in the system (Ryder, 2004). According to ANT, actants are mobile in a sense that they are rearranged, reconfigured through the network of places and agencies, via the process of 'translation' (Thompson, 2003: 72-73).

---

[34] See the national examples below (Chapter 4) about the general significance of social and political trust in the democratisation of society, and how it has been influenced (boosted and eroded) by recent developments in Finland and Hungary. The growing realisation of its crucial role in sustaining both democracy and economic growth, is evident from the immense literature that has emerged since the mid-nineties discussing social and political trust in the

These features of social organisation are also the prerequisites for communication and good networking, while they (i.e. the stock of social capital) are (re)produced through the same networking practices. In their 'governance-approach' to regional policies, a group of Nordic scholars applied the *Social Capital Theory* (especially Bourdieu's more spatially relevant approach). They prove in their case studies that utilisation and reproduction of social capital in socio-spatial practices are central to the 'coping strategies' of small communities and peripheral regions (see books and studies by Bærenholdt and Aarsæther 2001, 2002). On the one hand, the locally internal networks represent and enhance '*bonding*' (Bourdieu: 'social field' of insiders): strengthen shared identity; yet also, can give rise to exclusivity, narrow-mindedness, hostility for 'the other'. There are territorial and mobile forms of bonding: placed-bound communities are examples for the former, virtual communities and international NGOs represent the latter. On the other hand, *bridging* practices are usually combinations of territoriality and mobility. External linkages create bridges between the different social fields: a reach to new resources or markets; opportunities to receive information, fresh ideas, and to encounter different techniques and culture; and possibilities for diversification and co-operation. Yet they can open up a

community more, to external threats, too, and so increase its vulnerability.

Not surprisingly, ICTs have great potentials for the networking dimension of local/regional coping strategies. These technologies have the capacity to make ways of communication easier, cheaper, faster, more diverse and flexible – which attributes are increasingly important for remote and relatively sparsely populated areas. A group of Canadian researchers published much evidence for the impact of Internet[35] on social capital: it proved supplementary in terms of social network contact, and it seemed to increase organisational and political 'participatory capital' (Wellman et. al., 2001 and 2002). Although Internet does not necessarily affect the general sense of community (territorial bonding), it at least, supports new forms of belonging, such as on-line (virtual) communities (mobile bonding). ICTs may be a special tool to form and present to the outside world an image of the place or a product (on-line 'marketing'), as well as it can facilitate the reproduction of social capital through 'mobility' and 'autonomy' of human beings, things and information (territorial and mobile bridging).

Finally, there is an interesting connection between bridging and bonding as regards ICTs and communities. Wellman and his colleagues claim that the use of Internet does not seem to cause feelings of alienation from the community, but it can

---

disciplines of sociology, anthropology, political science and theory, economics, psychology, history, philosophy, management and organisation studies. (See for instance, Delhey and Newton, 2003 for a concise summary of theories about social trust).

---

[35] Barry Wellman and his colleagues at the University of Toronto carried out a survey among North Americans in 2000 to explore the effect of Internet on the accumulation and reproduction of social capital.

indirectly strengthen a sense of common identity by encouraging participation of social actors, and improving associational synergy and integrity of organisations (i.e. bonding) within. This aspect is especially crucial when fending off sudden external threats, when emergency decisions have to be made, and it is also important to the efficiency of representing common interests. In short, "social networks in cyberspace" complement, and interact with (i.e. build on, and extend the reach of) 'traditional' social networks; and offer social capital that may transcend time and space (Lin, 2001:212).

Social networks are ever-changing configurations of governing power. They tend to be more horizontal than vertical, they are usually non-hierarchical and decentralised, at least as opposed to 'ordinary' government structures. They are also unstable and difficult-to-pin-down because they are relational: the flows in the network continuously alter the relations between the members, who may also disconnect or reconnect almost at any time. The civil sector or civil society is one major arena where self-organised networks are essential[36] and are based on mutual and transactional trust among members: its strength is inclusiveness, fast adaptation and reconfiguration; its weaknesses are

instability, unaccountability and unreliability.

Through their positive network externalities (defined above in 2.3.2), beyond a certain mass of users, the networks facilitated by ICTs increase in values not only in economic but in social terms. Certainly, it is easy to presume the amalgamation of social and ICT networks just by imagining human beings (social actors, organisations) at terminals, hubs and nodes. Social actors improve and extend the technological net according to their needs and add their human network(s) to it, while the ICTs reinforce and broaden the social web. The result is a nearly organic system of man and technology with rich flows of information, ideas and knowledge along the connections. At least, in theory: because though undoubtedly, social and technological networks co-exist, their inclusiveness, complementariness and co-functioning also depends very much on the completeness of 'access' (in its intricate meaning discussed above) across society and space, which gives rise to further questions.

2.3.4 Geographical digital divides[37]

It is often revealed that global changes have led to higher risks of

---

[36] However, in some Post-Socialist countries, it has been observed that not all kinds of networking strengthen the role of civil organisations. The very autonomy of civil society (i.e. its confidence in its own power towards the political society, and its ability to cooperate with the political society) can be corrupted by embedded elitism which is tightly linked to the tradition of drawing on *informal networks* by individuals, instead of using institutions in pursuit of interests (see more on this below in 4.3.1 and Korkut, 2005).

[37] Some arguments in this section have been drawn from the theoretical introduction of my study titled Social Capital and ICTs in Local Development: The Case of the Hungarian Telecottage Movement, published in Marginality in the 21st Century: Theory, Methodology and Contemporary Challenges (eds. Jones, Leimgruber and Nel, 2006).

exclusion, or at least increased disadvantages for those fragments of society and places / regions / countries which for some reason or other have been switched off from the network (e.g. Castells, 1996/2000). Inequalities and competition in terms of 'information economy and society' occur on different regional levels. The global network of flows (of information, knowledge, innovation, wealth and power) have different densities in space because some nodes and prominent hubs are more able to facilitate links and can utilise the flows more than other places / economies according to their better features of access (in its full meaning).

In the course of many positive feedback mechanisms, the digital divides can be widening between the developed and developing parts of the world, the rural and the urban, as well as between privileged and deprived groups within societies, accumulating on already existing disparities in wealth, political power, innovation capacity, education, etc. In the new economy, connectivity and inclusion mean adaptability and advantages, while disconnectedness and exclusion result in vulnerability and deprivation. Parts of the hinterlands of major network nodes of 'informational development' may stay isolated and peripheral despite their geographical proximity to centres of dynamics due to having no (socio-economically and not just infrastructure-wise) functioning network-links with those centres. The assumption that advantages 'trickle down' to the poor and the peripheral can only be justified to a limited extent (Wyatt et al. 2000).

As a consequence of a neo-liberal global market, some metropolises are bound to grow in size and in their relative importance as hubs of the networked world economy. On the other hand, there are regions on all possible territorial scale from neighbourhoods to major parts of continents, where neither the basic physical infrastructure nor the human resources are close to being sufficient for integration into the global flows of information, innovation and wealth – pushing them further back in development relative to the rest of the world.

2.3.5 Scales and actors

Since spatial and social inequalities had become widely prominent, academic and political attention started to be more concerned with the idea of a socially and environmentally sustainable and 'fair' I.S. The problem in economic (and regional) development policy, although it has recently been posed in a globalising context, has not changed much since the mid-twentieth century: to what extent and by what means need market processes be controlled, regulated, interfered with?[38]   Different

---

[38] Consider, for instance the polarised theories by two influential economists of the 20th century, John M. Keynes and Milton Friedman on free market and public intervention. Based on the experience of the Great Depression in the 1930s, Keynes could not trust market forces left alone, while Friedman argued that governments should have limited rights to interfere. Though neither ideological strand has been completely justified or excluded since, there have been certain phases of economic development when one or the other was given more legitimacy by policies. For instance, the recent globalisation of markets has given more momentum to this

regions and places can be characterised with specific combinations of relatively mobile and more immobile and place-bound development factors, or assets.

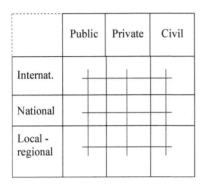

	Public	Private	Civil
Internat.			
National			
Local - regional			

Figure 4. Geographical scales and actors.

From among those which are especially connected to ICT- and knowledge-based developments, investment in the physical and technological infrastructure represent the former type, while the latter include the spatially (historically, culturally) embedded features, such as social capital. My assumption is that these two categories, even if not in a clear-cut way, can provide some guideline to define responsibilities of development policies on different spatial (administrative) levels concerning ICTs.

Besides the entire vertical of political-administrative levels, public, private and civil actors on each scale have their special interests and roles in developing ICTs, information flows and capacities in knowledge production. I

assume that their cooperation is especially vital for the functionality of networks and for the efficient operation of the decision-making vertical.

One of the central issues investigated in this dissertation is the possible cooperation and the division of work between these levels and actors for the enhancement of access and a spatially balanced development of the I.S. Therefore, when looking at the examples chosen to represent each geographical scale, the linkages defined in Figure 4 above are important aspects for analysis.

2.4 Summary and the elaboration of hypotheses

The introduction starts with the general and more abstract enquiry:

"How can the benefits of information and communication technologies (ICTs) and the so-called, 'information society' (I.S.) be extended to rural-peripheral regions and communities?"

This matter is elaborated further, divided into four concrete research questions focussed more on the actual case studies:

RQ 1:   What are the factors behind the differentiation in access, the emergence of digital divides concerning the rural peripheries of developed countries?

RQ 2:   What are the suitable points of intervention to help resolve digital divides? What are the different actors' roles and responsibilities at a) the international or

---

debate which in part, has led to questioning nation-state competence and a call for stronger sub- and supranational entities.

38

European, b) the national and c) the regional/local levels in order to achieve a spatially more inclusive I.S.?

RQ 3: Is the diffusion of ICTs or the emergence of an I.S. making horizontal interactions and flows more powerful, and thus administration and decision making more transparent and democratic?

RQ 4: What can Hungary learn from the achievements of the "Finnish model"?

The four RQs however, work with the complex ideas, the so-called analytical tools of access and network, and the concepts of geographical scales and actors, using them in the context of rural-peripheral areas.

Therefore, the aims of the theoretical explanations above were:

• to define the fundamental notions behind these concepts (knowledge, information, technologies);
• to show how the different conceptualisations of the I.S. use these fundamental notions; and
• to clarify the meanings of the analytical tools, which provide the linkages between the abstract, theoretical and the particular, empirical investigations about the development of I.S. in this book.

A brief summary of the results of these investigations – also indicating the directions towards answering the general theoretical question – is attempted below.

Information and *knowledge* have always been regarded as critical assets *and* processes in society, and their meanings have always been contested and, confused.

Yet along with the emergence of the new *technologies* to process, collect and very flexibly, cheaply and efficiently, distribute them, they have become more influential to socio-economic development or at least, their impact have become more conspicuous. Yet, the new technological hype has not helped much to clarify the meanings and the import of these two concepts. On the contrary, it mystifies them further, either equating them with each other and with the technologies themselves, or elevating them to a level beyond all other social and human factors. Nevertheless, the fact that these concepts have drawn so much attention and discussion indicates that there is something intriguing about them, and their relationships with each other.

No matter whether taking a technocratic or a cultural-humanistic perspective to the issue, developments related to the I.S. in general are inevitably divergent in society and across geographical space because all the factors behind '*access*' are unevenly available or given.

Furthermore, the development and utilisation of ICTs are expected to be not merely about regions and countries trying to keep pace and prevent the digital divides from widening further (i.e. about 'not being a looser'), but can be seen as a means to positively stick out and take over in the regional competition. This has to be recognised by *governments and other actors on different scales*, whose interest on the one hand, is to build competitive information- and knowledge based economies and societies, and on the other hand, face the fact of persistent inequalities.

Concerning both targets – efficiency and equality – *the necessity arises to measure* developments in order to understand, direct, react to, and monitor processes. Keywords are (e.g., the flow of) *information*, the (speed and diffusion of) *technological development*, and (the production and ownership of) *knowledge*, yet the selection of their units of measurement poses serious difficulties. The (at least) *four dimensions of 'access'* in the context of the I.S., require a more qualitative and differential-relational approach to the problem of *digital divides*.

Finally, *networks*, communication, and the reliance on ICTs are of significance on the one hand, to the whole I.S. concept in general, and on the other hand, in particular, to the joint (net)work of different social and other actors in shaping strategies, learning from each other, carrying out development projects (which in turn, may themselves aim at developing some aspects of I.S. in underserved regions, marginalised communities and social groups, etc.). Consequently, there must be a great variety and number of stake-holders, actors, drivers and interests in developing the I.S. on many spatial scales and political levels.

Territoriality – or geography – matters in the emerging I.S. so long as most of the factors that are attributive to the quality of access (to information, knowledge, ideas, welfare, services, etc.) are deeply embedded in culture and are therefore, place-bound. And they definitely, are.

Figure 5 indicates the relative measures of relevance of the key concepts (access, networks, scales and actors) to the individual research questions.

	Access	Scales & actors	Networks
1) Factors behind access and divides	O	∘	∘
2) Division of responsibilities	O	O	∘
3) I.S./ICTs and horizontal networking	∘	O	O
4) Learning from practices – Fin. and Hun.	O	O	O

Figure 5. The relationships between the main research questions and the key concepts.

2.5 Research design and methodology

The design of this research may be described either with a focus on its *outcome* (Figure 6), or with a consideration of the *process* itself (Figure 7).

In line with the above perspectives, and in order to answer the RQs, my research has evolved into a special *multiple-case study design*, where developments, institutions and practices *on different geographical scales* represent the units of analysis. As it is indicated in Figure 6, the material can be distributed into bigger and smaller 'boxes' ranked along these spatial (and political-administrative) scales, the former ones containing, and serving as contexts to, the latter.

40

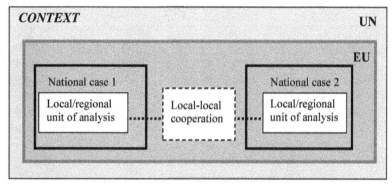

(Source: modified after K. Yin, 2003:40)

Figure 6. Case study design: "embedded multiple units of analysis"

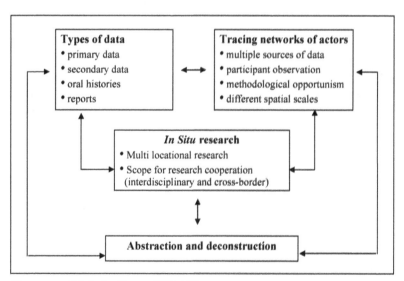

(Source: modified after Yeung, 2003:454)

Figure 7. Process-based methodological framework.

Following a discussion of international approaches to the I.S. phenomenon (the guidelines set by the United Nations and the European Union, in Chapter 3), I introduce two national case studies in Chapter 4: the visions, strategies, institutions and policies in Finland and Hungary, and the actual national developments concerning their advance towards or in, the information society. Finland and Hungary have reached different levels in I.S. development along in some way, dissimilar paths, which has an impact on their presentation in this work: the Finnish case is portrayed mainly *through its institutional framework* (the national innovation system), while the developments in Hungary are shown more in *a sequential manner*, showing the different phases of political recognition and commitment to the I.S. project.

In Chapter 5, the national studies are followed by accounts of regional-local 'bottom-up' initiatives to improve the spatial equality of access in both countries, seeking possible points of connection within their respective national and international agendas. This latter aspect is especially relevant to the last section of this chapter (5.4) where the planning of a joint project by local activists in Hungary and Finland is described and analysed.

There are some aspects of my work which are difficult to present by means of this relatively simple and static model, however. As the example of the Finnish-Hungarian co-operative efforts indicates, local-regional I.S.-innovations can have direct linkages to European programmes and networks and local actors have the opportunity to work together even across national borders. Also, the relevant forums of the United Nations, the European Union, the states of Hungary and Finland, and the examined regions and communities within can be seen in several respects as partners and actors in a more horizontal way, complementing each other in competence.

Besides, the five-six years of research to 'track down' such an evolving phenomenon as the I.S. is, involved much going back and forth between the different scales, cases and projects; it was a gradual and non-linear process. Preliminary results inevitably led me to shift my focus to different scales and to take up new perspectives, approaches, methods, and even, to formulate some new questions.

Therefore, as indicated in Figure 7, a *process-based methodological framework* describes the research done for this dissertation better: it shows the dynamic relationships between concrete sources, methods, and the positions taken up by the researcher.

Due to the epistemological shift (i.e. from a more positivist and quantitative to a rather subjective and qualitative approach), the style of my writing and the method of presenting my research results also vary: towards the end of the dissertation, there are more boxes of descriptive or narrative text, as well as more photos inserted in the dissertation.

Regarding the diversity of the units of analysis, a multitude of different sources and methods were necessary. *Political manifestos, visions* and *strategies* were as important as statistics and rankings were; and were sources of information especially

42

in the research presented in Chapters 3 and 4 (i.e. the international and the national studies). *Numerical facts* related to ICT-supply and -usage, published by companies and other organisations are plentiful especially on the national spatial level. Nevertheless, the speed of technological change, and the confidentiality of information about ICT take-up make it difficult to maintain standardised methods of data collection and analysis across the many geographical scales of investigation. Figures (maps) and tables of ranking are inserted in this work primarily to describe some of the recent tendencies, general digital divides, and the relative positions of the examined regions and countries. They are presented also for the purpose of underlining the ambiguities and problems that occur in measurement and quantification, faced by policy-makers themselves.

Questionnaire-based surveys, personal interviews (much supported by the ICTs themselves), were employed especially in the local-regional case studies (Chapter 5), i.e. researching bottom-up initiatives and projects. These were useful to make up for missing information from written publications, as well as to find more actors involved. They were used also for the purpose of triangulation with findings from other sources and in the (inter)national case studies (e.g. the small survey of European telecom decision-makers). *Local narratives*

were relied on to find evidence of more delicate networks; and to understand the influence exerted by higher levels of coordination, regulation and intervention into different aspects of the I.S.-developments. Learning *in situ* about specific practicalities, the limitations and opportunities in project development was also crucial: personal observation and some *action research* (for the last section of Chapter 5) helped better understand the human factors underlying the developments, and the functioning of socio-technological networks.

The process-based framework also indicates a continual abstraction-deconstruction of meaning and evidence; the outcome of which is the formation of the final conclusions.

So, the following three chapters present the empirical work done within this multi-scalar and process-based framework: the description of the international concerns and processes (Chapter 3); then, the presentation of the national developments in Finland and Hungary (4); following this, a report on regional and local strategies and projects, particularly in the rural peripheries of these two countries, concluded with a special personal account on the joint plans and efforts of two (Hungarian and Finnish) groups of local innovators for ICT-tooled community development (Chapter 5).

3 BEYOND NATIONS: TEN YEARS OF PROMOTING AN 'I.S. FOR ALL'

3.1 Introduction: approaches and methods

Given its complexity, and the multitude of definitions and stakeholders in the subject, a wide range of methods can be implemented researching the I.S. In this chapter, I present three lines of study that use different sources and techniques, yet which are linked together in order to answer:

a) What shifts in objectives can be recognised in the international and especially, the European guidelines to promote the development of an inclusive I.S., particularly in terms of access and digital divides?

b) When and in what forms did the local and regional dimension enter the global and European perceptions of the I.S.?

c) What functions have these international organisations, and especially, the EU, taken up in developing the I.S.? What is the best way to define their roles?

A major digital divide has existed on the global scale between the developed and the developing world which urged the United Nations to initiate a global forum for the I.S.: the World Summit of the Information Society has included a wide assortment of participants, not only the leaders of transnational ICT businesses and national governments, but representatives of sub-national regions and civil groups, too. I start with a brief account on the emergence, the limitations, and especially, the importance of this forum on the international level. Following this, I give a more detailed description of the development of the I.S. debate within the European integration reflecting both its competitiveness and the equality goals, and the available tools for the EU to exert its influence on its Members in this domain. So this first section is a presentation of conflicting interests, the changes in perspective, focus and political rhetoric, and an analytical account of the most influential forums, institutions, decisions and strategic papers, especially from the last ten years, and with particular concern to the spatial diversities and the territorial inclusiveness of the I.S.

Next, I employ a spatially descriptive-statistical method relying mainly on secondary data collected between 2000-2004 on the divergent *national* developments in terms of many variables that can be closely or loosely related to the diffusion of ICTs, as well as to the more broadly defined I.S. Without any intention to be comprehensive in the selection of maps presented, I highlight some advantages and limitations of this approach, which in fact, is customary in the exploratory material backing up political documents and decisions.

The final part of this chapter in a way connects the European to the national, and the sub-national: it reports on the purpose, the circumstances and the results of a survey turning attention directly to policy-makers and telecom regulators in different individual European states. It is an attempt to analyse the differences and commonalities in their opinions and actions regarding the *subnational* territorial inequalities in the diffusion of ICTs, and to contrast the findings to overall national performances in I.S. developments, as well as with the prospect of integrating national I.S. policy frameworks on the European level.

The foci of the different studies are nevertheless, related; they are complementary: some common conclusions are provided at the end of this chapter with regards to access, networks and actors, and answering the three questions above.

3.2 The global context: the UN World Summit of the Information Society

There have been two distinct strands of discussion concerning ICTs and the socio-economic developments in the 'information age' which had led to the *World Summit of the Information Society in Geneva* (WSIS, 2003), a UN forum under the co-ordination of the ITU[39]. One is focussed on the technological infrastructures[40], the other includes a much broader set of issues such as the ownership and use of knowledge, media and communication. The origins of the former may be traced back to the 1970s while the latter started in the early eighties.

Ó Siochrú, spokesman of the CRIS Campaign[41] argues in a critical article that despite the fact that much of the academic debate already handled the ICTs as tools, and not as determinants of social change, "means and ends were getting confused" in the field of policy from the 1980s onwards: the "corporate-driven modernist notion that technological innovation would solve social problems took hold in the sector" (2004:3). Certainly, the global urge to privatise and liberalise the telecommunications sector has found good justification in this approach. Yet ultimately, it has subjected technological development to profit-making "irrespective of the impact on social development and inequities" (*ibid.*) Global disparities in access nonetheless, had become obvious by the mid-nineties, and so for instance, the term 'digital divide'[42] was coined. The political paradigm was still not changed; instead, further liberalisation was assumed to bring the cure eventually.

The other strand of debate leading to Geneva was more concerned with communication (and its subjects and objects, its regulation, its freedom, etc.), as well as in its special stress on human rights – which, embedded in the context of global geopolitical tensions, triggered this movement on the international level in the first place. In the years around the turn of the 1970/80s, the widespread debate among governments

---

[39] The International Telecommunication Union is an organization within the UN where governments and the private sector coordinate global telecommu-nications networks and services. Its headquarters are in Geneva, Switzerland.

[40] See the description of esp. the technological and economic lines of thinking on I.S. in 2.2.2.

[41] CRIS: Communication Rights in the Information Society. CRIS is a civil movement with the purpose to help communication about the WSIS among civil society entities and "to ensure that communication rights are fully incorporated into the WSIS process, agenda and output." (www.crisinfo.org)

[42] See also 2.3.2 and 2.3.4.

concerning media and communication exhibited an unprecedented diversity of opinion, partly due to the rising voice of less developed countries in the UN, and their concerns about cultural and media imperialism (NWICO)[43]. This communication-strand recognises that information and communication have an important role not only in terms of the economy, but also culture and politics[44]; i.e. in society in general. Therefore its focus is not the tools, but the circumstances of their application, their owners and users, and *the content* communicated through them.

Unsurprisingly, these cultural issues had to be put off the agenda due to pressure by private media industries and powerful lobbies. Nevertheless, some journalists' organisations and the academia kept the discussion up (the *MacBride Round Table*, 1989-1999), drawing civil society actors into it (e.g. CRIS). Besides, a great number of other NGOs started to raise

---

[43] '*The New World Information and Communication Order*' constituted a forum about media representations of the developing world. Its central element was the a report by the 'MacBride Commission' (*Many Voices One World*, 1980) which analysed problems related to mass media and news, and suggested a new communication order to enhance peace and human development (Brown-Syed, 1993; Padovani and Nordenstreng, 2005).

[44] This strand in political thinking is closer to the cultural conceptualisations of the information age (2.2.2), and embraces issues which are often stressed as the difference between the meanings of the 'information' and the 'knowledge(-based) societies', for instance. 'Communication society' or 'interactive society' (e.g. Farkas, 2002:25, 137) is probably the most recent response to the technocratic rhetoric, emphasizing even more the importance of the human agent, and the dynamics inherent to the whole problem.

further questions concerning internet surveillance, the concentration of media ownership, commercial censorship, and so on. (Ó Siochrú, 2004)

At last, the Geneva WSIS in 2003 provided an opportunity for the convergence of these two perspectives, and room for interaction between a diverse set of civil actors and those organisations and governments who were drawn to the meeting by the technological interests in the I.S. In planning the WSIS event, the ITU still adopted the old ideologically-driven claims, i.e. the concept of an I.S. utopia based merely on the extension of ICT infrastructure, regarding the latter as the core issue of information and knowledge dissemination. However, provoked by this the civil society used the event to point out the faults in this way of thinking and policy making. The WSIS in Geneva therefore was forced to deal with a broad set of issues, and to depart, at least in its *Declaration of Principles*, from the mainly technocratic approach (see Box 1).

The recognition of the need to respect spatial diversity and to deal with inequalities on various scales is indicated also in the WSIS *Plan of Action*, which delegated certain tasks to be done by 2005 (the Tunis Summit) by designated actors from different sectors and various administrative-political levels. National governments were asked to create *showcase examples of public-private or multi-sector partnership* and to draft their *national e-strategies*. They were also advised to be early adopters themselves as *model users of ICTs* in their own administration and practices. International organisations and financing institutions were called on to develop their own strategies, and to report

- The establishment of ICT public access points;
- different (free, open source, proprietary) software models to ensure affordable access to everyone;
- assistive technologies to access public domain information;
- the promotion of awareness and literacy in ICTs;
- integrating social groups with special needs into the I.S.;
- capacity building to ensure a sustainable I.S.;
- a "global culture of cyber-security";
- "supportive, transparent, pro-competitive, technologically neutral and predictable policy and regulatory framework reflecting national realities" for a "people-centred I.S.";
- government intervention to correct market failures in underserved rural-peripheral areas;
- efficiency gains for SMEs (small and medium sized enterprises) via the deployment of ICTs;
- the protection of intellectual property and the dissemination of knowledge to encourage creativity and innovation;
- the adoption of "open, inter-operable, non-discriminatory and demand-driven" international standards in ICTs;
- a multilateral and democratic management of Internet, as a global and multilingual facility;
- the responsibility of local authorities in providing applications that are user-friendly and adapted to local needs;
- local/regional digital content representing and promoting cultural diversity and heritage;
- the independence and pluralism of the media;
- raising a 'Digital Solidarity Fund'.

Box 1. Major issues in the Declaration at the WSIS in Geneva (WSIS/D, 2003).

their experiences of *mainstreaming ICTs*. The UN Secretary-General was asked to establish a special working group on *Internet Governance* for "an open and inclusive process that ensures a mechanism for the full and active participation of governments, the private sector and civil society" (WSIS/P.A., 2003:6). Also, the *Digital Solidarity Agenda* was put forward: a call for mobilising resources in the developed world and the private sector, in order to give the poor countries the necessary technical and financial assistance for capacity building, technology transfer, and their cooperation in R&D, etc. Finally, the need was emphasized for international cooperation in research to define benchmarking indicators to measure the magnitude of the digital divide, and to construct and launch a *"composite ICT Development (Digital Opportunity) Index"* which would facilitate the monitoring of international progress in terms of the implementation of the key principles and actions of the WSIS (WSIS/P.A., 2003:13).[45]

There is much criticism about the WSIS failing in terms of concrete suggestions for viable solutions, in terms of clear formal commitments (Ó Siochrú, 2004), and that its documents paint "a wholly utopian picture of an 'Information Society' that grossly oversimplifies and generalizes a complex issue", because their vision was "technologically deterministic" as they 'fetishized' ICTs by using, for instance, the *e*-prefix as often as possible (Pyati, 2005)[46].

---

[45] This was carried out by a consortium called the Digital Opportunity Platform, who formulated the Digital Opportunity Index (DOI) to track progress in 180 economies, using data from 2004/2005.

[46] Pyati uses a textual-analytical approach to interpret the *Declaration of Principles* and the

One should however, be wary of exaggerated anticipations. Global summits like the WSIS cannot but result mostly in generalisations, guidelines and key principles, no-one can reasonably expect them to prescribe concrete measures, solutions for problems on every political and regional level, especially considering the complexity of the I.S. debate. The language of these documents is accordingly visionary, metaphoric, relying on emblematic expressions, not necessarily meaning that there is no real content, research and rationale behind the statements.

There are only few issues that can be dealt with in considerable depth on the global level. The situation of the highly indebted poor countries is such, as well as the international management of the Internet. Actions concerning these two were in fact more elaborated by the Summit than others: the subjects of 'digital solidarity' and 'Internet governance' were pushed forward to the next phase in Tunis (WSIS, 2005).

On the other hand, there are some statements in the texts which, above and beyond the evocative style and syntax, more

directly express a positivist attitude concerning social and technological developments; for example, in the introduction of the Plan of Action: "The Information Society is an evolving concept that has reached different levels across the world, reflecting the different stages of development" (2003:1). It is not explained what those levels and stages are; neither are the aspects and units of measurement specified based on which the positions of individual countries should be monitored.

Instead, it is implied that the progress towards a fully developed I.S. is a certain and single process, during which ICTs are adopted by a society to an ever growing extent. Still, just three points below, a perspective is articulated which indeed, differentiates between individual states and their social developments: it is proposed that specific targets for the I.S. need to be established "as appropriate, at the national level... taking into account the different national circumstances" in order to facilitate the assessment of progress; i.e. more relative to the given country's position rather than to be compared internationally.

All things considered, the most essential achievement of the WSIS has been the extensive and visible participation of civil organisations and their encounter with public and private actors in the discussions of I.S.-related problems. The WSIS provided space for inter-regional and inter-cultural discussions and the clashing of diverse interests between sectors, international, national and subnational actors. Also, it meant a significant step towards creating a more balanced political debate somewhere halfway between the over-politicised NWICO

Plan of Actions of the Geneva Summit. The author measures the frequency and place of use of certain fundamental terminology, such as *I.S.*, *inclusive*, *people-centred*, *knowledge society*, *ICTs* and *digital opportunity*; and points out that most of these are either not at all or ambiguously defined in these documents; and says this is a sign of oversimplification and technological determinism. However, similar observations may be made concerning most of the international manifestos, about any other sector of the economy or field of social life. Pyati's argument that "language is a powerful conveyer of biases, viewpoints, and values" cannot be acceptable as a reliable ground for such conclusions unless one ignores the context and the purpose of the communication.

movement and the private sector dominated technocratic perspective.

The fact that the produced documents bear some ambiguities and traces of conflicting view-points may well be the outcome of this. Almost certainly, the most interesting discussions, and much of the knowledge-transfer and networking were happening anyway, in the many parallel thematic workshops of the Summit; as well as the meetings, forums and publications that prepared and followed the event. The following lines from a member of one of the 1,740 participant organisations in Tunis[47] indicate the significance of this:

ICTs can only be seen as one of many tools available to promote sustainable human development. (…) Regional and global networks offer opportunities for exchanging information, learning from each other and joint actions at local level. The specific talents of each participating organisation contribute to an overall greater impact than if a single organisation or regional network worked alone. If we really manage to work in synergy with each other, developing a system to manage knowledge, both local and regional projects will benefit immeasurably. (…) Global networks, such as the GKP have the ability to support policy development at local level by sharing knowledge and experiences. Singly we are weak; together we can make an impact. (GKP --

---

[47] At the Tunis WSIS, more than a third of the partaking organisations were NGOs and civil society entities, i.e. over 6,000 people of the total, almost 20,000 participants (WSIS/T. 2005). GKP is Global Knowledge Partnership, defining themselves as "the world's first multi-stakeholder network promoting innovation and advancement in Knowledge for Development (K4D) and Information and Communication Technologies for Development (ICT4D)" (GKP portal).

member K. Delgadillo, Executive President of Fundación ChasquiNet)

3.3 Information Society under EU guidance

3.3.1 From Bangemann to Lisbon and the e-Europe Action Plans

In the course of the 1990s, the idea of the 'information society' was undoubtedly becoming a key consideration in economic political decisions in Europe, as well; both in the individual countries and on the level of integration. The first initiatives for the construction of the physical network infrastructures were made by major technology manufacturers and telecommunications service provider companies. Later, the states having recognised the significant potential for economic development offered by the sector, started the liberalisation of the national ICT markets. Yet, this was carried out in very heterogeneous, country-specific ways (starting at different times, carried on with varying impetus, and accomplished to different degrees.) At the same time, most of the European countries raised their R&D budgets and implemented regulative and subsidising instruments to enhance the readiness and receptiveness of their human resources. In several cases these measures were systematically incorporated in national 'I.S. strategies'.

During the second half of the decade, the European Union, then of 15 Member States, took up I.S.-related regulative and strategy making tasks, too. This was based on the general recognition that information and knowledge-based development is the only way for Europe and its individual states to retain and strengthen their competitiveness as opposed to the USA and the Asian rivals. In this regard, *urgent* action was demanded.

So, on the threshold of the emergence of the world-wide Internet, (and ten years ahead of the launch of the WSIS) in its Brussels meeting of December 1993, the European Council placed an appeal that a report should be prepared by a High-Level Group on the Information Society, made up of twenty international experts and headed by Martin Bangemann, for the Council's meeting on 24-25 June 1994 in Corfu about this problematic issue.

To sum up just the main messages of the *Bangemann Report*, some thoughts are worth to select in connection with what roles and significance were linked to 1) the ICTs, 2) the people, 3) the market and 4) the EU in the up-and-coming Information Age; and what benefits and risks were envisioned. (See also the list of contents of the Bangemann Report in Appendix 1).

Firstly, as to the nature of the *technological revolution*, the Report suggested that it was "a revolutionary tide, sweeping through economic and social life"; it would add "huge new capacities to human intelligence", and would change "the way we work together and the way we live together". This was a rather deterministic way to express the complexity of relationships between technologies and social development, yet there were some indication of a less direct connection in the statement that "(t)he information revolution prompts profound changes in the way we view our societies and also in their organisation and structure." (Bangemann, 1994: Ch. 1)

Secondly, and in my view, more importantly, it was declared that "(t)oday technology is in search of application" while "societies are searching for solutions to problems based on intelligent information." The significance of this observation lies in its focus on *the human and social 'use' of the ICTs*: their *applications* that are invented by people help the solution of known problems in society.[48]

All things considered, "the added value brought by the new tools, and the overall success of the information society will depend on the input made by our people, both individually and in working together." These people represent a richness of culture and creative diversity (frequently referred to as a source of competitiveness for Europe in the world), which also, can be supported by the information infrastructure, which is: "an extraordinary instrument for serving the people of Europe and improving our society by fully reflecting the original and often unique values which underpin and give meaning to our lives." (*Ibid.*)

Thirdly, the authors urged the EU to put *confidence in market mechanisms* as the motive power to bring Europe into the Information Age. This meant a call for concrete actions on the parts of both the European and the national actors: the promotion of entrepreneurial mentality to enable the emergence of new dynamic sectors

---

[48] In fact, it has been since even more emphasized that ultimately, it is *the user* who shapes the applications, and more recently concrete forms of integrating clients' and customer's observations and recommendations have become a popular practice among software developers and public organisations alike in the more developed information societies, partly facilitated via the new media offered by ICTs.

of the economy; as well as the creation of a common regulatory framework in order to bring about a competitive European market for information services. By contrast, the Report openly rejects the continuation of more public money, financial assistance, subsidies or protectionism (Info Highway, 1994):

The Group believes the creation of the information society in Europe should be entrusted to the private sector and to market forces. (...) The market will drive, it will decide winners and losers. Given the power and pervasiveness of the technology, this market is global. The prime task of government is to safeguard competitive forces and ensure a strong and lasting political welcome for the information society, so that demand-pull can finance growth, here as elsewhere. (Bangemann, 1994: Chapter 1).

So the concrete recommendations to the Member States in order to speed up the ongoing process of liberalisation of the telecommunications sector were the following (*ibid.*: Ch. 2):

• infrastructure and services still in the monopoly area were to be opened up to competition;

• "non-commercial political burdens and budgetary constraints imposed on telecommunications operators" were to be eliminated; and

• clear timetables and deadlines are needed to be set for the implementation of the practical measures towards these goals.

Fourthly, some concern was expressed about *Europe's unity and cohesion* in taking measures and in developments: national approaches were still too inconsistent, and this could decrease anticipated benefits. The first countries to enter the I.S. would gain the most and be the ones to set the agenda for the followers. Europe had a lot of strength and good chances (having "major technological, entrepreneurial and creative capabilities" already). However, there was the question "*whether this will be a strategic creation for the whole Union, or a more fragmented and much less effective amalgam of individual initiatives by Member States*" (Bangemann 1994: Ch. 1). Besides, several issues had been elevated onto the common European level, with a lot of tasks entailed that needed to be tackled with a joint effort; and according to the Group, the I.S. was the means to achieve many of these objectives.

The Report outlined a vision of the benefits that the I.S. would bring to the citizens and the economy of Europe. For the *citizens*, it would be a 'more caring' society with a considerably higher quality of life with a greater choice of services. For the *content creators*, it was expected to offer new opportunities to make use of their creativity. *Europe's regions* would have new ways to strengthen and express their identities and cultural wealth; *peripheries* would find novel ways to solve problems caused by their geographical remoteness. *Administration*, services by governments would become transparent, efficient, and responsive to citizens' needs. *Business* in general and small and medium-sized enterprises (*SMEs*) in particular, would have better access to training and other services, as well as a new means to communicate with customers and suppliers; therefore they would be able to reform their organisations to become more efficient and competitive. *Telecom operators* and hardware / software suppliers, i.e. the *IT industries* of Europe would get a huge domestic market to supply, test, and develop their products and services in.

Finally, the experts warned that deep changes brought by the informational revolution would present Europe with a major challenge: "either we grasp the opportunities before us and master the risks, or we bow to them, together with all the uncertainties this may entail." So, the greatest *risk* perceived was that if no action was to be taken, Europe would probably *lose out in the global competitiveness game*, and its affluent markets could be snatched away by the competitors overseas. Another danger lurked in the possibility of the emergence of a *"two-tier society of haves and have-nots"*, "in which only a part of the population has access to the new technology, is comfortable using it and can fully enjoy its benefits" (*ibid.*, my italics). Attention was drawn to the fact that public awareness of ICTs was limited, and there was a risk that individuals would refuse to be part of the new information culture, and use its instruments. To avoid this, "(f)air access to the infrastructure will have to be guaranteed to all, as will provision of universal service, the definition of which must evolve in line with the technology." It is remarkable that it was already obvious to these experts that technological development would be so fast that the actual meaning of 'universal service' would have to be revised from time to time. Besides: "A great deal of effort must be put into securing

widespread public acceptance and actual use of the new technology. *Preparing Europeans for the advent of the information society is a priority task. ... Education, training and promotion will necessarily play a central role.*" (*Ibid.*, my italics.)

The claims in the Report made in 1994 are still relevant, despite the fact that it contains undoubtedly, much technological determinism (with more optimism than reservations concerning the impact of ICTs). From a distance of ten years, one cannot help but credit the Report for its great ability of foresight. In fact, very few new issues have emerged since; the problems brought up by the Bangemann Group have been recurrent in the succeeding political documents and manifestos in Europe (and as indicated above, in the UN), only differing from time to time in the stress put on each; and in fact, most of the problems have not been solved since.

The most straightforward and urgent requirement called for in Europe in the year 1994, was to liberalise the telecommunications market and let its forces work undisturbed. On the other hand, concerns with inclusive and useful social applications, and the problem with peripheries appeared in a nascent form, too – according to some analysts, as a peculiar feature of the European approach to I.S. as opposed to the American model.[49] However, only very vague

---

[49] According to Malagrinò, the terms of 'Information Highway' and 'Information Society' are representatives of the American and the European approaches respectively, to the same problem. The US model lays the emphasis on the role of basic infrastructure, assuming that applications are a direct result of technological development, while the concept of I.S. used in EU policy stresses the need to push applications, considering the infrastructure 'just' as a tool, the

ideas were given as to the 'how' of public intervention and regulation for the sake of a fair I.S. The problem was known to the Bangemann Group and the necessity of some intervention by means of 'universal services obligation'[50] was also mentioned. Yet the issue of liberalisation was more imperative at the time for both Europe as a whole, to be competitive, and for the Members to achieve a harmonised, standard level in their telecommunications infrastructure and services. The private sector, without any doubt greeted these commitments with applause and expectations, and waited to see how legislation in the individual countries would fall in line with them.

The next major step in the development of the European I.S. policy was the so-called *Lisbon Strategy* in March 2000: the European Council embarked on a ten-year strategy "to make the EU the world's most dynamic and competitive economy." The economic, social and environmental renewal of the EU was seen as indispensable, so no wonder that the

eEurope initiative (implemented in June 2000)[51] was an integral part of this Strategy. It proclaimed its aims to bring '"every citizen, home and school, every business and administration into the digital age and online" (COM (99) 687), and to step up Europe's transition towards a knowledge based economy. It recognised and responded to "the need for the Union to set a clear strategic goal and agree a challenging programme for building knowledge infrastructures, enhancing innovation and economic reform, and modernising social welfare and education systems" (Lisbon European Council, Presidency Conclusions, par. 2).

Soon after, the *Action Plan* expressively labelled "*eEurope: Information Society for All*" was issued along the same lines of intention. It put great emphasis on the need for the developments to be *socially inclusive* and to help *diminish major disparities in living standards*. The eEurope initiative has been realised in two phases, with an important shift in focus according to how well the expected results had turned out. The *eEurope 2002 Action Plan* (agreed at the Feira European Council, June 2000) included a total of 64 targets to be achieved by the end of 2002, and concentrated much still on increasing connectivity ('quantitatively'; in order to exploit the advantages offered by the Internet). It was supplemented with *eEurope+* to cover the candidate countries.

However, the effective use of the Internet had not improved as fast as connectivity. Therefore, in March 2002, the European Council in Barcelona called on the

expansion of which inevitably depends on the requirements and demands coming from the applications themselves. (Malagrinò, 1998). As the applications are related more closely to specific social functions and needs than the narrowly interpreted technologies (i.e. the more physical forms of network infrastructures), the European approach is considered by some to be relatively more 'socially sensitive'.

[50] Universal service obligation (USO) is "an obligation imposed on one or more operators of electronic communications networks and/or services to provide a minimum set of services to all users, regardless of their geographical location within the national territory, at an affordable price." (EC portal, Summaries of the Union's legislation). See more on the importance of USO to regional development in 3.3.4.

[51] The source of the following information on the eEurope initiatives is the European Commission's I.S. portal (EC, 1995-2004).

Commission to draw up a new plan, and as a consequence, the *eEurope 2005 Action Plan* was adopted by the Council in December 2002. It centred on "the widespread availability and use of broadband networks throughout the Union by 2005 and the development of Internet protocol IPv6; [and] the security of networks and information, e-Government, e-Learning, e-Health and e-Business" (Barcelona European Council, Presidency Conclusions, par. 40). To some up, attention moved towards 'qualitative improvements': increasing the availability of high quality infrastructure, on-line content, attractive services and applications, and the encouragement of organisational change.

The above indicate a clear shift from the concerns related to competition in the telecom market and the provision of basic infrastructure towards the promotion of high-speed networks, intelligent applications, and the improvement of and investment into human 'infrastructures' or human capital, i.e. *upgrading the networking abilities of not just the technologies and applications, but of the people themselves.* Considering the fact that the latter, the human factors are to a great extent spatially bound, and differ across rural-urban, core-peripheral contexts, the 2002-2005 *e*Europe developments have had an important implication to regional development that surfaced in several European initiatives addressing inequalities in the I.S. (see examples in the following section).

3.3.2 European I.S. and the "open method of co-ordination"

In fact, *e*Europe has kept the 'rules of the game' established by the Bangemann Report despite this shift in focus. I.S. is not a self-contained common policy with a separate budget, and *e*Europe is not a public expenditure programme.

A reason for this may be that the major motive behind the *e*Europe initiatives has been to achieve efficiency for an increased global competitiveness, and so the EU is willing to take on little extra expenditure. Yet the expectations for both direct and indirect returns from the growth of a European I.S. are high. The argument was early established that besides the straight contribution by investments into ICTs to economic expansion, and the direct way technological progress in the information technology industries would increase growth through product and process innovation, the diffusion of ICTs would extend benefits to the rest of the economy (private firms and public services alike) and increase efficiency gains and savings there, too. Working methods and processes could be reorganised to make them much more proficient with the help of the new technologies, but it was also recognised that higher skills were an inevitable pre-condition for this, too.

Closely related to this, the other reason for not having a separate common I.S. policy on the European level is that I.S. development by nature can only be a cross-sectoral venture. There are funds and programmes already functioning which can be mobilised for enhancing the different components of access for certain purposes.

I.S. is not the only field of socio-economic development where there is a need for vertical and horizontal policy integration and "the identification of problems cutting across levels of government as well as sectors and institutional policy domains" (Faludi, 2004:1020). Urban policy, territorial cohesion, social protection, research and innovation are areas where novel governance modes and a 'post-regulatory' mode of planning (as opposed to the 'Community method') have been experimented with on the European level. These new approaches are referred to also as the 'open method of coordination' (OMC). Some features of OMC are (Ahonen, 2001; Faludi, 2004; Hodson and Maher, 2001):

• It complements top-down with *bottom up* approaches, yet the intricate and complex balance of power depend much on the *participation of social partners*.

• There are *guidelines* instead of regulation; political commitments instead of treaty obligations. It is a non-binding mode of operation.

• Its important tools are *benchmarking*, the *dissemination of best practices*, *mutual learning* and *peer pressure*.

• It is a manifestation of *multi-level governance*, decentralisation; demonopolisation of knowledge in terms of the relations between both EU and member states, and the nation state and its regions.

• It is applicable both in the European and a great variation of national set-ups.

Besides the non-binding and budgetless character of *e*Europe, there is further evidence for the European approach to I.S. being an example of the OMC. First, the Union aims at a construction for I.S. research and development within which one may operate supported by already existing budgets, such as the following:

• The Framework Programmes of the European Community: since the mid-eighties, the European Union (EC) has been conducting a policy of research and technological development based on multi-annual framework programmes since 1984.

• The *e*TEN, as a part of the broader trans-European network policy of the EU (TEN: since 1995), is designed to support the deployment of telecommunication networks based electronic services with a trans-European dimension. Its priority areas have been on-line government and health services, the participation of older people and the disabled in the I.S. (*e*Inclusion), on-line learning, increasing user confidence and security of e-services, and encouraging SMEs to participate in the e-economy. For instance, *e*TEN can provide up to 30% of costs of deployment in case of a new service; and it focuses on innovative projects which cannot be financed from private money, and which propose trans-European services. (EC portal: *e*TEN.)

Table 2. The European Community's Framework Programmes for R&D since 1994 and the weight of I.S.-related themes.
(*Source: EC CORDIS and DG for research*)

Notes: * Total budget here excludes Euratom, which has received around € 1 billion euros per programme period. **in addition to the priority themes, I.S. related research could also be funded in under parts of the FPs; e.g. in FP5, there were at least seven other related activities such as the Marie Curie Actions on 'Human resource and mobility', or programmes to develop research infrastructures (GÉANT and GridS).

	Total budget (billion €)	I.S. priority themes (programmes)*	Budget share of I.S. (%)
FP4 1994-1998	13.2	**ICTs** - information technologies (ESPIRIT) - telematics - advanced communication technologies and services (ACTS)	**28** 16 7 5
FP5 1998-2002	14.9	**User-friendly I.S. (IST)** - systems and services for the citizen; - new methods of work and electronic commerce; - multimedia content and tools, - essential technologies and infrastructures	**26**
FP6 2002-2006	16.3	**Information Society Technologies** - *applied IST research addressing major societal and economic challenges* - *communication, computing and software technologies* - *components and micro-systems* - *knowledge and interface technologies* - *IST future and emerging technologies*	24
		Citizens and governments in the knowledge-based society - *knowledge based society and social cohesion* - *citizenship, democracy and new forms of governance*	2
		In total:	**26**
FP7 2007-2011	50.5	Within "**Cooperation**" (1), - ICTs (1)	18
		Within "**Capacities**"(2): - *Regions of knowledge* - *Research infrastructure* - *Science in society* (and some more themes within with smaller budget)	6
		In total:	**24**

• The Structural Funds: an evaluation study published in 2002[52] confirmed that the Structural Funds make a significant contribution to promoting the I.S. For the period 2000-2006, their estimation of SF going to measures in this field was 10 billion euros, and half of the regions they surveyed gave priority to I.S. in their distribution of the Funds.

Political objectives have got increasingly complex and interrelated, reaching far beyond a single sector. Besides, with time, social-economic impacts started to surface, and from the interactions of different lines of policy, and from conflicting interests, new problems occurred. To understand and solve them, research and legislation concerning the I.S. have become increasingly important on the European level. Table 2 indicates the awareness of the former, and shows how the range of fundable I.S.-related research activities has got more diverse and demand- (ICT usage, content, social impacts) oriented in perspective within the successive EC Framework Programmes since the year of the Bangemann Report.

Research was in high demand concerning the territorial inequalities in terms of the different sides of access (which

task has caused much headache to every actor involved.)[53] Nevertheless, closely related to the eEurope initiatives, and financed under different ICT-related programmes of the European Commission, the SIBIS project (2001-2003) completed the task of developing innovative I.S. indicators that enable the monitoring of developments in the Member States; and BISER did the same for the regions of Europe (1998-2002). Both relied heavily on National Statistical Institutes and supra-national organisations (Eurostat, OECD); and they created indices focusing on several different domains of the I.S., and published their output in form of detailed handbooks.[54]

Consequently from the dispersed nature of funding sources across many different support schemes, there is a great need for forums and channels that connect actors to the possible resources and practical knowledge. Besides, as Malagrinò remarked in 1998, the regional dimension of developing the I.S. (which has been indeed, part of the 'grand visions', expressed in the Bangemann Report and the eEurope documents) was "independent of the context" to which these visions were applied (Malagrinò 1998). This vacuum has been since more or less filled in by initiatives started 'from below', by the regions themselves. Organisations such as Eris@ and its IANIS network have been successful in strengthening and networking of regions of Europe in order to help them find

---

[52] The study (Information Society and Economic and Social Cohesion – the role of the Structural Funds) was prepared for EC DG Regional Policy by a consortium with a diverse membership: a private company Technopolis Ltd, the Community programme IRISI, the non-profit organization eris@, (see more below about the later two) and a professor at the University of Athens. This is an example for both monitoring and the cooperation between different social partners and the Commission (See Technopolis Ltd. *et al.* 2002).

[53] Some of the difficulties which are likely to arise during such benchmarking ventures are introduced in 3.3.3 and 3.3.4.
[54] SIBIS: Statistical Indicators Benchmarking the Information Society; BISER: Benchmarking I.S. in European Regions. (See References).

their own ways and good practices in the 'information age'.

Important precedents (in addition to, of course, the Bangemann Report and other key initiatives by the Community) were activities launched by the European Commission in 1995 and 1997 involving sub-national authorities. The first one was a pre-pilot scheme named the *Inter-Regional Information Society Initiative* (IRISI) set up by six European regions[55] to promote I.S. on this spatial-administrative level. RISI gave support to 22 regions during the period of 1997-98 for the preparation of regional I.S. strategies. This assistance took the form of methodology workshops organised especially to train and inform regional managers and their consultants.[56]

Another important achievement was the recognition by the participating regions that there was "indeed much to gain through cooperation and collaboration in this field" (IANIS) on a longer term as well: they would therefore need to facilitate continuous debate about concrete applications and services and on key policy issues. Soon, in 1998, a non-profit organisation, Eris@ – *the European Regional Information Society Association* – was formed by 28 founding regions. Its membership has grown to 48 by early 2007 (including 45 regional members and 3 private companies).

IANIS is the *Innovative Actions Network for the Information Society*, a programme managed by Eris@. It is committed to "sustain and further develop inter-regional networking, ... widespread sharing of information, experience and good practice through an electronic communications platform, physical and virtual newsletters, workshops, seminars, annual conferences ...", "in the context of the I.S. and Structural Funds' investments for to design, develop, maintain, and provide access to an e-Region Hub with a Projects' Database..." (*ibid.*) These international networks and forums of sub-national I.S.-developing actors fulfil an important role in the dissemination of special know-how and best practices, and encourage engagement in partnerships and joint projects (see some examples in Chapter 5).

3.3.3 I.S.-disparities between countries in Europe

Soon after the Bangemann Report had been adopted, individual member states drew up their own *national information society strategies* one after the other echoing the EU guidelines and priorities[57]. Their advancements towards fulfilling the requirements of the Bangemann Report and its follow-ups ('Lisbon' and the *e*Europe initiative) have varied, however. The countries of the EU and wider Europe have taken or chosen different paths towards the I.S. Naturally, their demographic, economic,

---

[55] IRISI: North-West England, Sachsen, Nord Pas-de-Calais, Valencia, Central Macedonia and Piemonte.
[56] The Finnish North Karelian I.S. strategy was drafted within this support scheme, too. See 4.3 and Appendix 6 for details. The Paraddis programme of the West Finland Alliance was also granted support by RISI 1.

[57] Early (1994-1996) examples were: Finland, the Netherlands, Austria, Denmark, Germany, and Ireland.

physical-geographical, historical, political and cultural, etc. diversity has an important share in this.

As mentioned above, the EU has since the beginning been looking for the appropriate ways to *measure* what the rates of developments have been, and how individual countries differ from each other in their speed of progress 'on the road to the I.S.' On the national level, a more or less reliable set of statistical data on ICT-supply and take-up as well as data for variables related to human capital have been compiled and up-dated annually by the Eurostat and other organisations[58], mostly relying on information provided by national statistics institutes. Despite the limitations and ambiguities (i.e. concerning the relevance, standardisation of the indicators across fifteen or even more countries, and the problematic practice of quantifying certain socially complicated trends), these data could certainly provide more tangible evidence for the divergent nature of I.S. developments across the continent.

An early analysis[59] shows that already in the second half of the 1990s, the EU countries could be relatively easily categorised into sets of 'leaders', 'fast followers' and a group of those 'lagging behind' in technological and knowledge-related developments. A clear north-south division had emerged in both of these aspects within the EU15 space by the late-

nineties. The Nordic region was an obvious leader in ICT developments and take-up, as well as in investments into and some features of, the human resources. The southern Members on the other hand, were lagging behind considerably. Those countries which followed the 'leaders' relatively closely formed a rather heterogeneous group, each having strengths and weaknesses in different fields, and consequently, they were the least stable in their positions, their future perspectives probably being the most sensitive to national policy decisions that were to be made towards the end of the decade.

It is interesting to note also that the relative positions of the countries in the scales of both the 'ICT-' and 'knowledge-related' development did not correlate as much as one may expect with the levels of general economic development (GDP per capita); outliers were found especially among those towards the top of the lists (e.g. Finland and Sweden were positive outliers).

This allows for at least two assumptions. Certain aspects of individual national strategies and social-cultural systems can differentiate in terms of I.S.-development between countries of equal wealth. Besides, while high GDP does not necessary entail high values in ICT-related socio-economic developments, low GDP is usually a significant barrier to progress towards an I.S. (see for instance 4.3.2 about Hungary).

With the launch of the Lisbon Strategy and the introduction of the relevant action plans, more attention was paid to monitoring developments. This manifested also in the publication of more comparable I.S. / ICT-statistics during the first years of

---

[58] For some examples, see also 4.2.1 for Table 5 listing the top ten countries in 2004 according to the I.S. Index by IDC and the paragraphs on the Network Readiness Index and its components created by W.E.F.

[59] See the maps and diagrams in Németh, 2005: section II/1.A (Licentiate Thesis, University of Joensuu).

the new millennium: on a greater number of related variables (see for instance, Rédei, 2007a), and including also new EU-candidate countries in the comparisons. The series of thematic maps below present the situation across twenty-five countries of Europe, i.e. a 'hypothetical' EU15+10[60], *in this very crucial and eventful period both concerning technological progress and in terms of I.S. strategic developments.* They show the spatial inequalities according to just few selected variables from the available statistics that could fit into the categories of indicators describing a broadly defined I.S., proposed for instance, by Castells and Himanen (2001[61]; see a list of possible indicators in Appendix 2). These variables may be used to show the development towards an I.S. where:

- ICTs are widely used and accepted;

- which is also competitive, innovative, and intelligent;

- caring and equal in opportunities;

- free, open to the world, and trying to be environmentally friendly.[62]

Many, especially the last two sets of, these attributes are difficult to measure and compare across countries. The first group of variables, linked to the supply and take-up of ICTs, is perhaps relatively easier to 'map' in Europe based on numerical data, yet as it is illustrated below, their interpretations are still not straightforward.

First, the maps in Figures 8-11 show differences across Europe in terms of some of the factors behind *physical and financial access to ICTs*[63] (telephone and Internet services). Figures 8-10 indicate national disparities in a direct way, i.e. in telephone calls and Internet connection (subscription where the cost and/or dial-up) tariffs.[64] It is important to note that Figures 10 and 11 are in a way, complementary, and should be considered together. There are countries where Internet costs appear only in terms of subscription fees and others where it contains only the expense of a telephone call; yet in case of some countries, users are charged for the Internet connection in both ways.[65]

Figure 11 gives a similar message but indirectly via the levels of competition between Internet service providers (ISPs), since low competition most often means higher prices and less choice (i.e. lower quality of service) for the customers.

---

[60] 'EU15+10' means the old member states, eight of the accession states in 2004 (i.e. excluding Malta and Cyprus) and the most recent entrants, Romania and Bulgaria.
[61] See more about this work in Chapter 4.
[62] This is undoubtedly a rather utopian, or at least, optimistic approach as to the direction of the current social evolutions, yet at least it provides a vision to strive for; and matches the spirit of EU and UN manifestos.

[63] See 2.3.2 about the different dimensions of access to ICTs and information.

[64] In Fig. 8 and 10, the values are adjusted to national price levels, so they contain some information about the 'relative affordability' of these ICTs.

[65] It is difficult to interpret these two maps in detail, and make straight comparisons. The measures of the two variables are not convertible to match; Internet service can be of different Kbit/s rate and provided in different consumer packages; and it is not clear which ISPs – the incumbents or major competitors – provided the data.

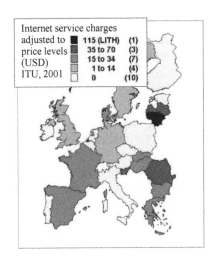

Figure 8. Charges by Internet service providers in EU15+10, 2001.

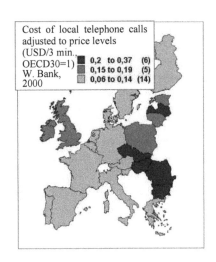

Figure 10. Local telephone call costs adjusted to national price levels in EU15+10, 2000.

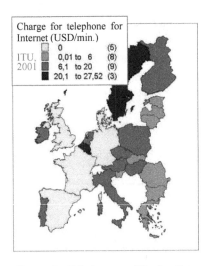

Figure 9. Telephone tariffs for Internet connection in EU15+10, 2001
(Note: not adjusted to price levels.)

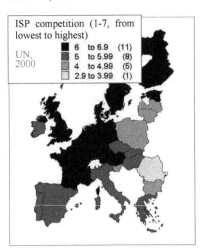

Figure 11. Level of competition among Internet service providers in EU15 +10, 2000.

62

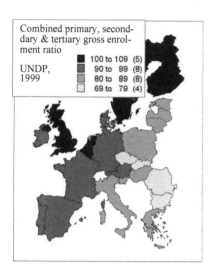

Figure 12. Combined gross enrolment in education in EU15+10, 1999.

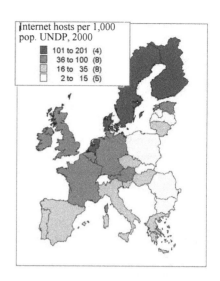

Figure 14. Internet hosts per 1,000 inhabitants in EU15+10, 2000.

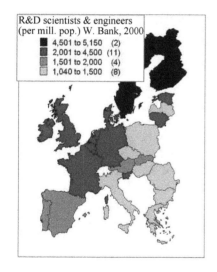

Figure 13. Number of scientists and engineers in R&D in EU15+10, 2000.

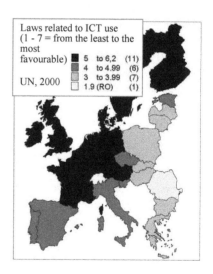

Figure 15. The quality of legislation of ICT use in EU15+10, 2000.

Despite the limitations to the interpretation of Figures 10-11, some observation may be made, for instance, concerning the group of East-Central European countries (with few exceptions[66]): where competition among ISPs is lower, Internet usage is more expensive, and therefore, as indicated in Figure 19 below, is less common.

High subscription fees surely discourage people from becoming users of ICTs, yet the material barrier is not the only one. Figures 12-13 represent European disparities in terms of two possible indicators of 'mental access' or the position and value of knowledge and technology in society. A generally higher educational level of the population and a technology-oriented profile of national R&D not only encourage the creation and diffusion of ICTs, but – coupled with wide-spread acceptance and use – they increase their utility to society.

Figure 14 maps Europe according to a popular indicator of the I.S.: the number of hosts in relation to the total population of a country. This only roughly represents the number of directly-connected computers in a country (ITU, 2006). Not all Internet host computers are identified by two-digit country codes (some bear three-digit codes, e.g. .org, .com, .int, reflecting the nature of the organization using the computer), so classifying hosts according to national economies is not a straightforward task. All hosts without national credentials are assigned to the United States. What is more,

hosts identified with country codes can easily be located physically in other countries. Therefore, the number of Internet hosts shown for each country can only be considered an approximation. Having acknowledged this, one can observe the general north-south and west-east divisions again, yet the additional diversity may or may not be indicative.

As mentioned above, legislation is an important pillar of I.S. policy (3.3.1), and is an important precondition of developing on-line content (2.3.2). With the diversification and expansion of electronic services, and with the convergence of the different media and the commercial and political activities, regulations concerning a great number of subjects are essential to make the usage of ICTs socially safe and functioning. Such issues are access to public information, audiovisual policy, competition, computer crime, consumer and data protection, digital signatures, domain names, electronic commerce, gender equality in access, intellectual property, minors and the Internet, international mobile roaming, etc. (Glatz, 2002; EC thematic portal).

What is more, I.S.-related legislation needs to be continuously and frequently reviewed, negotiated, harmonised and amended on both the European and the national levels due to the rapid technological developments. Figure 15 depicts the differences between the 25 countries in terms of their advancement in establishing a favourable legal control of these social-technological interactions.

Figure 16 indicates territorial inequalities according to another content-related indicator of the I.S.: the availability of on-line services provided by governments.

---

[66] According to the categories in the maps, exceptions from this regularity are Hungary and Slovakia, where competition among ISPs is higher than most of the CEECs, yet the percentage of users in the population is low.

This may be linked with the fashionable concept of e-democracy; though it can refer simply to "the use of information technology ... to overcome the physical bounds of traditional paper and physical based systems" (Pascual, 2003).

Since about 2000, the UN has been regularly ranking the countries of the world according to hundreds of features of e-government websites and services. Here again, the general pattern within Europe is confirmed.

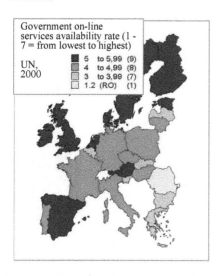

Figure 16. The level of government on-line services in EU15+10, 2000.

The European Commission has also been emphasizing the need to develop and monitor the availability of e-government services, especially since the *e*Europe 2002 initiative. The objective than was to achieve "generalized electronic access to main basic public services by 2003". Attention to this issue was kept up at the Seville European Council (2002), where the continuation of this initiative was ensured by *e*Europe 2005.

Then it was emphasized that these electronic services need to be *interactive, relevant,* and *accessible for all,* and should exploit the potentials of broadband networks and multi-platform access (Capgemini, 2006)[67].

Finally, Maps 17-19 present disparities in Europe in terms of demand and usage rather than ICT provision (supply). The aggregate number of fixed line and cellular subscriptions indicates the status of telephony in general. It covers up the internal dynamics between the two technologies, the occurrences of 'leapfrogging'[68]; but allows for figures higher than 100 per 100 inhabitants since some people can have both wireline and mobile subscriptions at the same time. Therefore, the information this picture conceals can be retrieved only from additional timeline data on both types of technologies. In some countries, mobile took over before wired telephones could diffuse more (e.g. Hungary); in others, after a close-to saturation point, the number of fixed line subscriptions decreased somewhat with the emergence of cellular technology (for instance, Sweden)[69]. Again, the lag of some new member states in the eastern peripheries was striking in this respect, where fixed line subscriptions started increasing from a very low level in the nineties, and mobile

---

[67] To date, there have been six annual reports on benchmarking the availability and sophistication of on-line public services across Europe, ordered by the European Commission's DG for Information Society and Media, for the purposes of the eEurope programme.
[68] By leapfrogging, in this context I mean mobile subscriptions by households that had no fixed line connections earlier.
[69] Main lines per 100 inhabitants in Sweden: 68.3 in 1994 and 63.4 in 2004 (Lumio, 2006:2).

telephony had not yet diffused widely by 2001.

Parallel with political declarations, while in 2001, only three benchmarking indicators were used and 17 countries were covered, the last benchmarking exercises relied on more complex models (see Figure 3 in 2.3.2) and added new indicators, covering 28 European states. These more recent results showed much development over the last five years in terms of both sophistication and availability of on-line public services. Yet considerable differences have remained between old and new EU member states (not that much between North and South, however), with the outstanding exceptions of Malta and Estonia.[70]

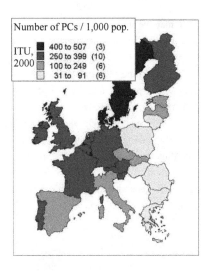

Figure 18. The number of personal computers per 100 inhabitants in EU10+15, 2000.

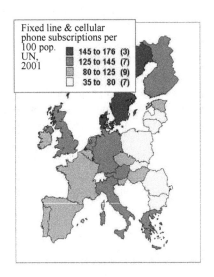

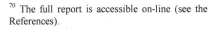

Figure 17. The number of fixed line and cellular telephone subscriptions per 100 inhabitants in EU15+10, 2001.

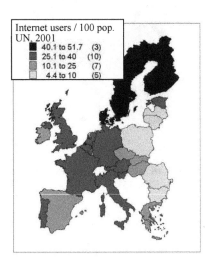

Figure 19. The number of Internet users per 100 inhabitants in EU15+10, 2001.

---

[70] The full report is accessible on-line (see the References).

The indicator 'Internet users per 100 inhabitants' covers a variety of different type of usage: access from work, home, school, public access points, etc. Also, as admitted by a UN benchmarking unit, surveys differ across countries in the age groups of users included, and in the time and frequency of usage they cover, which poses some problems in comparisons (UNCTAD, 2005).

In summary, the maps in Figures 8-19 indicate that there was still rather considerable differentiation between the EU15 and the 10 'enlargement countries' around the Millennium: generally, the North-South slope has remained, and a very prominent West-East dimension of disparities is added to it. Nevertheless, some diversity among accession countries can be seen, too, yet to account for the relative advantages of some states in the region like (in different aspects) Estonia, Slovenia, the Czech Republic and Hungary, necessitates further and more in-depth research.[71]

As the basic physical infrastructure (e.g. digitalisation of the fixed telephone network) and the penetration of certain basic applications and services (e.g. PCs and mobile phone subscriptions) in the society had approached their saturation levels in the higher tier countries, and there, some convergence had taken place, new questions came up:

Firstly, even within the countries more advanced in I.S., *subnational spatial*

and social inequalities have persisted to certain extent. Secondly, *attention shifted from the supply to the demand side of the technological infrastructure and services*, as well as to the diffusion and efficiency of such specialised applications as e-business, e-banking, flexible telework, the combination of ICTs and education, e-governance, and the on-line, network-supported forms of healthcare. Although these applications are mentioned in the WSIS Declaration and the EU guidelines, *national legislators have placed different emphases on them*. Thirdly, the different societies had accepted the new technologies with varying degrees of openness and 'readiness', according to their *cultural differences*. It is very probable that as a result of a combination of the cultural and policy-related specificities, some more or less distinct models of the I.S. have been taking shape. In the following, the findings from a survey with national legislators across Europe are summarised in support of these claims.

3.3.4 Actual and perceived sub-national disparities across Europe

Background information to the survey

In this section, some of the concerns and results of a survey are presented that was carried out during early 2004 to contribute to the project 1.2.2 of the ESPON programme[72] (see Box 2 for more information).

---

[71] Some understanding may be obtained below in Chapter 4.3 concerning Hungary. An account on the factors in the success of Estonia is provided in Frank and Németh, 2004 (see the References).

[72] The lead partner in the Transnational Project Group 1.2.2 was CURDS (Centre for Urban & Regional Studies) at the University of Newcastle (UK). The other partners were: the School of the Built Environment at Heriot-Watt University, Edinburgh (UK); CEIDET at the University of

The expansion of the telecommunications sector, the developments of ICT investments, networks and services are definitely a good example for the recent internationalisation of socio-economic processes; where there is an evident need for reform and the integration of, the national policy frameworks. So it is not a coincidence, that two ESPON research projects were directly related to ICTs and the I.S. in Europe.

Project no. 1.2.2 was the first in order, titled *Telecommunication services and networks: territorial trends.* Its tasks were to draw together and analyse spatial data on especially the supply side of the telecommunications sector in terms of both the mature ICTs (basic fixed voice telephony, mobile telephony, personal computers and the Internet) and the leading edge technologies (broadband technologies and Internet backbone networks). This was attempted not only at the macro- and meso-levels (i.e. concerning trends observed in terms of Northern / Southern / Western / Eastern Europe; and disparities between countries), but also on a micro-scale (sub-national regional developments).

Project no. 1.2.3, *Spatial aspects of the Information Society* looked at the performance of regions in terms of a more comprehensive definition of the I.S.: not only the readiness for and intensity of, using ICTs, but their impact on socio-economic development (shifting attention more to the demand side and the content-related

variables; see Appendix 5 about the index in). Figure 21 below includes the map produced in this project on the findings from the subnational analyses. (See also 5.2 for more results from ESPON 1.2.2 about Finland.)

However, data availability was a problem for the international research team, especially on the micro-level, i.e. about the sub-national territorial trends. Regional statistics were non-existent or information was commercially sensitive concerning particularly the demand for ICTs and network services. Assembling a standardised dataset on all three scales and for all the 29 countries very soon proved to be an impossible undertaking.

The researchers involved carried out a survey to obtain at least some of the missing information. Questionnaires were sent to the national authorities to find answers to some central questions. Do ministries and regulators of the telecommunications sector perceive regional inequalities in ICT-provision as a problem in their countries? Is there any centralised practice to monitor the sub-national trends in ICT supply and demand in these countries? Do national governments see it necessary and appropriate to interfere with market processes and if so, what tools of intervention they have in order to decrease sub-national disparities?

In addition, telecommunications companies were surveyed to get their perspectives on these same concerns.

Having no ministry and regulator responses from over half of the ESPON countries caused some problems for drawing more general conclusions. Yet, the private sector was even less responsive; therefore I

Aveiro (Portugal); and the Karelian Institute, University of Joensuu (Finland). As a member of the Finnish team, the author of this dissertation was personally responsible for analysing the completed questionnaires.

One of the major concerns of the EU has been its internal cohesion, as a condition for its ˡe, stability, growth and competitiveness. After several years of preparation, the **European Spatial Development Perspective (ESDP)** was approved in 1999 in Potsdam (EC, 1999; Faludi and Waterhout, 2002). Its aim has been to help eliminate the contradiction that while processes affecting territorial development are increasingly international and 'Europeanised', spatial planning has remained a strictly national affair. The ESDP offers a trans-sectoral and proactive approach to planning, and employs a spatial framework to co-ordinate a wide spectrum of policies placing great emphasis on sustainability and social cohesion. Though it is a legally non-binding document, and has no implementation instruments and funding mechanisms on its own, ESDP has had an influence on national developments by defining new concepts and perspectives to offer a way for some policy integration across Europe (Fritsch, 2006:9; ESDP 1999; Faludi, 2006).

To back up and apply the proposals for policy integration initiated in ESDP, much knowledge about the territorial structures and trends was needed. Therefore, the research programme **European Spatial Planning Observation Network (ESPON)** was launched in 2002 by the Commission. The objectives of ESPON were to carry out "applied research and studies on territorial development and spatial planning seen from a European perspective in support of policy development" (www.espon.eu, 2002-2006). It comprised over thirty research projects covering and involving the 29 countries of the 'ESPON space'.

Box 2. Basic information about the ESDP and ESPON.

give a brief account of the results based on the information given by ministries and regulators especially. (For the questionnaires and more detail on the exercise see Appendix 3 and ESPON, 2004: 1.2.2 Third Interim Report).

A summary of answers to the questionnaires

Based on the answers from thirteen European countries (a mere 44.8% response rate), the following observations can be made answering to the three main questions phrased above.

1 Perception of regional inequalities and their patterns

The respondents were greatly divided on the degree of subnational disparities in telecom networks and services, yet there is no regularity in terms of the

Small and wealthier states like Denmark and Switzerland naturally see territorial differences insignificant. (See Table 3 for more details.)

The territorial patterns of inequalities with respect to telecom networks and services were judged most concentrated in Norway, Finland, Austria, Greece, Hungary, Latvia and Romania, and relatively less concentrated in Estonia, Switzerland and Lithuania.[73] More precisely, patterns were defined as shown in Table 4.

---

[73] The Danish respondent did not answer the question, which might be a sign of no territorial perspective in telecommunications regulation there. Yet it is more probable that there have been strong territorial concerns and as a result, infrastructure is particularly spatially even, hence a territorial perspective is not needed any more in this regard. Is Denmark already making 'the next step' in development: trying to create more demand among the consumers after establishing physical access? The respondent from Malta argued that their country also, is too small to have territorial patterns.

Table 3. Perception of sub-national regional inequalities in the provision of telecommunications networks and services
(ESPON 1.2.2 survey results, March 2003)

Very uneven	Uneven	Generally even	Very even
Greece **Norway** (Ministry) Hungary Lithuania	**Austria**	**Finland** **Sweden** Estonia Lithuania Romania	**Denmark** **Switzerland** Malta

* Note that the scale is very subjective; it was not determined what uneven and even mean in absolute terms. Countries written in bold were EU Members at the time of the survey, and I added Norway and Switzerland to this group. The rest are the new accession states.

Table 4. Patterns of spatial divergence in telecommunications networks and services as perceived by national authorities in Europe
(ESPON 1.2.2 survey results, March 2003)

Patterns of inequalities	Respondents*
Capital *vs.* rest of the country	AT, HU, LV, EL; somewhat RO, NO, FI
Major cities *vs.* rest of the country:	LT, LV, NO, FI, S, HU, RO, EL, AT
Urban-rural / core-periphery dichotomy	EE, LT, FI, NO, RO, CH; somewhat AT, EL, HU
Natural obstacles (mountains, islands)	EE, AT
Rich *vs.* poor	stressed in RO, somewhat in LT and HU

* The ISO country codes represent either the Ministry or the regulating authority responsible for the telecommunications in the given country.

Answers varied also concerning the perceived factors causing these regional inequalities. However, reasons attributable to *market forces* prevailed:

• Since liberalisation, developments were reported to be getting more uneven in Norway, Austria and Hungary.

• The cost of service provision, scale of markets, lack of assured profit were factors listed by all respondents.

• The lack of competition was given as a reason in Estonia, Finland, Norway, Austria, Lithuania and Hungary (too much competition was not a problem anywhere).

The dominant role of market forces was much confirmed in the responses given by telecommunications companies. The catchment-population and business considerations were far the most important factors mentioned in their roll-out and network development decisions. Some companies clearly stated that they follow pure economic criteria (in Norway and Austria), others mentioned some more complex data-bases informing them about consumption patterns of their potential and existing clients.

There are less profitable regions. The companies labelled sparsely populated parts of countries (e.g. in Finland and

70

Norway) and rural areas far from back-bone and local nodes (in Austria), as well as regions outside clusters of attraction (Portugal) as less profitable. ADSL, high speed data access, optical fibre network, and in some cases even ISDN were services mentioned as not available in these regions because of low telephone density and consumption in these areas.

Returning to the ministries and regulators, the open question on the patterns of competition was not clear to half of the respondents. Those who understood it mentioned urban and densely populated regions *vs.* rural and peripheral areas, or residential as opposed to big consumers as main distinctions. The Greek respondent mentioned the fact that *different technologies show different patterns*: in case of mobile telephony, the level of competition does not differentiate between regions, while most of the telecom service providers concentrate on densely populated core regions. Generally, ICT investors aim to cover the whole country, but there are some services that are not available in certain regions. Also, telecom companies mentioned the fact that there was a territorial specialisation in certain alternative (yet not equivalent) technologies: ADSL is more concentrated in metropolitan areas, while some companies provide remote, sparsely populated regions with fixed wireless access. Finally, an important issue is the actual degree of competition in the TCT sector. In Denmark only, was competition assumed to be perfect. In Austria, Estonia, and maybe in Greece, it was claimed to be almost perfect across territories (except for some regions, or few obtrusive companies,

and at least in case of the more basic services). There were problems mentioned in Sweden and Hungary. In Finland and Norway competition was claimed to be not working across territories, as there were regions not benefiting from it at all. The Lithuanian and Romanian respondents did not give any account on this, for liberalisation of the sector had taken place a few months before the survey in both countries (1st Jan. 2003).

2 Any monitoring by the national governments?

Concerning monitoring and transparency, only two (Nordic) countries (Sweden and Norway) reported the existence of some practice of public monitoring and publication of territorial developments in telecommunications networks and services. Some spatial data on ICTs was published in Hungary, too, but it was not specified.[74]

As far as telecommunications companies and data provision were concerned, they expressed that country level data were certainly given and published; data on the regional and municipal levels, however, were not available to the public for business secrecy reasons generally. Two operators promised to provide information to the research team and emphasized that data could be utilised "only for non-commercial purposes." Others clearly denied it or referred to the fact that official data collection is done by the national regulator.

---

[74] In Hungary, ISDN and cable TV data are available at NUTS 3 level, published by the Central Statistical Office.

3 Any intervention necessary and done to reduce regional differences?

• Universal Service Obligation (USO), though respondents from member states referred to the relevant EU directives, was usually said to be limited to narrowband (basic fixed telephone services that enable cable + modem access). A bit more extended it might be in Norway, where leased lines were included, and in Denmark, where leased lines and ISDN were mentioned to be covered. In some accession states USO was very new or not yet in force (e.g. Romania) in early 2003.

Further liberalisation was men-tioned as a priority measure in Lithuania, Finland, Norway[75] and Austria; by contrast, liberalisation is not mentioned in Denmark, Sweden, Estonia and Hungary at all. Considering the fact that liberalisation in the sector took place at very different times in these countries, their reasons must vary. Nevertheless, this question divided the countries rather distinctly.

• More effective monitoring and regulation is considered to be a solution in Lithuania, Finland, Sweden and Norway, but not at all in Estonia, Denmark and Austria.

• Obligations imposed on telecom-munications companies concerning both territory and population coverage existed only in Lithuania, Switzerland, and Greece. There was a population coverage requirement in Sweden and Norway. In Austria, the Ministry claimed there was

obligation to cover rural areas in turn for urban licence, yet the Regulator did not make any mention of it. There were no coverage-obligations imposed on telecommunication companies in Finland and Denmark; and neither in Romania ("so far") but in fact all responses by its respondent gave the impression that things might happen in the future, which can be true, or can just indicate a sign of uncertainty, or optimism. Malta reported a "100%" obligation to cover the territory.

• The extension of USO to the broadband sub-sector, and funding to support USO were not mentioned as existing or possible tools for intervention in any countries but in Norway and Hungary. (Yet in Hungary, the answer to what extent USO had already been imposed was unclear.)

• Funding to support regional and local infrastructure projects was a concern in Sweden, Hungary and to some extent in Finland, but not elsewhere.

• Funding to stimulate demand locally is claimed to be a tool in Finland and Hungary only, and in Norway to some degree.

• Public-private partnership was mentioned by the respondent from Lithuania, and somewhat by the Norwegian and Hungarian authorities.

---

[75] Note the contradiction here, i.e. between this claim and that liberalisation was said to have caused further spatial divergence in Norway, and inequalities were seen as a problem.

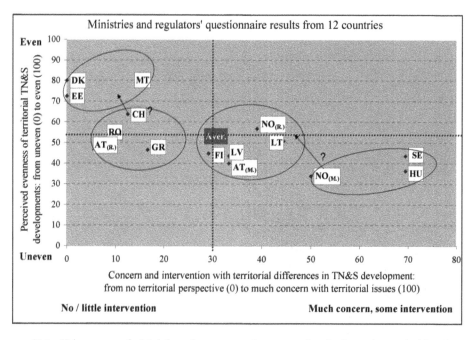

Note: Values were calculated from the responses by means of a simple scoring method based exclusively on the information given by the respondents. A$^{(R.)}$ and A$^{(M)}$ stand for the perspectives of the telecom regulator and the Federal Ministry of Economy and Transport in Austria, respectively. NO$^{(R.)}$ and NO$^{(M.)}$ indicate the telecom authority and the Ministry of Transport and Communications in Norway, respectively. Respondents from other countries were from either the regulators or the ministries (In total, there were 15 responses to the questionnaire, from 13 European countries.) Clustering of the countries is done based on visual (and subjective) judgement: the question marks indicate other possible ways of grouping.

(Németh in ESPON 1.2.2; survey results, March 2003).

Figure 20. The position of some European countries according to (y) the perceptions of inequalities in the provision of telecommunications networks and services (TN&S) and (x) the public will to intervene – as seen by their responsible national authorities

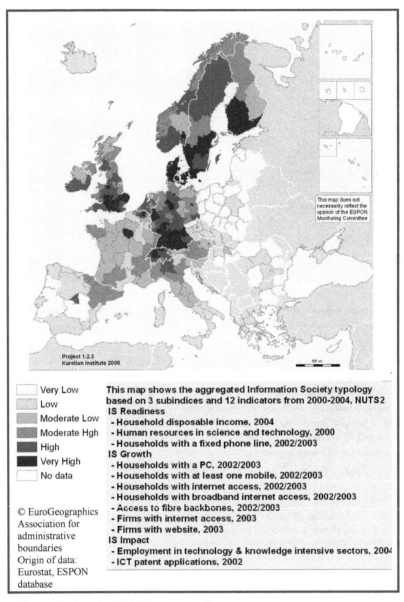

Very Low

Low

Moderate Low

Moderate Hgh

High

Very High

No data

© EuroGeographics
Association for
administrative
boundaries
Origin of data:
Eurostat, ESPON
database

**This map shows the aggregated Information Society typology
based on 3 subindices and 12 indicators from 2000-2004, NUTS2**
IS Readiness
 - **Household disposable income, 2004**
 - **Human resources in science and technology, 2000**
 - **Households with a fixed phone line, 2002/2003**
IS Growth
 - **Households with a PC, 2002/2003**
 - **Households with at least one mobile, 2002/2003**
 - **Households with internet access, 2002/2003**
 - **Households with broadband internet access, 2002/2003**
 - **Access to fibre backbones, 2002/2003**
 - **Firms with internet access, 2003**
 - **Firms with website, 2003**
IS Impact
 - **Employment in technology & knowledge intensive sectors, 2004**
 - **ICT patent applications, 2002**

(Source: Frank et al., 2006:115; re-arranged).

Figure 21. I.S. performance in NUTS 2 regions according to the ESPON 1.2.3 I.S. index

The question whether EU Structural Funds should be used to support investments into telecommunications networks and services brings out considerable differences between the respondent countries. Market forces were perceived basically sufficient in Estonia ("no SF can replace market forces"). By contrast, the relevance of the Structural Funds and national development plans was acknowledged in Lithuania, Sweden, Hungary, Malta, Romania, Greece and Austria. The Norwegian and Swiss authorities found this question not concerning them; the Finnish and Danish respondents gave no answer.

- Finally, there was no link mentioned at all between telecommunications policy and spatial planning in most of the countries. According to the respondents from Norway and Sweden, as well as from Hungary, some integration, cooperation exists in their countries. Yet the worth of and the necessity for, closer co-operation in policy making was expressed by several respondents.

The view of the private sector on what measures were necessary to decrease territorial differences was rather clear-cut and in general, contradicting the public perspective. Funding to support regional infrastructure projects and to stimulate demand locally, as well as public-private-partnership were among the important solutions listed, while further liberalization was almost not mentioned at all. Companies were generally aware of the diversity of demand, and even the necessity of investment to improve "mentalities" by means of education and subsidies to encourage electronic alternatives

(eGovernment) was mentioned. They understood that where service provision is not profitable, market forces and "universal" (national-level) intervention cannot help: but more targeted regional, local intervention is needed, and they all suggested the state should take responsibility for it.

In sum, the above may leave little doubt if any as to the difficulty of coming up with generalisations, typologies, clear examples. Even so, Figure 20 attempts at this by tracing a possible connection between perceptions of inequalities and the public will to interfere. Methodologically, this exercise combines qualitative and quantitative tools; the data was collected by means of questionnaires including both closed and open questions; assessing answers in 'quantified' categories can be at times problematic.

There were very few regulators and ministries who responded to the questionnaires and quite much uncertainty and subjectivity was communicated in those answers. In some cases where both the regulator and the ministry responded, there were clashing views and inconsistent information provided; and some incongruity within the answers by individual countries occurred, too. Besides, little information was gained as to the demand side (usage) of ICTs.

Still, it can be maintained that monitoring on the sub-national level was scarce at the most. However, due to the commercially sensitive nature of the information, it could only be a national authority trusted with the aggregation of data on the regional and municipal levels collected from different service providers –

as it was suggested by some respondents from the private sector, too.

Inequalities across national territory were recognised by most of the countries, yet there was none which had a concrete national policy framework to deal with it. However some regulative tools and targeted incentives were in use in a few cases, and acknowledged as important in others.

Most of the governments had done little in this field still, leaving much to the market to decide. On the other hand, the private telecom sector expected the public sector to handle the issues of social justice and regional development in terms of ICTs.

Besides shared tendencies and general problems, it is evident that the countries studied were (and generally, are) at different stages and on different routes in developing their ICT sector. They bear several individual traits which predetermine territorial relations, the weighing of these by policy-makers, as well as the possible scope of public intervention. Therefore, more in-depth *country studies* are needed to confirm these observations and to get a more detailed and inclusive picture of the interaction of ICT investments, government policy, and actual access in individual countries. The national level indeed, matters.

3.4 Summary

3.4.1 Summary in terms of access and the different perspectives on the I.S.

a) *"What shifts in objectives can be recognised in international guidelines to*

promote the development of an inclusive I.S., esp. in terms of access and digital divides?"

The global urge to privatise and liberalise the telecommunications sector in the early nineties found good justification in the standpoint that ICTs have currently been the determinants of social change. This chapter provided evidence of some hindrance both in the UN and in Europe to the shift from this technocratic-deterministic viewpoint to a more complex, people-centred and cultural approach towards the I.S. In rhetoric, seeds of a more culture-sensitive and inter-relational perspective appeared early, as well as concerns with social and regional inequalities in the benefits of technological developments. Yet it has taken many years for this view to be applied in practice both in the United Nations and the European Union.

Consequently, access was initially understood mostly in physical and financial terms, and hence investments into research for developing ICTs and the liberalisation of the telecommunications markets were the priorities set. Monitoring has been carried out by implementing indicators of physical access and basic take-up, and generally carried out on the macro- and meso-levels only.

As a result of escalating discussions between these international organisations and various social partners (i.e. the academia, and the civil society), a move in focus to the mental factors, and the content of access commenced. This has manifested in the promotion of new and relevant lines in research. Soon, along with some social problems surfacing, and assisted by better comprehension of the dynamics between society and ICTs, the need emerged for the construction of more complex indicators and models for benchmarking, as well as the necessity to look into the finer patterns of spatial inequalities in I.S. developments. Recent international summits and documents have indicated a concrete appeal to the national governments and their competent authorities to take up this task.

3.4.2 Actors and scales: international concern with micro-level inequalities and the regional dimension

b) "When and in what forms did the local and regional dimension enter the UN's and the EU's perceptions of the I.S.?"

Issues such as the *liability of national public authorities* to correct market failures in ICT-supply and to help underserved rural regions; *sub-national regional benchmarking* of I.S. developments; as well as the significance of the diversity and relevance of *local and regional digital content* were first introduced in the UN at the Geneva World Summit of the Information Society in 2003. There had been much international discourse preceding this, however, which can be described the simplest as the struggle between the 'traditional' technological, neo-liberal perspective maintained by the ITU and the major IT companies and their critique, a 'humanrightist', culturally sensitive movement of a very diverse set of public, private, civil organisations and representatives of the academia. It is

interesting to observe that these two strands of debate can be more or less identified via their focuses on different components of the access problem. While the former has been more preoccupied with the physical and commercial issues, the latter is calling for more attention to the mental readiness for the valuable use of ICTs, and to the problems related to content.

In the Bangemann Report in 1994, some concerns were expressed as to territorial divergence in the I.S. developments, but only between countries. Concerning the regions and the peripheries, the experts saw ICTs rather as a straightforward solution to many of their problems, such as geographical remoteness.

The regional dimension has got stronger in the European discourses along with the strengthening claims for multi-level governance; and with the realisation that as territorial cohesion is a precondition to the Lisbon 2000 objectives (growth and competitiveness), exploiting the local and regional potentials is a key to actually achieve these aims. As it was illustrated in 3.3.3, thematic maps based on national statistics (and dominating studies and political documents till very recently), failed to show the finer-grained spatial digital divides between urban and rural areas, for instance; neither could describe the degree of disparities within each country. The latter however is as much as a problem for overall national growth and stability as it is on the European level. The acknowledgement of these insufficiencies finally manifested in the Commission's appeal to national authorities for monitoring spatial processes within countries (little result of this could yet be seen in 2003, as indicated in 3.3.4); its own launch of benchmarking projects on the subnational level; its more conscious expansion of existing financial instruments for the benefit of regional I.S. development projects; as well as in its support to regional initiatives for networking and best practice dissemination.

3.4.3 Summary in terms of networks

c) What functions have the international organisations taken up regarding the development of the I.S.? What is the best way to define their role?

In both international examples, much pressure was exerted by actors outside the UN and EU political circles. Besides the private sector, the civil society has been rather active in pushing the organisers of the WSIS and the European Commission in a direction that would give them more voice in shaping the political agendas of the I.S. Networks of regional and local projects could work their ways into the broad policy framework of the EU as recognised partners and experts in the field of I.S. development practices.

These networks and forums of different social partners are a great asset to the Commission. They participate in research, help to attain regular benchmarking, monitoring and the diffusion of socio-technological innovations. In sum, they are channels to invest the efforts and the funds available from the common budget efficiently and 'in place'. Furthermore, the propositions by the international communities suggest that national governments are important players in this context, as well: they can and should promote, support, organise and draw information and other resources from, these networks.

At a fast glance, the EU has much in common with the UN in its approach to I.S. It gives guidelines and sets objectives, organises strategic forums, performs benchmarking, publishes statistics (ranks its countries, implementing the 'name and shame' incentive), supports the dissemination of best practices, orders and finances research, and gives a voice in policy-shaping to the national, regional and local actors. Besides, the EU has established financial instruments which can be drawn on by local I.S. development projects, too. Though there is still much to do in all these terms, it seems that I.S. policy in Europe is taking up the form of some 'open method of co-ordination' where the Community leaves quite much space for the bottom-up initiatives to express their virtuosity, yet takes up the role of a knowledgeable and carefully listening conductor.

4 THE NATIONAL LEVEL: TWO EXAMPLES

4.1 Introduction: choices, questions, methods

Information societies in different countries evolve along divergent paths, and are shaped by special national characteristics.[76] These characteristics are on the one hand, cultural and economic features that have evolved throughout decades and centuries, embedded in individual historical contexts and geographies; and on the other hand, they can be more directly linked to current visions, policy strategies and practical decisions and measures to attain a competitive and socially-economically sustainable I.S.

Naturally, these factors (cultural, economic and policy related) are not entirely separate, as for instance, the former determines the action space (limitations and opportunities) for the latter; and political decisions and institutions influence societal behaviour and value system. Much evidence is presented for this in the following two examples, i.e. the national case studies of Finland and Hungary.

Nevertheless, cultural and historical legacies cannot be held responsible for all the achievements, nor for the flaws of national I.S. policies and intervention. This chapter also justifies the claim that national authorities do have an important and active role in shaping their information societies. In fact, strong political commitment is a critical condition, especially since I.S. development coincides with modernising the working mechanisms in the state itself.

4.1.1 The choice of Finland and Hungary

Conscious of the ostensibly redundant selections of these two countries (predestined by the author's origin and current residence), no systematic comparison is attempted here between the two countries, but some underlying regularities are highlighted concerning their part in the endeavours towards a both competitive and spatially / socially inclusive I.S.

Still, the similarities and differences between "Nordic" Finland and "Post-Socialist" Hungary are meaningful to the context of this research. As regards the parallel characteristics: both countries are relatively small in (concerning their populations especially); located at the eastern fringe of the current territory of the European Union, "between East and West" in culture; speaking languages characteristically incomprehensible for the rest of the world; with long-established, resource-based rural activities as organic parts of their national identities and images; and with traditions of centralised administration and relatively strong local governments. Yet, in terms of their population densities, physical geographical features, the engines of their economies, their recent political histories and inherited legacies, the levels of and disparities in, for instance, the living standards and technological infrastructures; as well as considering several aspects of social attitude to (e.g. trust in), state power,

---

[76] Németh, S. 2005.

institutions and civil action, Finland and Hungary are rather dissimilar.

The meaning of the term 'information society' may be delineated in many ways and for several different purposes (see above in 2.2), and its development can be measured via a diverse set of variables. There have been many attempts to follow these developments over the past decade or so and rank the countries of the world or Europe.[77] Drawing on these statistics, the maps in Chapter 3 show considerable territorial differentiation between some characteristic groups of countries in Europe, and a little diversity within those groups as well.

It seems that the Nordic countries are closer than others to realising the information society. Finland is among them, and in fact, this small nation situated in the north-eastern periphery of the continent has been recently referred to as a kind of a special 'model' of the I.S., to be followed, or at least, critically learn from.

Some justify the existence of a Finnish I.S. by a simple reference to Nokia, the world leader in mobile communications. This company, however 'global' it has become in terms of its markets and its networks of sites and partners involved in its production and development activities, is of Finnish 'nationality'. Also, it seems that Nokia has a well distinguished place in the heart and sense of pride of the Finnish society and economy. Others accentuate the extensive usage of network technologies and interactive applications in public services for the benefit of the people. More arguments speak of the high computer and Internet literacy ('network readiness') among the Finnish population, or the internationally recognised excellence and technologically oriented nature of the Finnish education system. Fewer accounts inform us about a unique techno-culture and spirit as some sort of Finnish hacker legacy, as well as some remarkable innovative bottom-up developments in this country which aim at making the I.S. more inclusive and socially equal than it would be otherwise. In 4.2, I give an overview of most of these aspects, summarising some of the academic, political and more popular accounts on the features and the assumed origins of the Finnish I.S.

Next, the conditions in Hungary for building an I.S. are described. In the case of this country, a more detailed explanation is necessary concerning the impacts of the transition on the social and political-cultural environment; as the latter constitute the foundation and the action space for the creation of the I.S. The stressful and unstable times since Hungary's (re-)entrance to Capitalism, Democracy and her first experiences of being part of an increasingly globalised world did not allow for a consistent and continuous political development in terms of any sector. This is even the more valid regarding the establishment of a national I.S., which needs to be integrative and cross-sectoral by nature, and built on relatively dependable social interactions. Also, since I.S. as a national programme entered political thinking in this country later, basically with her prospects of accession to the European Union coming closer, real political commitment and implementation has reached lower levels than in Finland.

---

[77] See 3.3.3, and Table 5 below for IDC ISI; or Eurostat, ITU, OECD, WEF and UN rankings.

Nevertheless, Hungary has made the initial steps, showed some of her unique potentials and interest in information and knowledge based progress, and has had the first experiences of both success and failure on her way towards the I.S.

4.1.2 Questions and methods

Consequently, the central questions calling for answers in this chapter are:

a) What are the main and specific elements of the Finnish I.S. model, and how has the implementation of the national strategy progressed?

b) How have the governments of Hungary perceived the way towards the I.S. and where has implementation of concrete programmes taken this country in the past approximately 10-15 years? Is there an evolving 'Hungarian model' of the I.S.?

And at last, as a link between national and local/regional issues and competencies in these two countries, it is interesting to see:

c) How much concern is expressed in the national I.S.-related documents and actual programmes in these two countries about territorial inequalities and the regional development of the I.S.?

As mentioned earlier (2.5, and 3.3-4), country and region specific historical and cultural characteristics result in the emergence of different national types, or models of the I.S., so do Finland and

Hungary vary in terms of their paths taken and their results achieved. Consequently, I use two different methods of presentation. I take a mostly institutional approach to the Finnish I.S., and a more chronological perspective to the Hungarian national developments, indicating that the Hungarian I.S. is based on less established structures and mechanisms, and is featured by more discontinuities compared with the more continuous evolution of the Finnish I.S.

Not mastering yet the exotic language of the Finns, I had some limitations in doing research about Finland. However, not too much. Most of the important national and regional policy documents I wanted to draw on are available in English, and so are the relevant publications and news online. Yet, I am also aware that information targeting international audience may contain some bias towards the success of the Finnish I.S. Then again, looking into academic accounts published (in English) by more informed Finnish and foreign researchers on the topic may compensate for this potential 'patriotic partiality'. It is also important to include here the fact that by living and working in Finland, as part of the Finnish I.S. myself, a first-and experience as a user, consumer, and actor has also contributed to the picture I provide.

Obtaining information about the national political developments in Hungary was naturally not restricted by language but was made difficult by my geographical distance, being located mainly in Finland in the period 2001-2007. Naturally, shorter and longer (yearly) visits home for actual field work, and contacts with Hungarian researchers working in the field compensated much for my general physical absence, and so did the increasingly available digital material published by competent national authorities and specialised research communities. Besides, I relied on online journals and newspapers, newsgroups and forums critically discussing the development of different types of access and the politics of I.S. in general.

4.2 Finland: a model of connectedness

According to a survey conducted by Statistics Finland from 15-74 years olds approximately 2.7 million Finns or circa 70% used the Internet since the beginning of January. (...) The number of users has grown among all age groups; however, the use among those over 50 years of age has increased the most. (...) In April 2004 nearly 2.4 million or 61% of 15-74 years old had their own e-mail address. Among the youth between 15-19 the percentage was 89%. (e.Finland and Statistics Finland, 20th August, 2004.)

People over fifty find that the Internet makes it easier and faster for them to take care of daily shopping and banking matters, as well as reducing related expenses. (...) ... they see the Internet as broadening their worldview and bringing new content into life. In their opinion, the Internet does not alienate people from their immediate surroundings; quite the contrary, what ever alienation there may be, it is due to other factors. (Tuorila, 2004.)

4.2.1 Finland ranking high

Finland is frequently mentioned as one of the most successfully and fastest developing information societies. There are few relevant variables according to which this country is not among the top five in European or in the top ten even in global rankings, despite its being situated in a geographical periphery, and having the lowest population density on the continent.

Table 5 shows the good positions of Finland in the world according to four composite variables and their summation in the I.S. index. Besides, Appendix 4 provides more detailed evidence in figures for the persistent Nordic accomplishments and Finland's particular lead concerning the development of diverse content, as well as the 'depths' to which online applications are exploited by society in order to achieve more efficient information flows.[78]

Another example is the *Network Readiness* report by the World Economic Forum, Finland topped the list of 82 nations in 2003 (having stepped up from the third position in 2001), preceding the U.S., Singapore and Sweden. Within the overall 'Readiness Component Index'[79], Finland's strongest results were in *mobile Internet and broadband access*, and the *quality of local IT training programmes*; and there were top scores in *public access to the Internet*,

---

[78] See also Figure 24 in 4.3.2 below for more comparisons within Europe concerning Internet usage.

[79] NRI (Network readiness Index) is defined as "the potential and degree of preparation of a community to participate in the networked world, participate in and benefit from the ICT development." The component indices are 'environment', 'readiness' and 'usage', which are all broken down into sub-indices on the levels of the individual, business and the government. Besides, telecommunications infrastructure and market, as well as the political and regulatory levels are assessed (WEF, 2001-2002; Skidén 2003).

Table 5. Ranking according to the 2003 figures of the Information Society Index and its four component 'infrastructure pillars'

(Source: IDC, 2004.)

ISI Top 10	Computer	Telecoms	Internet	Social	Total ISI
Denmark	3	9	8	5	1
Sweden	10	7	1	3	2
United States	1	20	10	9	3
Switzerland	2	15	9	13	4
Canada	5	24	2	7	5
Netherlands	4	12	15	10	6
Finland	14	10	4	1	7
Korea	20	1	5	23	8
Norway	11	19	3	4	9
United Kingdom	8	22	12	8	10

government online services, and the general *capacity for innovation*. Considering the 'Usage sub-index', Finland obviously showed its strength in the government area, and it was number one in terms of the *use of online payment systems*, of *Internet transactions with the government*, and also, the number of *company websites.* Based on these findings, the report pointed out Finland (along with Singapore and Korea), as a role model for other nations in their endeavours towards an ICT excellence (Skidén, 2003).

What is more, *the dynamics and innovation has been kept up*. Publications on market research show that the *diffusion of newer ICTs* have been increasingly replacing older ones: in 2004, the popularity of broadband (BB) connections in particular, has been growing rapidly, as modem and

ISDN customers have changed over to ADSL and other BB services, and new subscribers generally (Åkermarck, 2004; Tuomi, 2004).

4.2.2 The Finnish 'national I.S. model'

The Finnish success story or 'ICT miracle' has generated a lot of interest, and its foundations have been researched by many. Several theories have been formed and many authors emphasise some individual catalysing factors behind the developments (Paija, 2001). However, (keeping in mind also the arguments presented in Chapter 2 about the intricate relationships between technology, society, culture, time and space) it is true that "(a) nations natural, technological, financial, human and collectively shared resources and competencies, its economic activities and institutional features co-evolve" (Oinas, 2007:1228), so a comprehensive clarification of the Finnish question would be the most suitable.

A relatively inclusive explanation is sought for instance, in the work titled *"The Finnish Model of the Information Society"* (2001) by Castells and Himanen. It is a relatively comprehensive and synthesising attempt at revealing the unique aspects of and the drivers behind, the Finnish accomplishments. The authors use mainly the institutional and evolutionary approaches to shed light on Finland's latest transformation.

Castells and Himanen proposed that all societies can be considered *information* societies which are strong in *ICTs* (in terms of the infrastructure and the production of these technologies) and in *'knowledge'* (R&D, human capital). An *economy* can be regarded *dynamic* if it is internationally competitive and innovative, and if its business enterprises are successful. A *society* can be called an *open society* if it is so politically and towards the global processes, and if it has a strong and active civil sector. In these terms, the authors argue, Finland is an open and dynamic information society and economy (2001:6-14). Besides, Finland continues to be a welfare state, i.e., an egalitarian society with an extensive public sector and income redistribution (Kiander, 2004: 1).

However, the highly developed I.S. experienced in Finland today is a relatively recent phenomenon, and was directly preceded by a serious recession (e.g. Oinas, 2005). In the first half of the 1990s, Finland fell into an "exceptionally severe economic crisis", a situation comparable to that of the countries worst hit by the Great Depression in the 1930s (Kiander, 2000: 5).[80] Finnish GDP shrank by 10-12 percent between 1991-93 and the unemployment rate increased from about 3 percent in 1990 to 17-18 percent in 1994 (Kiander 2000, 2004a).

In socio-psychological terms, this crisis caused a sense of uncertainty linked with "the growing mismatch between the old mental frames, values and norms of people and their new experiences in the rapidly changing techno-economic environment" (Schienstock and Hämäläinen, 2001:34)[81]. Although the impact of the depression varied with different groups of people, as well as across regions and sectors (due to differences in wealth and labour market positions, and in economic and production structures respectively), the Finnish society had to face new problems: "a realisation of a systematic risk in banking, large scale long-term unemployment and social exclusion, and the question of the sustainability of advanced welfare provisions" (Kiander, 2000: 6).

Nevertheless, in the past years, Finland has shown remarkable development according to more general economic indicators. In the second half of the nineties the annual growth rate of the GDP exceeded

---

[80] Kiander (2000, 2004a,b) discusses the roots of the crisis in detail. It was partly due to the general recession in Europe (that was connected to the currency crisis in 1992), but it was also the after-effect of the economic 'bubble' that had grown from a debt-financed boom in the late eighties.

[81] See 4.3.1 for to some extent, similar uncertainties society faced in Hungary at the same time. Also, the conflict and compromises between freedom and security in 'liquid modernity', discussed for example, by Bauman, 2001 (2.2.2, Table 1).

5%, and based on a global competitiveness study by the World Economic Forum, Finland was first in 2001, 2003, and 2004; and second in 2006. (WEF)[82]

So what actually has happened in the last, roughly ten years? Is it really this recent and short period of time where the reasons for success should be looked for? There have been both longer *continuities* from earlier periods and more recent *disruptions* in the forms of reforms and new elements which dynamised the economy, together resulting in this remarkably fast recovery.

In the face of the economic shocks and the industrial restructuring, political governance and corporatist institutions in Finland could stay more or less stable: decision making continued to be based on consensus building; the structures of the welfare state (even after modifications which cut many privileges) were kept. The central labour market institutions (the strong trade unions and the centralized income policy) have been left almost unchanged. (Kiander, 2004a.)

Besides, structural changes, reorganisation of business processes, some cuts in public expenditures were necessary. These however, could not take place without public support: new behaviour patterns on the part of the citizens, who had to maintain their trust in each other and the State, and work even harder. In fact, Finland has been listed among the most trusting societies in recent studies, which could be in part explained by *subjective well-being* (i.e. by a generally high life satisfaction and relatively low levels of anxiety; Delhey and Newton, 2003, drawing on Euromodule 1999-2001; Inglehart, 1999).

Finally, it is very likely, that the rapid economic growth since the mid-nineties has occurred also on account of the expansion of the 'informational economy', the Finnish IT sector. Technological revolution of course, has its roots in earlier socio-economic developments; it also has its important continuities. In the following, these continuities and reforms, and their relations are described in some more detail.

Nokia, the networking company and a new business culture

It would be oversimplification to attribute the recent achievements by Finland exclusively to the success of the well-known mobile telecommunications company Nokia; or to assume that at the core of the Finnish I.S., the plain formula operates that the wealth created by this company covers the expenses of the Finnish welfare state.

Nevertheless, Nokia has obviously had an important and <u>direct role</u> in the exceptionally speedy economic growth in Finland in the second part of the 1990s. It had become the most valuable company in the EU by 1999, and was at the same time, ranked globally number 9 in this respect; besides, the *high-technological cluster* emerging around it (concentrated geographically mainly in the south-southwest), can justly be called the engine of the Finnish economy.

---

[82] Rankings for the years 2001-2002, 2003-2004, and 2004-2005.

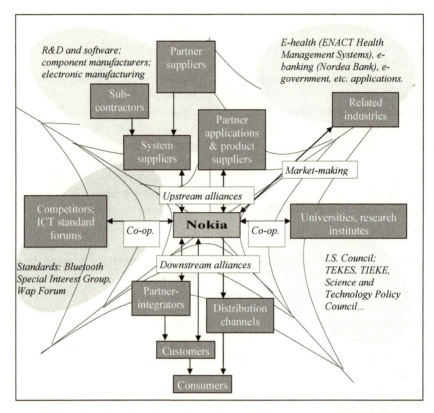

Figure 22. Nokia's network environment (based on Ali-Yrkkö, 2001:42; supplemented).

Indirect impacts, i.e. those reaching to the general business culture in Finland, might be even more important to the country's recovery. Nokia pioneered in Finland in intra-firm restructuring as well as inter-firm networking (Mäkinen, M. 1995; Ali-Yrkkö, 2001). Very much like the entire national economy, this company had to face crisis in the early nineties. It could be saved from bankruptcy only by its comprehensive and innovative reconstruction, i.e. by introducing a new business model, new

organisational and production structure, new financial basis, and by shifting its product markets (see more detailed descriptions on this and the Nokia Values in Castells and Himanen 2001: 15-27; Mäkinen, 1995; Ali-Yrkkö, 2001 and 2002; and Schienstock and Hämäläinen, 2001:75-151; Oinas, 2005; and Tukiainen, 2003).

As a result, the company conducts active *'alliance policy'*, puts much effort into improving its *networking* capacities. The number of its inter-firm alliances has increased considerably in the past decade or so: the web around Nokia comprises "'horizontal' alliances between competitors, 'diagonal' alliances between companies in different industries and 'vertical' alliances between buyers and suppliers" (Ali-Yrkkö, 2001:12; see Figure 22 for Nokia's network environment).

In fact, it is the very nature of Nokia's industrial profile that pushes it to network extensively: timed-based competition (i.e. short product life cycles and terms of delivery times), and uncertainties (the difficulties of forecasting demand and future [technological] development) require obtaining information and knowledge incessantly. This can be done most ingeniously through cooperation with other companies and organisations; even with competitors.

Regardless of the degree and nature of their linkage to Nokia and the ICT-production sector, sub-contracting and supplying partners, and competitors had to reorganise their business processes, internationalise their operation in a like fashion and under the same restructuring pressures. They started to exploit ICTs to increase the efficiency of knowledge flows, established R&D units abroad, and globalised their services and markets[83]. By networking, they all could gain much from the know-how existing within the *Finnish ICT cluster* (Ali-Yrkkö, 2001).

In sum, a wider transformation of business culture took place in the early nineties, in which Nokia was a "flagship corporation", perhaps a crucial initiator: a *paradigm shift in the use of ICTs* by firms matched with the establishment of a *trustful environment* facilitating knowledge sharing; *new organisation forms* flattening hierarchies and introducing horizontally connected and semi-independent work groups, and *increasing inter-firm cooperation* (Schienstock and Hämäläinen, 2001).

The network economy however, does not stop at the borders of the business sector.

The Finnish national innovation system: interactive frameworks and creative atmosphere

Institutional embeddedness and *social welfare* are vital to the sustenance of innovation and growth in the private sector. The network logic, quite predictably, can be traced in the whole social system.

The 'Finnish model' is a much more complex organism than to depend on the well-being of a single, though influential, company, or an industrial cluster. At the basis of its existence, there lies a much broader foundation which is to be found in wider social relations, and the national innovation system (NIS). The intentional creation of the Finnish NIS started in the mid-1960s. Finland was the first country to implement the NIS concept (initiated and promoted by the OECD) as a fundamental category of its science and technology policy (Oinas, 2005:1235).

Naturally, the profound and strategic deployment of the ICTs themselves plays an important role in the efficient

[83] In 2006, Nokia had eight production unites outside Europe: in Brasil, Mexico, the USA, and in two in India, two in China, and one in South Korea (NOKIA website).

performance of this 'organism'. What makes the Finnish I.S. particular is the intricate ways in which the functions of the welfare state are interconnected with the new, knowledge-intensive economy emerging along with the 'informational' developments.

This is the feature distinguishing Finland from other relatively distinct types of the I.S., such as the more 'authoritarian' one developing in Singapore, and the market-oriented and more 'capitalist' I.S. model of the Silicon Valley, USA. It is not surprising therefore, that Finland has come out as world leader in the 'society' pillar of IDC's Information Society Index (see Table 5 above; and note in what aspects the US, Korea, Sweden are at no. 1 positions).

Castells and Himanen present a complicated diagram to demonstrate how the services and functions of the welfare state are thought to supply the foundation for the rather complex structure which can be referred to as the Finnish 'national innovation system', 'innovation milieu', or, actually, the Finnish model of the I.S. (2001:95). It suggests in fact, that everything is connected to everything else, which may cause some doubts. On the other hand, it is evident that Nokia itself is engaged not only in business alliances but in important non-business partnerships, too (App. 6). Some more detailed explanation in the following may help to overcome disbelief.

At the core of the Finnish innovation system, there is <u>a highly connected set of centrally funded national educational and R&D institutions</u>, and related public organisations; and <u>high-quality and free of charge public and tertiary education</u>, with an enhanced system of universities.

The Finnish success in Pisa (2000, 2003), a three-year international survey of the knowledge and skills of 15-year-olds carried out in every three years in the main industrialised countries, is another frequent fact brought up in the context of human capital.[84] Besides Finland's top scores in reading, mathematical and scientific literacy, the high level of equality and the underlying equal opportunities are striking features of Finnish education in international comparison. Actually, the results were a source of "great joy but at the same time a somewhat puzzling experience to all those responsible for and making decisions about education in Finland" (Välijärvi et al., 2002:3).

The findings encouraged education researchers to reflect upon the possible reasons. The outcome was the general

---

[84] PISA assessed young people's capacity to use their knowledge and skills in order to meet real-life challenges, measured literacy in three domains, reading, mathematics and science. In 2000, reading literacy was given a special priority; in 2003 the main domain was mathematical literacy. Students had to comprehend key concepts, and to apply knowledge and skills in different authentic situations. Besides, information was also collected on student attitudes and approaches to learning. Finnish students' ranked no. 1 in 2000 in reading literacy (interpreting texts, retrieving information) matched with a high level of equality (i.e. low standard deviation); no. 4 in mathematical literacy (understanding change and relationships, and space and shape) also very equally distributed, and were positioned no. 3 in mean performance of scientific literacy (life and health, earth and environment., technology). (Välijärvi et al., 2002; e-Finland 2004a, b.)

conclusion that "there is, … no one single explanation for the result" but "a web of interrelated factors having to do with comprehensive pedagogy, students' own interests and leisure activities, the structure of the education system, teacher education, school practices and, in the end, Finnish culture" (*ibid.*). In any case, Finland has taken up the role of a model in this regard, inviting foreign experts to study their system, and exporting it to such geographically and culturally distant countries as China, for instance (e.Finland, 2004c).

The financial situation of the educational sector in Finland started to improve considerably with the decision and guidance of the Science Policy Council and the funds from the Finnish Academy in the 1960s. As a result, already in the 1970s, twenty universities were functioning in the country (while in the fifties, there had been only two towns in Finland with comprehensive universities). This had important implication to a regionally more even distribution of jobs and development potentials, too.[85]

There are technologically oriented universities in Helsinki, Oulu, Lappeenranta and Tampere. Compared internationally, *the cooperation between universities and state-owned research institutes, and the business sector* is more widespread than it is elsewhere (Paija & Rouvinen, 2004).

Since the late 1960s, several key institutions have been founded or renewed.

A national institutional and financial infrastructure has grown to provide the foundation for the development of education, basic and strategic research and innovation in Finland. The most significant of these institutions and some of the important linkages and complementarities between them are given a more detailed account in the following.[86]

The Science and Technology Policy Council (founded in 1986, *Valtion Tiede- ja Teknologianeuvosto*) is the prime source of R&D policy of the government. It gives advice concerning the national R&D budget and the medium/long term goals in the strategic development and coordination of Finnish science and technology policy. It is also responsible for the functioning of the national innovation system as a whole. The Council is a serious and rather influential body in international comparison, organised directly under the Prime Minister. It is made up of "the main cluster actors around the same table" (Paija, 2001:52) including basically all imaginable interested parties: eight key ministers, ten high-level representatives from universities, key personalities from Finnish industries (e.g. Nokia's CEO), leaders of the *Academy* and *Tekes* (see below), and directors of the employers' and employees' organisations.

The Academy of Finland (*Suomen Akatemia*) operates under the administration of the Ministry of Education; it was reformed in 1969. The Academy gives long-term funding for high-quality scientific

---

[85] See more concerning regional dynamics in 4.3.1.

[86] The main sources I rely in this section: Castells and Himanen, 2001; Paija, 2001; Markkula, 2003, and the Internet pages of the organisations.

research, and acts as an expert body in science policy. It also ensures reliable evaluation and promotes extensive *international co-operation*. Besides its Board and Administrative Office, it is made up of four thematic Research Councils responsible for the main fields: Biosciences and Environment, Culture and Society, Health, and Natural Sciences and Engineering.

Sitra (*Suomen Itsenäisyyden Juhlarahasto*), the **National Fund for Research and Development** was founded in 1967. It is "an independent public foundation under the supervision of the Finnish Parliament... (whose) activities are designed to promote the economic prosperity of the Finnish people" (Sitra web site). Castells and Himanen call it the "Public Capitalist" (2001:32) because it does not give funds for technology R&D *per se* but it is more like a venture capitalist organisation financing promising and innovative start-ups in *co-operation with another fund* (*Tekes*). Sitra had a major share in drawing up the second, revised national information society strategies, too (1998).

Between 1994 and 1998, a noticeable and conscious shift in focus took place in national I.S. thinking and policy: the first version of the **national I.S. strategy** published in early 1995 was concentrating on technologies and the economy, while the revised strategy published in Dec. 1998, was titled *Quality of Life, Knowledge and Competitiveness*, and was composed of spearhead-projects such as electronic transactions, telework, sustainable I.S., personal navigation, e-learning, local I.S.,

content industry, and knowledge-intensive work (Hanhike and Nupponen, 2000).

More than 140 measures with the participation of several Ministries and the Prime Minister's Office, 2003-2007.

- Implementation of the broadband strategy so that fast and reasonably priced connections are provided to all citizens by 2005.
- Reforming Government Information Management.
- Developing the interoperability of information management in public administration and cooperation related to information society.
- Information campaign promoting general awareness of electronic services.
- Information society cooperation between large cities.
- Raising the level of public sector funding of R&D.
- Common platform for 'eIdentification' and 'ePayment'.

Box 3. Examples of projects in the Finnish National I.S. Programme, 2003-2007. (Source: Gov. Policy Programmes / I.S., 2006).

The strategy work has been coordinated by the **Information Society Council** (*Tietoyhteiskuntaneuvosto*) since 2003, and the latest (third) strategy, for the period of 2007-2015 was published in September 2006 (see Figure 24 below). The I.S. Council chaired by the Prime Minister, replaced the former "Consultative Committee on I.S.". It is "a negotiation body ... for coordinating cooperation between administrative branches and between administration, organisations and business life" involved in developing the I.S. Its appointment is connected to Matti Vanhanen's term as Prime Minister, who also chairs this body. It meets three times a year, and monitors policy impact and efficiency, puts forward proposals on I.S. policy, and has been reporting on the progress of the **National I.S. Programme** (2003-2007; see Box 3) to the Government. (I.S. Council, website.)

Tekes or the **National Technology Agency** (*Teknologian kehittämiskeskus*) is „the main channel for business-oriented public research and development finance" (Castells and Himanen, 2001:31). Established in 1983, it focuses especially on developing enterprises which produce exportable products and services. Tekes maintains *close links with both the Academy and Sitra*, yet it preserves significant autonomy from ministries (which is a unique feature in comparison with similar institutions internationally). The Agency has funded several successful Finnish technology firms, and played an important role in Nokia's development, too. Tekes *proactively* initiates joint research and technological programmes with universities and the private sector, and also provides financial support to industrial projects and individual projects in research institutes in a *reactive* way if they come up to certain criteria: esp. if they are innovative and risk-intensive.[87]

One other important quality rewarded by the Agency is the ability and extent of *networking* between the various participants who are engaged in particular R&D projects. To promote this idea, the Agency often *recommends partners* – also from abroad[88] - for particular themes and purposes, and it also carries out continuous monitoring and evaluation of the programmes and projects undertaken. So Tekes can be justly called the "'weaver' of networks and 'godfather' to new ICT companies" (Paija, 2001:53).

TIEKE, the **Finnish I.S. Development Centre** (*Tietoyhteiskunnan kehittämiskeskus ry*) is a non-profit and neutral organisation defining itself as the "meeting point for I.S. developers". Its mission is to network its members for the enhancement of I.S. expertise and tools. It has two main strengths. One is its *wide membership*, which "mirrors an entire spectrum of Finnish society and all key players in the information society": over a hundred companies in ICT development, manufacture, marketing, and organisations who deploy these technologies and services,

---

[87] An ambitious goal of Tekes' has been the *FinnWell* technology programme which aspires to develop Finland's healthcare system into Europe's best. To achieve this goal, the FinnWell projects aim to strengthen the linkages between healthcare organisations and technology companies. *iWell*, a previous

healthcare-oriented programme initiated by the Agency, which ended in 2003, addressed health from the viewpoint of service users, while FinnWell combines the interests and needs of organisations, service providers and clients (Virta and Tekes, 2004; Tekes website). This course shows a very conscious developing strategy.

[88] Just one interesting example for the international role Finnish Tekes has taken up, is its activities in China: it opened its Shanghai office in Sept. 2004, committed to strengthen the cooperation between these key technology players in these two, very different-sized, and geographically as well as culturally rather distant countries. (See e.Finland 08.10.2004).

as well as several ministries and public agencies. The other is the *flexibility* of its focus and aims, which "reflect the rapidly changing ICT environment ... (changing its) course from time to time according to need". *Networking and interoperability* are perceived to be the main requirements at the moment, so they have been currently in TIEKE's focus, too (see also the section on e.Finland below).

The Finnish government has a firm belief in developing the I.S., since they see that it is the way to guarantee future economic success for the nation. So finally, there needs to be a mention here of a Parliamentary organ that supports politicians in this resolution of theirs. It is the **Committee for the Future**[89] (*Tulevaisuus-valiokunta – TuV*), which is responsible for 'inventing the future', and as such, is considered a "truly unique Finnish innovation" (Markkula, 2003). It formulates and evaluates the Government's regularly submitted reports on the 5-15 years' future of Finland, prepares recommendations on various future related questions, and

---

[89] The origin of the Committee dates back to the midst of the severe socio-economic crisis (1992), when the majority of the MPs approved a legislation suggesting the Government should provide them with a report about the country's long-term development trends and options. Consequently, the Parliament appointed a 'Committee for the Future' on a temporary basis for this purpose, and the first report was submitted in October 1993. Soon after, the Parliament decided that the Government should present them a 'Futures Report' at least once in each electoral period. In late 1999, along with the revision of the Constitution, the Committee for the Future was granted a permanent status, starting from March 2000 (Parliament of Finland website; Markkula, 2003).

assesses technological development and its societal consequences.

With a regard to I.S., which is indeed a key vision and strategy for the future of Finland, the Committee have *advocated certain crucial measures*. The applications and opportunities offered by ICTs must be within everyone's reach in order to help a faster development of on-line services in the public sector, and for this research has to be stepped up as a joint project shared by the government, municipalities, and the companies operating in the field. The Committee has had also an important role in the high levels of central R&D financing. Besides, public support of creative projects that have the potential to enrich *regional innovation systems* and local economies has been urged.

Not surprisingly, the Committee itself *cooperates widely*, basically with all institutions mentioned above, and naturally, with the Finnish Government and Ministries. Also, it works together with various foreign parliaments and other international organisations and institutions specialising in the survey of future development trends and options, and civic organisations (see: the Committee's website).

The State has for long enabled and encouraged innovation and growth in the ICT industry and market.

Some initial advantages were rooted in special historical situations matched well with public sector responses favouring competitive and innovative markets and the build-up of technological expertise. Besides, there has been a more consciously planned course of telecom liberalisation and deregulation policy followed by the State.

Finland's success with ICTs should not be perceived to be exclusively an internal phenomenon of this specific sector. It is rather the "context of a cross-sector cluster" (Paija, 2001:51; my highlights) that is at the heart of the remarkable growth of the Finnish telecommunications industry. As a rule, the competitiveness of a cluster depends on the political, institutional and cultural environment in which it functions. A very important aspect of this context is the fact that *the cooperation network of the ICT companies extend into other industries, as well as into spheres of research and universities.* Very recently, this networking has increased suddenly. Reasons for this could be the requirements to spread the risk that is so typical of the sector and to take advantage of external expertise and information.[90] Compared internationally, the collaboration between Finnish private firms and public research institutes has been outstandingly broad.

There is "a long self-strengthening and complex development process that started in institutions, organisations and throughout society as far back as the eighteen hundreds" (Paija, 2001:51). It seems that in Finland it was a set of certain successive and *'enabling'* public sector decisions – not all deliberate and part of a conscious strategy, though – which ignited development processes. Four examples of this follow here.

First of all, *the structure of the Finnish telecom markets* was unique already

at its earliest decades (from the late 19th century) because it encouraged interaction between operators and equipment suppliers: the Finnish Senate, then under the Russian Empire, created many private licences for telecommunications activities to get round Russian telegraph regulations. Therefore, there was no such monopoly situation in Finland as in other countries; *competition was inherent* to the telecom market from the start.

After gaining independence in 1917, the state telecom operator was established to keep up the telegraph and army telephone networks that were left behind by the Russians. Thus a duopoly of private and public telecom markets emerged in Finland, which secured a good basis for equal competition once liberalisation took place in the 1990s. Elsewhere in the world, difficult regulation was needed to guarantee conditions for fair competition when monopoly markets were disclosed; Finland was spared this problem.

Secondly, *foreign equipment suppliers* could freely enter the Finnish markets, unlike in other countries, where national suppliers had the benefit of a monopoly position. This secured further sources of *technological innovation and learning.* There were over 800 operators in Finland in the 1930s. They attracted innovative equipment dealers from abroad, too, who were pleased to test their latest technology in Finland (e.g. Sölvell & Porter, 2002; *Finnfacts*).

Thirdly, and as a consequence of the above, the operators were compelled to build up *technological expertise* of their own that could enable them to integrate the

---

[90] As mentioned above concerning 'Nokia's web'.

different manufacturers' network components, and so could make them "expert customer" (Paija, 2001:52). This *knowledge* was later utilized by the nascent domestic component industry, the precursors of Nokia, in fact.

Finally, this *expertise was uncovered and activated by the State* again. This was done through calls for tenders announced for to find technological solutions matching the requirements of different public institutions, e.g. the National Defence, the State Railways (VR), and the Border Guard. Hence the Finnish domestic telecommunications component industry came into being in the sixties through the *co-operation between the public and the private sector.* The peak of this partnership was the establishment of the Nordic Mobile Telecommunications (NMT) network in the seventies. Once again, the standards of the NMT were made open to boost competition in the market, which resulted in the Nordic region becoming the largest mobile communications market in the world by the early 1980s. (Paija, 2001:51-52).

It was in the eighties when information technology started to get some emphasis in political circles (see also above the years of foundation of *Tekes* and the *Science and Technology Policy Council*). Around this time, *liberalisation* was a key driver of further progress, it brought about a revolution in digital and wireless communications. This time the push came from the side of the private sector. Originally the analogue NMT licence was the monopoly of the public telecom company, to which the private network providers responded by setting up local and regional radio telephone networks, which was, on the other hand, within their legal rights. So the private sector was operating without country-wide licences first, hoping that a national licence would be granted to them soon.

After some more pressure and political struggle, these hopes were realised, and private telecom companies could take great and perfectly timed advantage of digitalisation.[91] By 1994, old laws on data transfer rights had been reformed, and the *telecommunications market had been fully liberalised.* Finland was one of the first countries in the world to achieve this. The opening of markets has covered the whole Finnish telecommunications sector since, resulting in strong competition, considerably low prices and a wide selection of high-quality services (ESPON, 2002-04).

In addition, the liberalisation of the capital markets provided an extra source of risk capital, the lack of which had been a major barrier to new business activity up till the 1990s. This measure also ensured a further momentum to the growth, diversifycation and internationalisation of the Finnish ICT cluster, and for instance, helped Nokia also, to become a dominant actor in the global market (Paija, 2001:53).

---

[91] In Finland, telecommunications operations were opened up for competition in the early 1990s: in 1990, the markets of GSM networks and data transfer were liberalised, and "full-fledged competition in local, trunk and international telecommunications began in 1994" already. Nowadays, one only needs to notify the Ministry of Transport and Communications to establish telecom services in Finland, and only the construction of cellular networks requires a government licence (Tuomi, 2004: 8; Cairncross, 1995).

Direct public R&D funds have been upgraded gradually since the early 1980s.

As early as in 1982, the Finnish Government decided to raise national research and development expenditure from 1.2 per cent to 2.2 per cent of the GDP. In 1996 a further increase to 2.9 per cent of the GDP was resolved to achieve by 1999, despite the fact that the Finnish economy had hardly started to recover from its deep recession period. This later goal was fulfilled already in 1998, so yet a higher rate of growth was set to be accomplished by 2000/01, by which time R&D budget had reached 3.2 per cent of the GDP. (Castells and Himanen, 2001). By 2005, this figure had grown to 3.5 per cent (see Figure 23 below).

Finland's determined investment in technological development even during the economic downturn in the early nineties may be credited to the joint vision and determination of the members of the Council to get "Finland back on its feet through know-how" (Paija, 2001:53), as well as the political influence and dedication of the Committee mentioned above.

State organisations and public services have set an example in using ICTs and central funding aims at the promotion of best practices.

In Finland, "the general societal view is that national parliaments should generate preconditions for efficient, innovative activities by citizens and communities, and show examples of such activities in their own work, with the overall purpose being to improve the quality of life" (Markkula, 2003).

More generally, this requirement has been fulfilled in terms of providing a high-quality and 'welfare' educations system encouraging lifelong learning (Rédei, 2007a), a favourable environment for business, investments and innovation, the promotion and extensive support of research, and establishing a virtually all-inclusive framework for flexible networking and cooperation.

In addition, more concretely, public and governmental organisations themselves have led the way in using and providing services via ICTs. Various user-friendly solutions have been implemented ranging from innovative e-governance and e-democracy practices; ICTs applied extensively in both traditional and 'virtual' education, in public libraries, by public transportation companies; organisational, municipal and regional authorities' websites and portals, community intranets, etc.

The existence of such a portal as "e.Finland - Technology Serving People / The Window to Finnish I.S." (www.e.finland.fi), together with the incredible amount of up-to-date information available at its site, is more than convincing. eFinland.fi is constructed and maintained "in wide cooperation with several ministries and national promoters of information society."[92] Its purpose is "to provide all interested parties a single site offering a concentration of Finland's information

---

[92] Members of the consortium are: the Ministries for Foreign Affairs, of Finance, of Transport and Communications, the National Technology Agency (Tekes), the Finnish Information Society Development Centre (TIEKE).

society activities, thus eliminating the need to search for information from several sources." It shows a tremendous national interest in promoting best practices, the latest technological applications and IT know-how. Significantly, it is the embodiment of a deliberate advertisement of Finland to the world as "a country where Information Society of tomorrow is a reality today".[93]

In 2004, the Finnish Prime Minister's Best Practices Award, and the competition for high-quality Internet services in public administration announced by the Ministry of Finance had 266 entries. The most popular divisions were *training and studies*, *social welfare and health*, and *electronic commerce*, and a total of 68 Internet services from the central government, local authorities and public administration participated. The idea of giving out such prizes comes from the deliberation to increase public awareness of I.S.-related best practices, to "showcase top-quality Internet services and solutions that are functional and useful from the point of view of citizens", and to promote their diffusion throughout the entire community. Innovation and further development of current practices are expected to gain impetus as a consequence, and such competitions are also hoped to make it easier for innovations to reach the international market (Ahonen and Ala-Harja, 2004).

There have been substantial investments into innovation by the private sector, too.

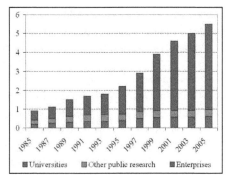

(Source of data: Tekes & Statistics Finland.)

Figure 23. Investments into R&D in Finland, billion euros

Besides the generous public support of R&D, re-investment by the private sector into their research and development activities remains significant (In fact, private R&D expenditure has exceeded the amount of total funding by the state.) In 2005, for example, over 70 per cent of the total investments into these activities in Finland were by the private sector (by comparison, the same figure was 57 per cent in 1991; Castells-Himanen 2001: 34; see also Figure 23.) Nokia is the major player in private R&D investments.

Some special historical conditions encouraged telecom innovation.

Not all developments have been the results of the conscious strategy and planning of the past couple of decades: 'good fortune' and lucky timing also have played a significant part (Paija 2001:53).

---

[93] This claim can be found in the introductory article of the eFinland portal (see References).

Two instances of unplanned but lucky events have been mentioned above already, which had further consequences. The political dependence of Finland within the Russian Empire until 1917 created the situation that (despite repeated requests by the Finnish Senate,) telegraph lines constructed on their territory remained under Russian control (surely, for their military strategic importance). So when just a year after the invention of the telephone (1877) the first telephone line was laid in the Grand Duchy of Finland, the Senate perceived a chance for achieving national independence embodied in the creation of several *private* licences for telephony *separate* from the Russian telegraph infrastructure.

The other interesting incident of several coincidences was set off by a 'fossilised' imperial regulation about data transmission rights, and the 'short-sightedness' of policy-makers wrangling over the GSM licence till the early 1990s. As a result, private telecom companies were refused the analogue NMT network licence in the 1980s, and consequently, they responded by creating their own regional radio telephone networks, and just a few years after, as new market entrants they could take full advantage of the digital GSM licence (e.g. Radiolinja Ltd.). The timing was, by chance, perfect: adequate networks and competition in the market had already been given, *and* just by the same time, the suitable mobile phone technology had become available, too (e.g. Nokia, and several competitors).

Surely, there is always continuity behind changes, so the NIS and recent policy innovations in Finland are also rooted in more enduring, cultural-historical aspects. Explicit and long-standing features of the broader Finnish society have increased the nation's capacity to transform. Oinas (2005) mentions the relatively tight social networks and cross-sectoral linkages that have been permitted by the small size of the population, and the legacy of a "forest sector society"; as well as social cohesion coming from diverse sources such as the free public school system, the summer cottage tradition, student union politics, the unique national language, and arenas that link cross-sectoral elites. These later, i.e. the 'discursive institutions', Oinas argues, helped to establish strong commitment by the government to technology-driven development from the 1960s, as well as facilitated the policy-institutional changes in the early 1990s. Forums of cross-sectoral elites have been crucial in the coordination of the current emergence of a "state-enhanced, innovation-oriented system where firms play a more prominent role" than before (ibid: 1237).

Besides, Finnish national identity has been an interesting question for a long time, in the contexts of their long historical struggle for independence, their strong sense of survival in biological-climatic, as well as in economic and political terms, their emphasized wish to belong to the 'West', their relatively recent accession to the European Union and their successful integration into the global economy. According to some authors (e.g. Castells and Himanen, 2001:84-93; Oinas, 2005) these features of a unique historical heritage, geographical and geopolitical situation partly explains why the new knowledge-based, information society is becoming probably the latest 'national project' or self-definition of this people, both through more natural socio-psychological processes as well as a result of some deliberate identity-shaping by the state.

The creative Finnish hacker culture and values have been prompting wider 'social innovation'.

The term 'hackers' do not necessarily stand for computer criminals operating on-line (the later sort might better be called 'cracker' to make the difference explicit), but simply for "individuals, who believe in their ideas and start to realise them with passion ... who love programming and networking with others to do it" (Castells and Himanen 2001:38). They are usually students who emerge from departments of informatics at technological universities, and who are often driven by the mere excitement they get from problem solving and not by an interest in profit (at least in the beginning, which generosity has been made possible by the right for free study and an advantageous student grant system in Finland; Paija, 2001:53-54). Besides, Patomäki notes that an interesting driver of early hackerism in Finland was the country's peculiar geo-political position and closeness to the Soviet Union which "forced technology-freaks to be creative when ready-made solutions were available to others in the West" (2007:144). (Allowing access to high-tech innovations to countries so dangerously near to the Communist Bloc was considered a risk. This concern played an important role in the

1980s in the case of Hungary and the young computer enthusiasts there, too; see below.)

Often, hackers train themselves further in some special field, and later, launch some private enterprise based on software they have developed themselves, or start working for a telecom giant. Yet in any case, they stick to the concept of open-source, rely on mutual trust and a sense of fair play among their professional society, so they make their results and ideas public in order to let their colleagues all over the world, develop their software or other inventions further. Famous Finnish hackers are: *Johan Helsingius*, who operated the world's most popular anonymous re-mailer (and had some problems with the Finnish police consequently); *Tatu Ylönen*, the inventor of the SSH encryption software (1995); *Jarkko Oikarinen*, the developer of the Internet Relay Chat, *Linus Torvalds*, one of the most genuinely respected hackers in history and the 'father' of the Linux operation system (1991)[94]; *Ari Lemmke*, who has supervised the work of a group of Helsinki students who developed the first network browser with a graphical interface called 'Erwise'.

However, the most significant innovation coming from Finnish hackers was not a technological but a social one. Their example has been inspiring for many of the young, not exclusively computer-minded innovators. Other bottom-up developments have been realised based on

---

[94] The Linux operating system is in fact, gaining popularity: between 2001-2004, It doubled its share of home and office computer op. systems in the world, and in 2004, in its 'place of birth', the University of Helsinki, Linux is being introduced as an *alternative* to Windows (Nurminen, 2004).

How depressing it was to step off the Finnair plane, still enthused by the experience of a prosperous society of mass scholars, inventing the future at their leisure, and walk into the pre-election brutalities of New Labour. Everyone to work, says the chancellor Gordon Brown, no matter what the job entails, no matter how pointless it is. For in the land of New Labour, the soul's play-day is still the Devil's work-day; and idleness delivers the poor onto his scaly hands.

For it's the soulful, playful, scholarly "idleness" of hackers... All those world-changing, freely-gifted innovations produced - HTTP, TCP/IP, Perl, Apache, Sendmail, and Linux - have provided the very backbone for the network economy. ...

Rather than coercing the poor into their brain-destroying Mc Jobs, perhaps the chancellor should be thinking about how to make them all ethical hackers. (...)

(I)f you're knowledge-rich and facilities-rich as well then experimentation and creative play become your vocation. Look at pop music, fuelled by passion, technology and a lot of unspecific fiddling around. Hackers and rockers are spun from the same ethical DNA.

So it's possible that some unemployable, disaffected kid, glommed on to a PC for days, nights and months on end, supported by free education and decent social support, could come up with the next geek miracle for Britain. But as long as the Protestant work ethic dominates government thinking, targeting resources to shape a nation of dutiful workers instead of a nation of unruly players and creators, that's an unlikely scenario.

(Pat Kane, 2001.)

Box 4. Impressions by a foreigner: Finland as a nation of "unruly players and creators." (S.: Kane, in *The Guardian*, 29.03.2001.)

co-operative networking and the open-source model which are not necessarily taking advantage of the latest technologies.

Himanen has famously termed the quintessence of all these as 'social hackerism' in his book titled *The Hacker Ethic and the Spirit of the Information Age* (2001).[95]

An interesting 'outsider's account' on the Finnish hacker culture and its special social context justifies Himanen's view, which is given by a journalist in the well-known British daily, *The Guardian* (see Box 4). He expresses admiration and even some envy for this phenomenon, which is so "un-American", and drawing a bitter comparison between the Finnish 'hacker ethic' and the 'British Protestant ethic'. It seems that the former is a more viable strategy in the 'information age' than the later, which is known to have been the driver behind industrial revolution.

Mr. Kane had surely been much influenced by Himanen's work and some other similar accounts on the lives and work of hackers and the Finnish education system. Also, the title of Himanen's book evokes a clear and intended association or implication to Max Weber's *The Protestant Ethic and the Spirit of Capitalism* (1902), so the comparison above between the British and the Finnish structures and attitudes is certainly not a coincidence. Nevertheless, this view 'from outside' may be an indication of the fact that culturally embedded attitudes do make a difference, as well as that there is a certain 'spirit' behind

---

[95] The hacker values: "promote passionate and freely rhythmed work; the belief that individuals can create great things by joining forces in imaginative ways; and the need to maintain our existing ethical ideals, such as privacy and equality, in our new, increasingly technologized society." (Himanen, 2001: iv).

the growth of anadvanced I.S. This spirit may be just natural to those who share it, yet rather alien, incomprehensible, yet often enviable to those who do not.

Finally, I quote some thoughts from Paija and Markkula (with my own highlights added to words I consider to be of key importance.) The citation from the former author, I reckon, may refer to *all* the above factors and actors – ranging from collaboration in research and development, shared interests in market liberalisation, historic coincidences and opportunities taken advantage of, through funding mechanisms based on complementariness, the role of the state and public policies, to the Finnish networking spirit and hacker ethic fostering the legendary open-source model. The later quote in fact, has the same message complemented with an indication how I.S. should be rather considered as striving to realise a 'knowledge society', and accentuates the importance of networking, cooperation, the abilities to trust, to understand, and communicate with each other.

The development of the **competitiveness** of a country and its companies is closely bound up with the operating **environment** and its internal dynamics. ... There is no such thing as a universally applicable 'cluster policy'. The best way to encourage more innovation and competitiveness is to create a **framework** for uninhabited **interaction** between cluster operators, both private and public. *(Paija 2001:54.)*

Human capital has extremely close connections with **social capital**, due to the fact that **learning** is a highly communal event and **joint process**, in addition to its strongly individual aspects.

Social capital is generated by an **intellectual culture** ... Essential components of social capital include **networks**, work processes, **atmospheres**, **shared values** and work methods, **trust**, and the capacity to think and **interact** with other people. (...) Innovativeness generates innovativeness – but only in a **trustworthy and trusting growth environment**. To be reliable, one must rely on others. (...) In an innovative environment, working relationships are often networks and networks "emerge" from the environment. (...) **Educating** people in **creativity** and **responsibility** from early childhood is a serious challenge to an information society. To achieve this goal, we must aim for a knowledge society. (...) Knowledge is something that we already have within our reach. What will be required next are the **capabilities to apply and to exploit knowledge**, to **get along and learn together** with people from different cultural backgrounds, and to learn to use and develop further responsible and effective knowledge management on both personal and societal levels. *(Markkula, 2003)*

In sum, see Figure 24: it clearly reflects the central ideas expressed in the citations above. It is drawn from the national vision of the I.S. in Finland for the coming eight years (the third I.S. strategy period: 2007-2015). The focus has shifted from an ICT-utilising to a knowledge-based society, and the objective of a socially and spatially equal I.S. has become more pronounced as an important foundation. Certainly, the construction of the building blocks has started already, and Finland's intention to continue on the same path is obvious: towards a "people-centred and competitive knowledge and service society".

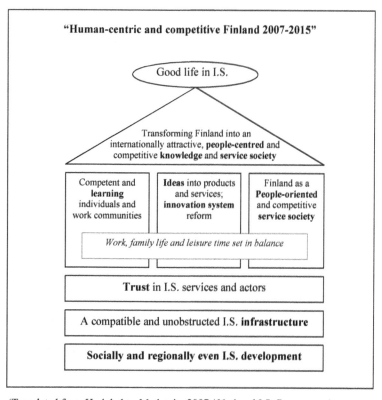

(Translated from Harjuhahto-Madetoja, 2007 / National I.S. Programme)

Figure 24. The construction of the National Knowledge Society for Finland, 2007-2015

4.3 Hungary: building an I.S. under pressures

With an area of 93,000 km² and a population of approx. 10 million, Hungary is a small-to-medium sized country in its more immediate region, Central and Eastern Europe (CEE). Central in Europe may it be geographically, Hungary is currently a periphery in economic and political terms; and is a rather insignificant player in global economy. Still, this country has attracted much attention in the past few decades by trying to break out of this position and to hit a confident and independent, yet not isolated path of development.

Abandoning old habits and structures, however, and finding an 'own way' always take a long time. An obvious sign of this is that since the change of its political regime in 1989/90, Hungary has been most frequently referred to as a former Socialist (or Communist) country, a former Eastern Bloc country, and transition economy, etc.

Economic, social and political transition has taken place in divergent ways in the CEE region. Hungary has also shown some specific traits, which are discussed by scholars and analysts in an ever expanding literature since the early 1990s. Not going into all the detail, I give a brief account first, on what I find especially important about the developments in the past almost two decades. I explain some of the *aspects of the transition process* which have *contributed to a particular social environment* or *'social quality' in Hungary.*[96] The social environment is essential to understand when looking at the development of the I.S. in its fullest meaning, i.e. in its non-technocentric, cultural interpretation (see 2.2.2), or as a communication society (see e.g. the international developments of I.S. discourses in 3.2.1). (Post-)transition Hungarian phenomena such as the missing democratic channels for interest articulation and poor transparency of political decisions are indeed, aspects that deserve some attention here.

Afterwards, telecommunications and I.S.-related policy developments are described along several important phases and episodes: the continuities from before transition, the privatisation and liberalisation process and some other education and content related issues in the nineties; awakening political vision and commitment around 2000-2003; and the developments during the years after EU accession. Along these lines, I present an overview of access-development and compare Hungary's (changing) positions to the rest of Europe (and Finland) when possible.

Clearly, the approach here is less institutional than in the above description of the Finnish I.S., and instead, it is more sequential due to the fact that the direction of I.S. developments in Hungary has been only recently established, and the necessary institutions are just evolving. However, by the end of this section, the shape of some sort of a special 'Hungarian model' will emerge.

---

[96] Social quality is composed of four major conditions: socio-economic security, social inclusion, social cohesion, and social empowerment (Altorjai & Bukodi, 2005).

"We could become the southernmost Scandinavian country, but if political destructiveness, the limitless hunger of the elites, resigned apathy, the praise of ignorance, and the absence of the performance principle will dominate, we easily could become the northernmost Balkan state." (Dessewffy, 2006; translated by S.N.)

Hungary is known for having been one of the first among the countries under Soviet influence to introduce a few reforms already from the late 1960s; and then to actually carry out a 'peaceful revolution' in 1989/90 introducing a democratic multi-party system, and a market economy. In historical retrospect, this latter event, i.e. the 'regime change', was just one important step along the longer path of *transition*[97]. Besides this major turn in 1989, the transition from State Socialism to democracy and market economy has been both pushed on by, and loaded with, embedded *social-historical continuities,* path-dependencies. These continuities were either proactively helping or disturbing social adjustment to the upcoming new circumstances and challenges, depending on the context, the specific aspect, and the phase of the transformation.[98]

In the early 1990s, Hungary had some obvious advantages over other Eastern Bloc countries since some experimentation with economic reforms and the initial steps in democratisation had already taken place decades before the actual change of the system[99]. For example, "gradual marketisation" (Laki and Szalai, 2006:323) in the 1970-80s had resulted also in an 'entrepreneurial boom' in the early 1990s; (ibid; and Nemes-Nagy, 1995:7), as well as in a relatively speedy development of a new entrepreneurial strata.[100] Also, as Adair puts it, "the process of democratisation in Hungary was initiated by Communist-era networks of technocrats and intellectuals" (2002:52), which began to democratise the

---

[97] I am inclined to use *transition* as an equivalent of *transformation* (e.g. as in Kornai, 2006); and I use *regime change* or *system change* when I refer to the concrete event of 1989/90.

[98] See for example accounts in: Adair, 2002; Delhey and Newton, 2003; Győrffy, 2006; Herrschell, 2007; Kozma, 2005; Laki and Szalai, 2006; and the more concrete individual references below.

[99] The first such reforms were carried out already in the late 50s, when the kolkhoz system and the use of obligatory targets in agricultural production were abandoned. In 1968, the launch of the New Economic Mechanism put a definite end to command planning and introduced some profit oriented incentives. As the state itself, started to persuade people to rely more on themselves, a sizeable second economy had emerged by the 1980s which operated through market mechanisms. This had resulted in relatively higher living standards (compared to other countries of the Eastern Bloc); and a spontaneous privatisation (i.e. without public control) that facilitated a gradual liberalisation of exchange and interest rates by 1989. These helped an easy shift to market economy, making hyperinflation and "macroeconomic shock therapy" unnecessary in Hungary. (Győrffy, 2003:240-241)

[100] Laki and Szalai give several examples in their study for the benefits of early reforms on entrepreneurship after transition. An important link between past and future was the "peculiar process of 'learning by doing' in the uncontrollable conditions of the planned economy ... in the difficult years of their private business start-ups" which later "enabled the new entrepreneurs to promptly invent and apply innovative solutions in response to the sequence of sudden difficulties they faced..." (2006:339).

one-party regime already between 1985 and 1989; and hence there was a peaceful reorganisation of the system.

Nonetheless, besides these positive aspects, continuities in the transformation process have had drawbacks and negative implications to stabilisation, modernisation, and democratisation.

First, Hungary's famous "Goulash Communism" (*gulyás-kommunizmus*) could only be maintained by considerable overspending by the state and consequent *debt accumulation*, which latter was accelerated by the oil crises in the 1970s. Gross debt had reached USD 21 billion or 65% of the GDP by 1989 (OECD, 1991:37), which was exceptional among the Socialist countries at that time.

Second, the legacy of the past seems to last in forms of certain routines, like that of *public overspending*. Though some crucial measures by the first democratic government (1990-94) could nearly balance the national budget, keeping the fiscal policy tight (e.g. the introduction of several taxes, decreasing redistribution and welfare services) for a longer period of time was difficult not only because of a coinciding global recession, but also 'politically' (e.g. Győrffy, 2006). The government could not face the prospect of the whole country turning against them because of *the stern social costs* of the reforms.[101] Society already was paying a

high price: structural unemployment rose from virtually, zero to close to 20% nationally in two-three years. The previously less noticeable inequalities in income suddenly became very obvious across the Hungarian society and the national territory, and continued to increase during the transition years (e.g. Csaba, 2000; Kornai, 1994 and 2006; Nemes-Nagy 1995, 1996; Horváth, 2000; see also 5.3.1 below).

The old routine of overspending, unfortunately, has been kept up by the succeeding governments, regardless of their party-affiliation. An exception to this was a 'stabilisation package' introduced in March 1995. The set of reforms (named '*Bokros-package*' after the Minister of Finance) was a combination of extremely harsh monetary, fiscal and income policies which caused a lot of controversy and made its inventor the most unpopular figure of his country (Keay, 1996), as well as much likely, cost the socialist Government (1994-1998) its next term. It came as a surprise (as it had been drafted in complete secrecy), and it was a real shock to society; but it saved the country from financial collapse, and returned her international credibility (Győrffy, 2006: 245).[102]

---

[101] The inability to deal with disagreements and with 'being despised' seems to be present on many levels. Hollander (2006:36) says that "genuine and durable political pluralism requires a capacity to tolerate the strains of disagreement, to coexist peacefully with those we deeply disagree with about important public-political

matters and social values" and adds, that "even highly educated Hungarians ... find such disagreements alarming and difficult to live with... They are stunned and uneasy when free expression brings to the surface nasty, divisive sentiments."

[102] Somewhat typical of the political culture, Mr. Bokros was forced to resign in mid-term, by his own government, as soon as the threat was gone. As an article in International Herald Tribune pointed out: "...his proposals to raise the retirement age and restructure the pension system, bringing in the private sector -- a first in post-Communist Central Europe" were ahead of

It is important to note that the likes of the Bokros-package could not be a plausible routine solution in the future. Firstly, because it was the threat of imminent crisis in 1995 that finally forced all major political actors to recognise the need for this sharp intervention. Secondly, "long-term sustainability cannot be based on exceptional leaders", but on an institutional framework where "people do not have to be wiser or more trustworthy than they are to make the system work" (ibid: 255). The unfortunate fact is, that personalisation (instead of institutionalisation) of politics is indeed, a known trait of Hungarian people's attitude to policy decisions and their outcomes (Korkut, 2005). Third, "a culture of stability cannot be established on surprise elements" (Győrffy, 2006: 256); but on transparency, i.e. people's continuous information about, involvement in, and their understanding of the necessity for certain critical decisions, and reforms.

From about 1997, Hungary started to show again an improvement in her macroeconomic performance. In a relatively short period of time, most of the initial structural problems were solved; post-Socialist Hungary seemed to have managed to enter not only Capitalism, but liberal and global Capitalism. As a promising pioneer, much faith was invested in the continuation of her progress. In terms of GDP per capita and its annual growth, decreasing unemployment rates and incoming foreign direct investment, Hungary was among the most successful of the Central and Eastern European (CEE) countries (following only Slovenia and the Czech Republic; e.g. UN statistics).

Hungary was the first in the CEE region to apply for European Union membership[103] (1994); and by the end of the decade, her accession had become more realistic and was supported in Hungary both by the major political parties and the population. The "need to revise Hungarian identity so that it can respond to the demands of the modern world" emerged; and it did not only in the political rhetoric, but as an "essential requirement for guaranteeing the relevance of the undertaking in the minds of Hungarian citizens" (Kosztolányi, 2000).

Importantly, EU accession was, however, generally perceived not as a threat but as a guarantee of national survival (progress, preservation of distinctiveness, language, material and cultural prosperity, and stability), and as the antipode to the dangers of "staying outside in the Era of Globalisation" (ibid). After 1989/90, the event of the EU accession in 2004 was the second "emphatic experience of the 'kairos'" (i.e. a decisive historical momentum; "the right time to do something"; adopted from Kozma, 2005:491, 497) for the Hungarian people; a

his time; and "'(c)learly, it was all too much for the left of the party, which felt that the man widely viewed as the 'most unpopular in Hungary' was too much of an electoral liability."

[103] Yet this was not the first time for Hungary to show interest in the E.C.: at secret negotiations in the mid-1980s, political and economic leaders in Hungary applied for membership in the European Economic Community, and then, it was rejected. However, shortly after the collapse of the old regime, Hungary entered diplomatic relations with the E.C., and the association agreement was signed at the end of 1991.

feeling of achievement coupled with rising hope.

Nevertheless, difficulties re-emerged after the turn of the millennia, which could be attributed to external (global economic) and internal (policy-related) factors, and as a consequence, much of the earned comparative advantage was lost in the course of a few years. "As the hopes of the transition for better living standards remained unfulfilled, people became increasingly distrustful of political institutions and disillusioned with the political elite" (Győrffy, 2006:251). Unsatisfied expectations (concerning the results of both the transition process and EU accession) sowed the seeds of social conflicts that would spring up again and again in the consequent years and even, decades.

Indeed, after a short period of stabilisation in Hungary (ca. 1997-2000), old routines of overspending continued. The tight macroeconomic policies were loosened again without much consideration of perhaps, the bad timing (i.e. another global recession). The approaching new elections in 2002 increased spending, and the new Government had very little space for cutting it after having promised the contrary in the election campaign. Higher the deficit was rising, the less transparent public finances became (ibid: 247). The combination of *keeping information back concerning the actual situation, and promising higher living standards* has been brazenly used in order to win public support in political struggles.

For the purposes of the present study, a rather persistent problem has to be underlined here, which lies behind many of the weaknesses of current societal relations in Hungary, hindering their development and corrupting their functions, and thus holding back economic stabilisation and further democratisation. It is something which no single governing party or coalition can be rationally expected to have the means and the power to eliminate in its four-year term. It concerns *social and political trust*, and the "difficulties in the orientation of interests" (Tóth, 1998:8), an inherent feature of this post-Socialist and yet, pre-modernised society.

Transition in Hungary, indeed, did not take place in a few months; and it had not been accomplished even by the accession to the European Union in 2004. It was, or rather, has been a lengthy and weary process of some ten-fifteen (or more) years, complex with upheavals and setbacks, crises along the way. It has worn out society and societal relations to an extent which may undermine the further stages of democratisation.

The economic and political developments described above, not surprisingly, were accompanied by increasing social and political distrust, and pessimism. Especially, the lack of trust in political institutions, in the political elite, and in politics in general has to be stressed. This is a problem deeper than and far beyond, the first disillusionments after the initial "sense of euphoria and triumphalism" (EBRD, 1999) over the system change. Many refer to the situation in the recent years as a "moral crisis", and an environment "fertile for populism"

(Győrffy, 2006:251, Hollander, 2006:35-36[104]).

In his work titled *Spheres of Interest after the Political Transition in Hungarian Society* (1998), Tóth argues that social-political transition is always an evolutionary and multidimensional process of several different continuities and interruptions, from a stage left behind, to a new system not yet attained. This causes many discrepancies to the system of social institutions. Despite the introduction of parliamentary democracy, some hierarchical structures from State Socialism have prevailed in Hungary after 1990, and transition in fact, has been taking place more or less through the elite's interest-bargains, "above the heads" of the masses. *Distrust* in state power is almost an inevitable outcome of this situation (Dombi, 2001; Korkut, 2005 on 'elitism'; Marková, 2004).

Moreover, Tóth explains, that there are "silent pursuits of interests", which are voiceless because they do not even appear in the "sphere of interest articulation", since society on the whole, is 'not ready' in terms of *institutions, culture and mentality*, for their presentation, aggregation and communication" (ibid: 9, translation and italics by S.N.). The author referred to the early nineties when saying:

Today's Hungarian society, in a "blissful" state of pre-modernisation, is still characterised by a state of inconsistent recognition and awareness of self-interest. This is primarily because of the lack of state resources for the establishment and especially the maintenance of a public field for exercising political power as well as a middle-level for the harmonisation of interests, and last but not least, for comprehensive social-economic agreements. (Tóth, 1998: 11; translated by S.N.)

Nevertheless, the absence and / or the underdeveloped nature of suitable institutions and the missing channels for the articulation of interests were a critical problem not only directly following the system change, but they are unfortunately, valid to the current state of affairs in Hungary, almost two decades later. The actual leadership, the political elite needs to take more responsibility for this situation and as Dombi puts it, "politics-makers sooner or later should realise that although, they may own power temporarily, they are first and foremost servants of the common people, not their masters" (2001:9).

In sum, *elitism, the personalisation of politics, populist tendencies,* as well as *poor transparency* have characterised political developments in Hungary since the 1990s. Besides, the continuing *search for and the many conflicts around, national identity,* the *lack of trust* in the leadership, and the *missing democratic channels for interest articulation* are aspects that are especially relevant to the development of an information society in Hungary.

As indicated in the previous chapters (in relation to processes both internationally, and in Finland), I.S. is being increasingly defined as a 'network society',

---

[104] Referring to a concrete incident of this moral crisis in 2006, Hollander claims that "Hungarians were more outraged by the lies of their high-ranking officials than by their politics (and the objective conditions resulting from them)" and he concludes that moral indignation is a more powerful force in political conflicts than material interest" (2006:36). This at least, suggests that pragmatism may not be among the most important features of either the leading elite or the general public in this country; and I myself see a point in this claim.

and more importantly, as a 'communication society' or an 'interactive society' (e.g. Dombi, 2001; Farkas, 2002; Pyati, 2005): social networks are strongly associated with institutions and trust-relationships; the promotion of e-government, the provision of interactive digital services and information flows between the state and the citizens are imperative elements of both on-line content development[105] and democratic transparency.

Therefore, in addition to the enquiries worded above, two further questions *specific* to the 'Hungarian model' (see question b) above) call for some investigation, or at least, consideration:

b/1 How have ICTs and the promotion of digital content been employed to improve the channels of interest articulation in Hungary?

b/2 How much have the old legacies in institutions, culture and mentality been making the application of these new technologies difficult?

4.3.2 I.S. in Hungary

The forming of an information society in Hungary is not a political issue dependent on terms of government. With a collective effort, we have to achieve our goals within ten years!
(HISS: the Hungarian Information Society Strategy, 2003: 3)

Along with the tasks directly related to the transition process, the 1990s presented another challenge to Hungary: the

necessity to join and be an active participant of, the 'new economy', the global I.S. and the related innovation processes. More than fifteen years had to pass from the first attempts to establish the fundamentals of these developments by means of sectoral policies until the emergence of some political commitment and a more integrated, comprehensive approach to the I.S. taken up by the state. In the following, this progress is described in two, more or less distinct phases, focusing especially on the role of the central government, but also with some implications to the involvement of other actors. (However, the latter are given more emphasis in 5.3).

I start with the more immediate pre-transition period and the first ten years after the change, highlighting *some* of the legacies, continuities, as well as interruptions and reforms which have been relevant, for instance, to the social acceptance of the new technologies, or to the initial infrastructural disadvantages in Hungary. Then I describe the main foci of policy attention, as well as the achievements and the difficulties since about 2000, right before and after Hungary's EU accession. The latter incident divided the past 6-7 years into two phases that roughly represented the preparation and the first steps in the implementation, of a national I.S. strategy.

Continuities and reforms (1990s)

The basics of mental access: affinity for using ICTs

During the 1980s, inevitable changes took place in Hungary (and in the Eastern Bloc in general), a few of which

---

[105] See the discussion above in 2.3.2 for instance, the UN and EU guidelines, as well as the example of Finland.

were linked in some way or another to the informational-technological developments in the West. The collapse of the Socialist regime itself could be associated with at least two technologically related facts.

Firstly, some essential ICTs were increasingly available in the Eastern Bloc (television, photo copying machines, fax, and the first PCs), which made state control over the flows of information in society more and more difficult. Communication had indeed a high political value for the reason also that authoritarian structures in the last few decades, had been able to uphold their status quo only by the regulation, filtering and the deliberate shaping of social and political information networks. Therefore, it is no wonder that, as Tamás argues: "the increased access to social information, the liberation of communication from under earlier controls, and the disputes over the relationship between the new publicity and regulation ... produced the most serious political conflicts of the decade following the establishment of the new democratic political order" (2001:61-62).

Secondly, the pre-transition blunder is often referred to in retrospect that while in the West, 'the revolution of chips' was being prepared, in Hungary a 'country of iron and steel' was under construction even in information technology (consider for instance, hardware dependency, as well as the dominance of electric engineering and programming in technological training; Magyar & Z. Karvalics 2000:511). Isolated from the global processes and without the function of market mechanisms, technological development was imposed on

society more as an exogenous and independent force than integrated with it and its actual needs, which resulted in a low efficiency of investments into R&D (Tamás, 2001:45). Socially relevant technological innovation had been *de facto* for many decades limited by the political and economic isolation of these countries from the West, i.e. by the CoCom embargo.[106] All these aspect had yielded in a considerable technological gap between the two worlds, making the Socialist economies incapable to compete with the market economies by the 1980s.

This problem, however, was recognized by the Socialist-Communist regime, and so they looked for ways to go around the CoCom limitations. These ways in fact, were offered by the societal processes themselves which were the outcome of the loosened state control on information about developments in the West. One way was the so-called 'private import' of technological goods (Dessewffy, 2002). Among the Socialist countries, Hungarians had the greatest freedom to travel to the West, and the neighbouring Austria was a favourite destination for their masses of tourist-shoppers. This was how the first personal computers were 'imported' semi-legally in parts or in one piece to be either resold domestically, or be kept by young techno-enthusiasts who gave rise to a self-educating 'Commodore-64 subculture'. They freely distributed programme codes broken for reuse; some of them became 'hackers', others set up private

---

[106] CoCom: Coordinating Committee for Multilateral Export Controls, placing embargo on exports from Western countries to the Socialist Bloc for the time of the Cold War.

enterprises or took up public employment in the information sector in the nineties. Meanwhile, the state at least, tolerated and did not try to officially prevent, this and other ways of diffusion of computer skills in the eighties (Dessewffy, 2002).

However, this growing affinity for ICTs had remained limited to these specific groups of the Hungarian society. Research found that the majority of the people were still unfamiliar and / or even, suspicious towards personal computers in the nineties (Csákó, 1998; BME-ITTK & TÁRKI, 2001), including those educators whose very task was to introduce ICTs in public schools and universities.

The first years of the 1990s might well have been the moment for public intervention to mobilise and efficiently organise this *existing* human capital and promote 'access' in educational institutions. However, for many understandable reasons (lack of resources and attention due to the confused condition of the country) this intervention happened only in the later nineties. Therefore, neither the development of e-literacy and openness among the general population, nor the emergence of domestic ICT innovations could occur in this early but rather crucial stage.

Another important and in a way, controversial legacy, as well as a factor significant both to the mental capacities (skills and openness) to use ICTs and to the access and creation of content on the global media, is language barriers or *linguistic incapacity*. Firstly, Hungarian content stays mostly incomprehensible and therefore, inaccessible to the rest of the world; the on-line presence of the national culture has a

rather limited audience globally. It is an even more important problem that only a very little percentage of Hungarians can make themselves understood in another language (Eurobarometer, 2005; Dessewffy, 2002), and therefore it is more difficult for them to be aware of and identify with, much of the world outside. The inability to understand English can already discourage or even completely block people from using the Internet. Neither can they easily communicate and network internationally and draw from resources that are potentially available via the World Wide Web.

In Hungary, the situation was especially bad in this respect in the early nineties, when most of the active population had no foreign language skills at all (except for some knowledge of Russian, 'on paper', included formerly in their public education as compulsory). With time, a new generation of young adults started to emerge who had some sufficient skills in English or German; yet Hungary is still lagging behind most of Europe in this respect.[107] Moreover, great disparities in language skills exist across the national territory, following urbanisation patterns and west-east divides (see also 5.3), and adding to other disadvantages in 'access' to information and knowledge. Linguistic incapacity has for

---

[107] In 2005, 71% of surveyed Hungarian population (aged 15 years and over) claimed to master only their mother tongue. This is contrary to the tendency that small EU member states (with not widely spoken national languages) have better foreign language skills in general. In this ranking, Finland was positioned much above the EU-25 average (50%) with its 66% of foreign language speakers (among which about two-thirds mentioned English as a second-third language). (Eurobarometer, 2005.)

long been a "barrier to Hungary's becoming a Knowledge Society" (Dessewffy, 2002); and it is partly the reason for info-pessimism, influencing motivation to use ICTs in Hungarian society.

Upgrading physical access: the national backbone network and the public telecommunications infrastructure

An important initiative in the late eighties (1986) was the launch of the National Information Infrastructure Development (NIIF) Program by the *Hungarian Academy of Sciences* and the *National Committee for Technological Development*. Its aim was the creation of a nation-wide computer network for R&D institutions, universities, collages, and public collections (libraries, archives), as well as some other major public institutions in Hungary, allowing them already in the immediate pre-transition years to access basic services such as e-mail, file-transfer, or remote log-in (NIIF). So by 1990, the basic elements of the domestic research network had been set up. Following the political change, and the establishment of Hungarnet (Hungarian Academic and Research Networking Association, 1991) representing the user communities, international connections could be formally created. All the relevant ministries and the *National Scientific Research Fund (Országos Tudományos Kutatási Alapprogramok; OTKA)* joined the Programme soon, and from 1992, regional networking centres were set up to integrate local services to the central ones. The number of users doubled yearly to reach almost 100,000 by 1995. Since, much technological development has taken place, international connectivity has increased further supported by various EU initiatives.[108]

Yet, having acknowledged the relative readiness of the backbone network for the intellectual and administrative elites and their activities, one should not forget about the poor state of the basic *telecommunications infrastructures* in the nineties. This was also associated with pre-transition processes. The old regime had been trying to keep up the short-term contentment of the society (by loosening control, and introducing some economic reforms, as mentioned above) in order to prevent insurgences. This could be maintained only at the cost of neglecting long-term investments (Tamás, 2001:61); i.e. into transportation, telecommunications and public utility networks. However, as a consequence, living standards were inclined to drop considerably on the long run.

So, the condition of the telecommunications infrastructure in Hungary was rather miserable in 1989, even in quantitative terms. An interesting point to make here is related to the fact that since the cycles of the different ICTs have been progressing rather fast in the world, the indicators to be used to see their development in a given country needs to be revised from time to time. In Hungary, this

---

[108] Access speeds and data transfer capacities of NIIF/HUNGARNET have been improved by for example, the TEN, QUANTUM, GEANT projects of the EU. By early 2006, over 600,000 users from about 500 institutions (ca. 6 % of the Hungarian population) has access to advanced infrastructure and services via the academic and research network. (NIIF)

has been even the more relevant because at the time of the system change (1989/90), the country's level of development could be described with indices such as the *number of fixed telephone lines per 100 inhabitants* and the length of waiting lists[109]. Then, the failure to meet even quantitative demand, and shortcomings concerning the very basic qualitative features were the sources of major problems.

However, the first post-Socialist government recognised early the urgent need to upgrade basic telecommunications infrastructure. This was achieved by a radical measure: through the prompt privatisation of the Hungarian Telecommunications Company, *Matáv*. It was sold to a German-American consortium, with a legally guaranteed monopoly in telephone services till 2001 to encourage fast results.

Consequently, fixed line telephony diffused remarkably fast. The telephone cable network was modernised and efficiently expanded to the whole national territory. The earlier indicators became more or less obsolete. Waiting lists virtually disappeared by the middle of the decade, as everyone who wanted a fixed line could get it fast. The diffusion of telephones in households reached its saturation point in mid-2002 (HIF, 2000-2007) as mobile telephony hit a faster rise; and then, even slightly dropped, just as it happened in most other countries.

The digitalisation of the fixed network commenced at a fast pace (the proportion of digital connections in the network reached up to over 91% by the end of 2000; TEP, 2000.) The physical foundations for a greater variety of telecom services had been created.

Rapid spread of mobiles and insufficient Internet diffusion at the end of the 1990s

The two ICT technologies in vogue in the latter nineties were mobile communications and the Internet. The diffusions of these two solutions in the society, with regards to subscription numbers and usage have been rather different in Hungary. The mobile network covered the whole country and included the majority of the population in a matter of a few years, while the network of Internet technologies diffused slowly and selectively (see also 5.3.1 about territorial tendencies). This has more or less been a trend in other countries, too, yet the gap between the growths of these two telecom sectors has grown bigger in Hungary; which can be attributed to some specific CEE or Hungarian traits. The expansion in the usage of mobile phones in society surpassed all expectations in Hungary. While forecasts in

---

[109] The number of fixed telephone lines per 100 people was 5.8 in 1980 and still below 10 in 1990 (TEP, 2000). At the end of the 1980s, one had to wait eight years on average for the installation of a new telephone line in Hungary (Dessewffy, 2002). There existed settlements without a single telephone connection.

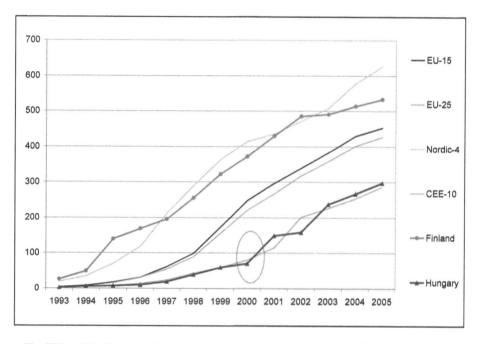

The CEE and Nordic regional data is calculated with national population weights.
(Source of data: CSO/KSH).

Figure 25. Estimated number of Internet users per 1000 inhabitants.

1994 (when GSM services were launched in the country) projected a maximum of 1 million subscribers (ca. 10% of the total population) by 2000, there were 2 million cell-phone users (20%) already by the middle of that year. This expansion even accelerated afterwards: 7 million subscriptions (70%) by early 2003 and over 10 million (100.4%) by early 2007 (100.4%; HIF 2000-2007).

There have been several factors driving the rapid diffusion of mobile phones in Hungary. Besides their fashionableness (i.e. that of a social status symbol); their practical utility, more precisely, the flexi-

bility and freedom they offer their users can be mentioned. Dessewffy (2002) emphasizes however, that individual freedom in the nineties was valued even higher among the Hungarian population (and in most of the CEE region) than by other, more mature democracies because of the low reliability of institutions and the state. Besides, in Hungary, this problem with trustworthiness has been not only a subjective or perceived one (which may be the case in some western societies) but based on experiences of everyday life. Low trust has been to a great extent rooted in objective circumstances in healthcare, public transportation, police, administration and other public services (see also the explanation above in 4.3.1). What is more, the success of mobile telephony in Hungary occurred in spite of the fact that mobile services (calls, text messaging) have stayed above the price levels in Western Europe.[110] This shows that trust in institutions has been so low and individual independence valued so high that people were ready to sacrifice even beyond their financial means for to secure the later.

Internet use is also likely to enhance individual freedom, yet its expansion in the society has been one of the greatest failures in the course of Hungarian I.S. development so far. Some of the reasons for this have already been discussed above (language and ICT skills). Nevertheless, the greatest barrier was a long lasting monopoly situation in telephone services and the provision of Internet services.

Although both the private sector and the European Union were urging telecom liberalisation from 1994 (Bangemann Report, see 3.3.1), in fixed line telephone services, it had not happened in Hungary till 2001 when the concession rights of the incumbent *Matáv* came to an end. As a result of the monopoly, prices continued to stay very high (esp. as compared to income levels in Hungary; see Figures 8-10 above). This was a major hindrance to the diffusion of Internet usage, in general, and to the spread of Internet into households in particular. Figure 25 indicates clearly the main point of divergence

between the diffusion trends in Hungary, the CEE and EU regions, and the Nordic countries. Indeed, after 2000, a sharp rise is observable in Internet usage in Hungary which was due to the liberalisation and a special discount package (named *'Mindenkinek'* – For Everybody; launched in April 2000) introduced by Matáv to boost off-peak usage and save its position in the market (Molnár, 2002).

Results from various researches and surveys in the late nineties (and early 2000s) indicated the general problem. If access was from home, it was still dominated by narrow- band solutions: analogue modem ('dial-up'), and ISDN technologies at the turn of the millennia. Usually, however, access to and usage of, the Internet was more likely to be from the workplace, the school and public access points set up especially by civil initiatives.[111] These later have been playing an important role especially in peripheral and underserved areas because both narrow- and broadband applications have been rolled-out unequally across the national territory, following existing disparities in economic growth, income levels and general living standards (see 5.3).

Other negative aspects of Internet in Hungary were the lack of regional co-operation in the CEE region in terms of infrastructure development (not to mention any harmonisation of services and joint content production). The interesting situation persisted that if an electronic message was targeted to a neighbouring

---

[110] In 2002, for example, mobile call tariffs in Hungary were equal to those in Finland, while average wages in manufacturing, for example, were only about 20-25% in Hungary of the Finnish figure (UN statistics).

[111] Probably, it was not a coincidence that it was then, in the late nineties, when the movement of the telecottages got a real momentum. (See 5.3.2 below.)

country, it had to travel via the United States (Dessewffy, 2002). Cooperation across the CEE occurred from the late nineties however, between civil society organisations, and among the different groups of the Hungarian minorities: they recognised the potentials of the ICTs to strengthen cultural links with the mother country and ease political and identity-related tensions in the regions. (Nevertheless, the EU accession of many of the CEE countries brought some improvement regarding collaboration between the states.)

Access in education by Sulinet ('phase 1)': the launch of a public initiative

Magyar and Z. Karvalics point out (2000) that education has always been considered a strategic sector in the CEE region. It was also the only field in which, Hungary was able to come quite close to the level of world standards (as it is indicated in brain-drain maps; see also Rédei, 2007b: 135-137). "Glorious and noble tradition is, however, in vain if school as an institution does not adjust to the informational challenges" (ibid: 518). The Hungarian government seemed to have recognised this relatively early when it initiated the *Sulinet* ('Schoolnet') *Programme* in 1996.

As mentioned above, schools have been one of the major sites of access to Internet since the late nineties. Sulinet has had many short and long-term aims touching on several (i.e. the physical-financial and infrastructural, mental, content-related)

aspects of access in education.[112] The first phase of the programme however, focussed almost exclusively on the physical-infrastructural integration of schools into a national network, to achieve a decentralised public education and equal opportunities in every region of Hungary (Nagy & Kanalas, 2003:40).

The Ministry of Culture and Education gave the task to a consortium made up of the incumbent *Matáv*, and two other bigger companies, who could then subcontract the construction of different parts of the network to local telephone operators. On a first, higher level, a backbone structure (2 Mbps) was built which was directly joined to the optical cable ring of *Matáv*, and which facilitated linkages to the regional nodes and international networks (via Hungarnet). On a second, lower level, the schools were connected to this backbone frame. From 1997, over 1,500 institutions were included in the common network: approximately 850 secondary schools (all secondary schools were linked before the end of 1998), 350 primary schools, hundreds of libraries and student housing complexes, and so on, from about 300 municipalities.[113] Initially, schools with more than 500 students received 64 Kbps ISDN connections, smaller ones were connected with telephone modem (dial-up). Capacities of the network on both levels have nevertheless, increased

---

[112] Information about the Sulinet programme is from: the Sulinet website; HVG, 2007; Magyar, 2001:224; Nagy & Kanalas, 2003:40-41; and Szekeres, 1998.

[113] The integration of primary schools, some 3,000 in total, has not been completed to date (09.2007).

after 2000, with the emergence of broadband solutions (but selectively, more probably in bigger secondary schools).

Surely, the creation of the physical network was to be followed with more steps that would improve especially the ICT skills among teachers, as well as networking and on-line content for educational activities (see Box 5); however, most of these measures were launched only after 2002.

- *Targeted financial encouragement* of demand for ICT tools (Sulinet Express, 2003-2006): with a focus on the younger generation, families with children, and teachers as well as other public and civil servants, through special tax allowances (i.e. for buying PCs and other digital tools, a tax allowance of ca. €250 or HUF 60,000).

- *Improving mental access* in target groups: organising training for teachers in specialised or general ICT skills, as well as in the specific ways of employing the technologies efficiently in teaching their particular subjects on different levels.

- *Developing relevant and useful content*: creating, collecting, and pooling modern curricula, on-line material, teaching aids, standardised databases, etc. to support the educators in their work; offering these resources on-line, and in other forms (multimedia packages).

- *Enhancing networking and interactive on-line information processes* between actors in the education sector: Sulinet portal, a virtual surface for the communication between the different communities involved (the Ministry of Education, the teachers, the students, and their parents), and experimentations with e-learning.

Box 5. Sulinet 'phase 2' ambitions.

Show of commitment (after 2000)

The advanced countries have, in the past five to ten years, experienced a dramatic expansion in the use of information-communication technologies, and Hungary has only succeeded in keeping pace with them in resolving the historically disastrous situation in the availability of fixed telephone lines and in the area of mobile telephone services.

In December 2002, only three tenth of Hungarian population used computer regularly or occasionally, and only 17 per cent used the Internet on a weekly basis at least. The vast majority of Internet users have never made a purchase via the Internet.

(HISS, 2003: 14, 12)

Taking stock

Internet diffusion in society remained one of the main targets of criticism after the turn of the millennia. Despite this, in early 2002, Matáv cancelled its 'For everybody' discount package, as well as its earlier '*150-forint*'[114] offer to use telephone connection for Internet during the night.[115]

---

[114] 150 Hungarian forints (HUF) were then equal to approximately 60 eurocents (05.2002).

[115] Matáv argued that these deals had caused them a deficit of several hundreds of thousands of euros. Yet in reality, since these had concerned the off-peak hours, they considerably *expanded* the use of the Matáv-network capacities, and therefore had meant increased revenues for the company. Molnár (2002) draws attention to the fact that Matáv implemented a unique accounting method: it compared its profits to a *potential* net income which would have occurred if the Mindenki-package customers had connected to the Internet within the more expensive peak-hours instead, paying the regular charge by minute.

These measures however, were followed by immediate reaction by the users: they either reduced their minutes spent on-line or withdrew their subscriptions from home altogether and looked for other alternatives to access Internet (i.e. from the workplace or libraries).[116] About 39 thousand households were affected by Matáv's decision, which represented 18% of all households that had had Internet connection (Molnár, 2002). The incumbent suggested that these households should switch to ADSL. However, at the time, ADSL services could not mean an attractive and feasible enough option for most of the people in Hungary because of their limited availability across the country (see 5.3.1 below; and e.g. Erdőháti, 2002; Molnár, 2002), and the fact that they all of a sudden, meant a huge leap in costs.[117] Rural areas especially, where incomes were lower, were left with little if any prospect, not to mention the fact that in villages and smaller towns, ADSL was not even technically available.

The conduct of Matáv also confirms the claim by some observers (e.g.

Fischer, 2005) that despite the fact that by 2002 competition had significantly improved in the telecommunications market, the monopoly behaviour of companies persisted. For several decades the rule had been that the service provider dictated the conditions and the consumers had only the "right to suffer" (*ibid*): this was the formula before the system change when people had to queue for telephone lines, and during the 1990s because of the monopoly granted to Matáv. It had produced a generation of consumers who were unaware of their consumer rights and the means to exercise those. So, even after liberalisation, these consumers stayed defenceless and confused in a multi-player market environment with complicated tariff systems, misleading and incomplete information in mobile and internet contracts (e.g. in loyalty contracts), and other rather unethical tricks used by companies in competing for customers.

The Sulinet Programme also slowed down significantly after its school network infrastructure had been more-or-less completed. The change in government in 1998 probably was one of the reasons for this. The programme was re-launched in 2003 with a next phase, the Sulinet Express initiative (see Box 5 above), but it was much criticised from the beginning. Evaluations were contradictory by the different political groups and stakeholders, and the whole issue became, like many other state initiatives in 'transitioning' Hungary, a political battlefield. It was mostly seen as inconsistent, irrelevant to its original purposes, irresponsibly costly to the state budget and not achieving even its quantitative targets (HVG, 2007). Many

---

[116] Many users returned to the rather slow and less reliable tariff-free Internet services (e.g. Freestart) which they accessed via telephone-modem kits again, facing the phenomenon of 'World Wide Waiting' (a cynical expression often used by irritated net-surfers) instead of the benefits of the World Wide Web.

[117] Matáv's 'Home ADSL' (introduced in mid-2002) cost an initial opening payment of 120 euros, and the monthly subscription fee of 61 or 53 euros per household, depending on the length of the contract (*Figyelőnet*, 2002). Considering the fact that the minimum wage in 2002 was around 200 euros (raised by a government decree in 2001 from about 100 euros) in Hungary, this was a price affordable to few families.

attacked the government for giving unfair privileges to certain companies within the *Sulinet Express* framework, to ones also, which were owned by politicians. However, the managing authorities felt that they had achieved a lot: by the end of 2005, 150 thousand new PCs had been purchased by households, half a million computers were upgraded and some 600 thousand families had bought different ICT tools, while public education institutions had received hardware worth almost 25 million euros (HVG, 2005).

Around the turn of the millennia, and on the threshold of EU accession, the political and academic elite evaluated the conditions in Hungary also in terms of its responses to the challenges and opportunities of the I.S. Besides the improvement in basic physical ICT networks, the nineties could be characterised by a few scattered and at least, partially successful initiatives by the state to promote 'mental' readiness of the population for these technologies. However, the different interventions were lacking co-ordination.

Most of the assessments in fact, were more negative than positive, and called for urgent action. Magyar[118] bitterly pointed out in 2001 that Hungary was not only lagging behind the West but many of the other formerly Socialist countries, who have taken over very fast: Estonia, Latvia, Slovenia, and in some respects, Lithuania and the Czech Republic had passed Hungary in I.S. developments (2001:223). "So, while the Hungarian political elite makes pride in referring to the richness of Hungary in

human capital, the conditions for this human capital to be actually utilized are missing" (ibid: 203, translation).

The most important observation by analysts was that there was *no coherent vision* available of a Hungarian I.S., and if there was any perspective, its main rhetoric was about the threat of becoming a *loser*, a country and economy lagging behind, or at least, about *the need to catch up*, and follow those more developed others (Pintér, 2000b; Z. Karvalics, 1998). Truly, this pessimism was rooted in numerical facts. Yet, importantly, there was no coherent political agenda showing a way out, no coherent national strategy, which linked the I.S. to the actual social-economic and cultural context in Hungary. The whole issue was very much an isolated political concept, without much meaning to the average citizen, and with little true understanding by the political community either.

A major change was much anticipated in the early 2000s, and it seemed to have arrived in 2002/2003, when some important legislative measures were taken (pressed by EU accession, for the most part), and professional and political debates had culminated in the drafting of the National Information Society Strategy. In the following, I provide a brief overview of this and two related documents published in 2003 and 2006.

Making a strategy: assessment, vision, implementation and monitoring

The Ministry of Informatics and Communications drafted a country report in late 2003, both in the Hungarian and English

---

[118] Bálint Magyar was the Minister of Education in Hungary during the periods 1996-1998 and 2002-2006.

languages, and much in the spirit of 'being ready for accession'. This 30 page long study, The Hungarian Information Society on the Eve of Accession to the European Union: snapshot and strategic objectives can be considered as a preface to the actual National Strategy. It gives a summary of the already existing foundations, as well as the shortcomings and the objectives of developing the I.S. in Hungary. Each *main dimension of access* is taken into consideration: physical and financial access (e.g. the backbone infrastructure, telecom market liberalisation and the fast diffusion of mobile telephones), investment into human capital (mental access; esp. the Sulinet Programme); and content development (e-commerce and distance work, e-government, on-line health care, the National Digital Data Bank, etc.)

Also, the most important I.S.-related legislative measures are mentioned that had been partly or fully realised by 2004. Already in 1998, Hungary agreed to adjust and streamline her legal system to fulfil the so-called *Acquis Communitaire*[119], and to bring national policies and programmes into line with the broader and even non-binding EU guidelines and recommendations. Naturally, this had been completed by 2004, and in terms of I.S., too. While the legal background for cost-based connection fees and universal service obligation still required some adjustment[120], the directives on e-commerce had been fully implemented, as well as the satellite and cable broadcasting *acquis*, the legislation on intellectual property rights and industrial property protection.

At several points in the discussions in this 'snapshot' paper, the problems with spatial inequalities, social inclusiveness, and content are mentioned. The following are probably the most important observations:

•   Half of the (already very low number of) connections to Internet from home were realised via analogue (dial-up) connections, while close to 30% had broadband.

•   However, more than 75% of the 14-17 years old were frequent users (partly due to *Sulinet.*) The usage rates of internet correlated with educational attainment in Hungary more than it did in the EU-15.

•   The digital divide was greater in Hungary than in the EU-15 countries in average; and the main reasons behind the gaps were both financial and cultural. Digital illiteracy, missing language skills, and the lack of attractive content were recognized shortcomings.

•   Spatially, there were considerable digital gaps between the major cities and the smaller municipalities; and differences

---

[119] The *Acquis Communitaire* is a body of EU regulations and practices to which candidate countries are expected to conform to be allowed to join the integration. For the enlargements in 2004 and 2007, it included 31 chapters, of which competition policy (6), education and training (18), telecom and information technologies (19), culture and audio-visual policies (20) were the most relevant to I.S.

[120] In 2003, a new telecommunications law was drafted to result in a drop in telephone call charges, as well as in the requirement imposed on companies to contribute to a national 'universal access fund'. It came into effect in 2004, the year of Hungary's accession to the EU.

could be observed also between greater regions.

• Market incentives could not be sufficient to bring infrastructure and services into under-served regions. However, policy intervention was seen as something that might itself create digital gaps by giving preference to one social group or type of region above the others.

• The positive role of telecottages (community access points) to help rural communities join the I.S. was given much credit to (see 5.3).

• While e-commerce had been developing relatively fast (also due to proper legislation), e-government was rather poor: about 40% of the public services could be accessed on-line but 85% of these were in the category of simple information provision.[121] Besides, efficient inner processes of administration, uniform data management, and the integration of services and applications in the government were still missing.

A much more thorough and complex document, the actual Hungarian Information Society Strategy (HISS, 2003) declares its main purpose as:

"to review and to systematise the tasks related to the formation of the information society in order to ensure that the responsibilities arising therefrom – to be fulfilled by the whole society – will take place in a *coordinated* manner"
(HISS, 2003:5, original emphasis).

The strategy-makers' awareness of the social and cultural problems, the former lack of a coherent approach, and the timing of their work is indicated also by the six objectives they defined (see Box 6), as well as by the fact that (beyond the usual rhetoric in I.S. documents (e.g. competitiveness, prosperity), they claim that the HISS is most of all *a social programme*, which requires a positive change in attitudes by everyone. The Government's responsibility is however, to take the initiative: set an example, and help other creative forces to unfold.

In its first section, the HISS describes rather realistically the current state of affairs in terms of: infrastructure, content, IT skills, legal and social environment, equal opportunities, R&D, the IT industry – and the shortcomings and challenges seen in all. Then, the document explains the current economic, political technological, cultural, and regulatory circumstances and tendencies that were expected to have an impact on the potentials to develop these fields.

Consequently, the vision of the future is outlined: *eHungary* standing on two major pillars, which are claimed to be in harmony with the EU programme 'eEurope 2005'. Even though this formula may imply some simplicity and a slightly technologically-deterministic approach, the Strategy is actually much aware of the interdependencies and cross-sectoral nature of the tasks involved in realising this vision. It defines two major horizontal objectives (R&D and equal opportunities) and four fields of intervention (content and services, infrastructure, knowledge and skills, and legal and social environment). All these six areas of I.S. policy contain actions that are

---

[121] I.e. the lowest level of government on-line see Figure 3 in 2.3.2).

relevant to both the 'informatisation' of processes (pillar 1), and the implementation of electronic services (pillar 2).

Without going into further detail about the content of the Strategy, I want to draw attention to some of its interesting features:

• The claim is clearly and often made in the text that this was the last chance to prevent a kind of 'national tragedy': now, or never. I.S. is "the only real alternative" (3) to "catch up and join the advanced European information societies" (11), because "we have lost our relatively good position we had in the '90s, we have fallen behind in the rankings" (12), etc.

• Surely, the timing is also relevant because of the approaching accession to the EU. Yet, it is finally understood and acknowledged that the lack of political consensus, integrity and continuity, as well as the lack of social awareness and public support had so far disrupted a continuous policy development and efficient implementation.

• As the third (best) scenario for Hungary, the following is included: "Learning from the Finnish or Irish example, for instance, it [i.e. Hungary or the Hungarian I.S.] attempts to develop more dynamically in several areas of the information age, and gain a better position

---

The six objectives of forming the national I.S. Strategy:

1) to make it clear to everyone that Hungary had no choice but "to enter the age of information, as intensely and innovatively as possible";
2) to present a comprehensive vision, complex and co-ordinated set of plans, and operative programmes for their realisation;
3) to ensure that these would promote the growth and competitiveness of the economy;
4) to prove that ICTs are effective tools, and thus establish the prestige of the IT sector;
5) to comply with the expectation from the EU with this document and so be entitled to community subsidies;
6) to offer a basic plan, a guiding principle and organizational scheme

eHungary
for a *modern European Hungarian Republic*: conscious and organized nation-development through the application of 'informatized' processes and the implementation of electronic services; mass accessibility of these services and development of a manifold and versatile information culture.

First pillar:	Second pillar:
"modernization of processes through the application of information and communication technologies."	"electronic services – modernization of services with the aid of information and communication technologies"

(Source: based on citations from HISS, 2003: 3,

Box 6. Six objectives and the strategic vision: eHungary on two pillars

among the European knowledge societies" (11). However, there is no mention in what way these examples should be followed, and what those areas are concretely where Hungary could achieve a competitive advantage. This leaves the impression in me that in fact, the strategy is more realistic than visionary, and it is 'content' with achieving the middle scenario, i.e. keeping the position of Hungary and not falling more behind other countries of Europe.

• It is recognised that I.S. is the only possible means to simultaneously attain both fundamental development goals: improving economic competitiveness, and a better living standard (social welfare) in the country. Since these two aims (as it was internalised in the Finnish developments; see in 4.2) also depend on each other, neither can be neglected, but they should be systematically *integrated*.

• Also, already on the first page, and then later in the assessment of the political and social environment and tendencies, the issue of low social / public and political trust is brought up. On the one hand, the strategists believe that "the widespread use of processes and services supported by the latest solutions of information technology, as well as social cooperation, will contribute to achieving social welfare and public trust." (3) And turning the table around, the lack of interest in using Internet had been partly due to "suspicion towards ... service providers, as well as distrust" (18). How to trigger positive changes in these aspects is still more of a question in the Strategy then an answer. Implicitly however, the state's initiative in to develop user-friendly and

interactive e-administration services is proposed as a solution to start with.

• The systematic way the Strategy organises the extremely complicated set of different problems, objectives and means of intervention demonstrates the effort to integrate and co-ordinate the vertical (sectoral) policies with the horizontal ones. The framework used in the document is rather practical for implementation: the different types of so-called 'high-priority programmes' were to be elaborated at the cross-sections of these vertical and horizontal lines and pillars.

• The Strategy itself, however, does not want to be more than a guiding principle and an organizational scheme; so it has few concrete examples to offer about ways of intervention. What is nevertheless expressed is that via concrete legal procedures programmes proposed by private, public and civil actors will be selected from, and then integrated into the HISS implementation scheme (of co-ordination, co-funding, and monitoring by the Ministry and its responsible institutions).

For the complex strategy making and co-ordination tasks, new and unconventional governmental institutions had to be created. First, in 2000, the Hungarian Government appointed a Commissioner for ICT (2000) within the office of the Prime Minister. In 2002, it was replaced by a separate Ministry of Informatics and Communications. However, establishing the *Interministerial Committee on Information Society* (ITKTB) within this Ministry in 2003 was a most essential decision: a co-ordinating body with a diverse membership and several professional sub-committees. Its 25 members with voting rights are the deputy state secretaries responsible for I.S. affairs at the different ministerial departments; and with consultation rights, 39 representatives are delegated from interested public authorities (for instance, the National Tax Office, and the National Health Insurance Fund), from related business, R&D and civil associations (e.g. the Hungarian Academy of Sciences, Hungarian Association of IT Companies, Janos von Neumann Computer Society Association, Hungarian Association of Content Industry). The creation, monitoring and the yearly revision of the national I.S. strategy and have been the main tasks of its Strategy Planning Subcommittee. Other subcommittees were established along the main lines of the strategic objectives and high-priority I.S. programmes: on e-administration (e-government), on the National Digital Content, on the Public Net (*KözHáló*) programme, on information systems security and on satellite navigation. The Development on I.S. Subcommittee is responsible for integrating I.S. development into the broad National Development Plan, as well as for promoting public-private partnerships.

During the first three years of implementation, different ministries and departments took charge of elaborating and launching various high-priority programmes under the supervision of the Interministerial Committee. The Centre for Electronic Government within the Prime Minister's Office has been responsible for *eKormányzat 2005.* The Ministry for

Economy and Transport has been managing the *KözHáló* (PublicNet) programme, which aims to set up a public utility ICT network that provides local governments and local public institutions as well as civil organisations with access to the Internet. By 2006, over 5,000 broadband terminals had been installed in schools, and the programme also supported the creation of 3,000 *eHungary points* (PIAPs, ICT and information centres, in some cases community access points built on existing telecottages, see in 5.3.2). After two years of preparation by the Ministry of Informatics and Communication, the *National Digital Data Base (NDA)* opened for the public in June 2004, and it has been continuously developed: a catalogue of Hungarian cultural content. Also, the digital knowledge base of the *Sulinet* network (curricula, tests, simulations and other education-supporting material on-line) expanded considerably in 2005-2006. Loosely connected to these major programmes, innovative initiatives emerged with the participation of the civil society such as the creation of the IT-mentor profession (e.g. to complement PIAPs with skilled assistants).

In 2006, the Interministerial Committee published a report on the implementation (2002-2006) and the impacts of the above mentioned and other key programmes. Despite the achievements, the main conclusion of the assessment was that since 2002, Hungary had managed only to keep its relative position in the world and in Europe with its I.S. development, and the only field where it had gained some advantage was e-government. Yet, because of the still low penetration rates, few people actually benefit from these services. Realising many of the ambitious plans was made more difficult by a political and financial crisis in 2006 that forced the Government to introduce budget-tightening reforms. Moreover, institutions closely related to I.S. policy kept on being replaced and reformed. The Ministry of Informatics and Communications itself was abolished in 2006 (most of its tasks related to I.S. were transferred to the Ministry of Economy and Transport.)

Since about 2000, the issue of creating an I.S. has been an object itself, of the competition between the major political parties in Hungary. They tried to win public attention and support by endorsing their own 'Tourist's Guides' to the I.S., by binding the cause (and the merits from its expected triumph) exclusively to themselves, i.e. to their governmental term(s) (Dessewffy, 2002). This has on the one hand, helped public awareness increase and invigorated political discourse about the I.S. On the other hand, it has also resulted in discontinuities, incoherence in plans and implementation, some steps backwards, as well as in scepticism appearing in academic and civil circles concerning the credibility of the national I.S. project. One of the weaknesses of the Hungarian national I.S. politics has been the fact that it was not reaching across the whole political society, and therefore it has not been so far embraced by the general public either.

Anyhow, the publication of the Hungarian Information Society Strategy (2003) was most probably a watershed. It was a crucial event not only as an externally pushed adoption and adaptation of the

corresponding documents and programmes in Europe, but also as a first show of commitment by the state to provide the necessary institutional coordination and support to the previously rather sporadic I.S. development initiatives.

(Own photo, 2005)

Figure 26. *e*Magyarország (*e*Hungary) point road sign.

4.4 Summary

In the following, I sum up the results from the above analyses based on the three question put in the introduction of the present chapter (4.1).

a) *"What are the main and specific elements of the Finnish I.S. model, and how has the implementation of the national strategy progressed?"*

In Finland, the construction of the I.S. can be seen partly as *a strategic choice* (deriving from the 1990s crisis), but also as a continuation of a long-term survival strategy; and linked to the investments into the *national innovation system.*

If we extend the interactions between companies and public authorities to the wider society, the basis of the Finnish I.S. model is essentially *a social innovation environment or a 'cross-sector cluster.'* It is a complicated and interconnected system of the corporate-business sector, the Finnish state and the universities, as well as the individual and 'civil' innovators. After over a decade of planning, the 'I.S. cause' has integrated into the wider national development strategy.

In sum, Finland can be considered an advanced and socially rather inclusive information society. This observation is based on a deeper analysis of interactions, and not only indicated by the clear-cut figures in global ranking lists. The *wide acceptance and ultimate use of technology* (in everyday life, and of ICT as being at the centre of political debates and budgetary decisions) come from both *a general sense of social security and trust in the state, as well as practical individual experience of the usefulness and ease of the new technologies.* Trust is an important focus of the coming National I.S. Programme, too, where it is also understood as the basis for people's willingness to rely on I.S. services and actors.

Whether the Finnish I.S. model can stay a leading 'best practice' depends much on how it can retain this implication to welfare as well as its relevance to economic competitiveness. This on the other hand, is a matter of the self-innovating capacity of the national innovation system.

b) "How have the governments of Hungary perceived the way towards the I.S. and where has implementation of concrete programmes taken this country in the past *approximately ten-fifteen years? Is there an evolving 'Hungarian model' of the I.S.?"*

While in Finland, we can talk about several revisions of I.S. strategies and an arsenal of networked institutions and some crystallised routines to invent, organise, implement and monitor those, the Hungarian developments towards an I.S. are quite recent and in a flux, therefore they may be described best in a chronological manner.

Hungary has inherited *substantial infrastructural weaknesses* from the Socialist Era. It is understandable therefore, that the focus of policy in the early nineties was to bring this very basic infrastructure to level with the western standards. The little resources and attention available were focussed on this most urgent challenge.

Also, some unfavourable legacies of the old era as well as *the transition process* itself have *created a special social environment* or *'social quality' in Hungary* which has not been particularly supportive of carrying through a national vision, a practical and integrated cross-sectoral strategy and programming of such a venture as the development of a "European Hungarian" information society. Still, efforts have not been completely unsuccessful: building on positive continuities and introducing a few timely reforms in the nineties helped the country overcome some of the most important shortcomings in basic physical and mental access. This however is not sufficient for Hungary to become and stay competitive. *The strategic moment was evidently missed in the nineties*, though not without some understandable and objective reasons.

One can talk about real political commitment only from around 2000-2003. The moment then, however, was less coupled with the sense of 'kairos' and confidence than with that of *urgency and fear*: the prospective of acting too late (and thus being taken over even by the other CEE countries) was felt almost as a threat to national survival.

Yet then, the I.S. strategy was accepted by the Government as a *cross-sectoral strategy and a social programme*. Remarkably, it paid attention to all components of access, and it recognised the *crucial interrelationships between (the lack of) social / public trust, and the (insufficient) usage of ICT-supported services* by people and institutions.

In the circles of the Hungarian 'I.S. elite' (researchers, strategists, journalists, politicians, etc. discussing this problem), the awareness of a Scandinavian (or more appropriately, a Nordic) model has many interesting implications. First, they distinguished between different types of I.S. even within Europe. Second, they realised that many similarities exist between these countries and Hungary (size, geopolitical positions, cultural resources, etc.) Thirdly, and probably most importantly, the Nordic I.S. is seen as a model to adopt (with some inevitable modifications) since it successfully and naturally integrates those two main goals which cause much of the headache for Hungary since transition: *better life for citizens and a consequently greater social and political trust, and increasing competitiveness of the economy.*

In view of the above, the Hungarian I.S. Strategy has all what it takes except for maybe three important issues:

1   There has recently been slightly more confidence among the political and intellectual elite concerning the results from implementing the Strategy. *The question is whether they can help the broader society internalise this sense of purpose, and acknowledge the importance of the 'I.S. cause' as something that is in their own interest, and not just a political show, and a way for the rich to get richer…*

2   To achieve this, the development of on-line interactive content serving administrative procedures between citizens and the public institutions has got much attention in the recent years. However, actual usage of these services (the Internet subscription rate) is still low, restraining their upgrading and customisation through feedback, and preventing the development of an on-line culture (see questions *b/1* and *b/2*). *The special invention Hungary should come up with to her own benefit and helping also other transitioning countries, is the method to break the vicious circle around distrust.* The problem is pointed out in the Strategy, but no clear directions to solve it are indicated.

3   Finally, financial depression and the yet weak and rather changeable institutional background keep on inhibiting the realisation of the strategic ambitions. *Probably, implementation would be more efficient if the limited resources were invested first in a more concentrated way,*

i.e. into a specific but decisive field that could be a Hungarian 'strength', and which then could work as a catalyst for the expansion of other areas. However, I.S. involves all strategic sectors (education, telecommunications, healthcare, state administration), which are not only underfinanced, but have a highly politicised nature, not to mention the horizontal components of the national I.S. strategy, regional development, and R&D. Among these circumstances and the sharpening regional competition, Hungary is still challenged to find her 'own way', her own model not just in the meaning of 'type', but 'good example'.

c) "How much concern is expressed in the national I.S.-related documents and actual programmes in these two countries about territorial inequalities and the regional development of the I.S.?"

In the case of Finland, regional inequalities in the diffusion of ICTs have been a rising issue with the second version of the strategy, and it has been receiving more attention since. It is found in the foundation of the 'edifice' of the National Knowledge Society (Fig. 24). The actual way to tend to them is not interfering with the market processes directly, but encouraging public-private-partnerships and networking, by promoting competition between good-practices (particularly the local solutions in specialised services such as e-health), by granting special awards, by supporting research, evaluation studies, and by dissemination via the on-line media itself.

In the case of Hungary, many revised international examples had been already available to rely on by the time of the national I.S. strategy was drafted; so it is not surprising that the issue of elevating spatial inequalities was incorporated as a horizontal objective. However, even before, there had been considerable awareness in general, of the rapidly escalating regional inequalities and social disparities since 1990. This understanding was also projected to the technological-infrastructural aspects of the I.S. (see also Figure 20 in 3.3.4 above), as well as concerning related skills, and available content. As a solution, market incentives are considered, but more importantly, the encouragement of public-private partnerships (a special work group is devoted to this within the Interministerial Committee for I.S.). A working example for the later is the cooperation between the state's *KözHáló* and eHungary programmes and the civil association of telecottages. According to the report in 2006, disparities have not decreased according to most aspects of access, so equal opportunities will have to be a high priority in the future, too.

5 THE REGIONAL AND LOCAL DIMENSIONS OF THE I.S.: EXAMPLES FROM FINLAND AND HUNGARY

5.1 Introduction: questions, approaches and methods

Some aspects in the cases of Finland and Hungary described above imply that from the perspective of I.S. strategies, achieving social inclusiveness of economic growth is as important a goal (and as fundamental a precondition) as the expansion and efficiency of the national economy is. The national authorities in most of the European countries, as well as the European Union (as shown in 3.3.4 and 3.3.1) acknowledge that social inequalities in terms of access in the I.S. have obvious manifestations in the geographical space, too. Relatively irrespective of the actual stage of I.S. development the countries have reached, national governments are aware of the emerging territorial disparities in the possible and accomplished benefits from ICTs,[122] and the regional inequalities in citizens' prospects of becoming a full member of the I.S.

As already suggested in different sections above, as a logical assumption and as findings from policy documents, surveys and interviews, spatial patterns of development are not changing considerably in the 'information age'. Micro- and meso-scale patterns of territorial digital divides in terms of the different components of access and their various, reciprocally reinforcing combinations tend to emerge along traditional spatial inequalities within countries. One of the aims of this chapter is to show clearer evidence for these statements, and answer this question:

a)   Are the long-standing centre-periphery relations and the urban-rural divides reproduced in course of the diffusion of ICTs and their valuable applications?

Besides presenting the regional inequalities in access to ICTs within Finland and Hungary, the focus of this study shifts to the *sub-national actors*. Concerning them, the question I try to answer is:

b)   What interactions have been in the Finnish and Hungarian local cases between the bottom-up initiatives and the top-down policies of the national actors?

Locally instigated and (at least, in their respective regions) innovative I.S.-solutions in Finland and Hungary are presented below: a community intranet well embedded into the regional and national ambitions for an I.S.; and the telecottages in Hungary mushrooming from the mid-nineties to serve especially the smaller village communities which faced accumulated social-economic disadvantages during the transition years.

---

[122] In line with my definition of 'access' (see 2.3.2 above), by potential benefits, I mean the existence of physical and financial access to ICTs as tools. By accomplished benefits I mean the actual value gained from the constructive usage of these tools which require higher levels of openness, language skills, and digital literacy ('mental' access), as well as relevant and reliable content and services on-line.

Some actors who are involved in these examples, of course, are familiar already from the previous two chapters: telecommunications companies, international agencies, the nation state and its institutions of research and education, professional and civil networks, and the local people as both 'users' and innovators. Nevertheless, it is interesting to see:

c)   how these actors can handle the task of improving access to ICTs and utilise their benefits for local / regional development.

Concerning the methods and sources of information, in researching the Finnish, North Karelian regional and local developments, I relied much on the related policy documents and the available spatial statistical data and scientific articles, evaluation studies written by well-informed researchers at the Karelian Institute, Joensuu. However, to get also some first-hand experience and personal impression, I carried out own empirical field work in the region (in the autumn of 2003, and during shorter visits later): interviews with actors at both the Regional Council in Joensuu, and in some of the rural communities in the province where the studied intranet project was introduced.

During my work I found little linguistic barrier. Although some local publications, newspaper articles and detailed project plans were only available in Finnish, I could always find ways to get closer to the content with some help from my interviewees and colleagues. The managers of the *Oppiva Pohjois-Karjala* project granted me unlimited personal access to the community intranet itself, allowing me to observe its functions directly.

In my investigations about general and ICT-related territorial developments in Hungary, I relied on available spatial statistical data and review scientific articles and thematic volumes written since 1990 by Hungarian experts of the topic. Concerning the evolution of the Hungarian telecottage movement, I used first of all interviews with key actors tracked down via a 'snowball method'. I performed some fieldwork both in the physical and virtual environments. I paid visits to the Budapest headquarters of the Telecottage Association, as well as to several telecentres in the Hungarian countryside; participated in some of their meetings and conferences. I carried out an on-line survey of telecentres in a selected rural region. I regularly visited their on-line locations, forums, and debates to stay up-dated with the developments as much as possible. Besides, over a period of 3-4 years (2003-2006), I received much information in print or in digital form from them and other Hungarian researchers involved in the movement or at least, in this topic: books and scientific studies, training materials, newspaper articles, and links to useful Internet websites and forums.

The last case study in this chapter, and in the dissertation, is unique in the way that it does not only connect the Finnish and Hungarian local / regional case studies, but, from the local actors' point of view, brings together many of the processes and perspectives discussed in terms of international I.S. guidelines and institutions (Chapter 32), and the respective national developments (Chapter 4). It helps answering both questions a) and b). In producing this final study, half by chance and half intentionally, I took on the role of a participant observer, or even, action researcher. The details and circumstances of this method are presented in 5.4.

5.2 Sub-national developments in the Finnish information society

5.2.1 General and ICT-related inequalities in Finland

Finland has shown many positive results and advantages in both the technological and the social-human 'infrastructures' of the information and network society. Nevertheless, some challenges and problems exist; "important reservations" are added even by Castells and Himanen in their description of the Finnish I.S. model that concern mainly spatial dynamics, more specifically, inequalities across the national territory (2001:62).

This might sound strange in view of the inclusiveness of the Finnish welfare system and especially to those who are familiar with the situation in some other parts of the world. However, Finland has territorial disparities and relatively marginalised or disadvantaged regions as opposed to the south and south-western economic 'core' of the country. This centre-periphery relation is observable on different regional scales in the country, in terms of economic dynamics, employment opportunities, and to some extent, infrastructure, as well as in living standards and consequent migration patterns.

In a so sparsely populated country as Finland, regional socio-economic processes may be followed easiest through observing migration patterns over time. The implication of population densities is perhaps stronger here than elsewhere: economic growth attracts labour, and inhabitants are the essential foundation and the precondition for further growth, investments and the continuation of public services in a region (Gløersen et al. 2005).

Migration patterns have changed many times since the Second World War in Finland, particularly from the point of view of rural areas, semi-peripheries and smaller municipal centres. The post-war settlement policy helped rural growth, but then, from the mid-1960s, the fast growth of the national economy triggered migration from the rural areas to both the major urban nodes and the urban-rural fringe, as an increasing number of people could be employed in manufacturing and the service sector. Besides towns, the 400 centres of rural municipalities could benefit from the new jobs created by the expansion of the welfare state. During the recovery phase of the 1990s, migration accelerated again, but in the opposite direction, following more the spatial logic of the 'new economy': it targeted especially the major cities in the S-SW core area, and not the outlying rural-provincial centres. After, in the prosperous and more stable late-nineties, the semi-peripheries became attractive again for a time. (Tykkyläinen, 2006:153.) Most recently, migration increased again into the southern bigger urban centres and the spatial re-concentration of public sector jobs is

131

expected to start to some extent due to national economic efficiency considerations.

Overall, the rural peripheries, i.e. very sparsely populated regions dependent on their relatively distant rural centres (the "intensely rural" areas: most of Northern Finland excluding Oulu, and vast areas of Eastern Finland) have been loosing population for many decades. However, the regional 'urban' centres of these peripheries have had to adjust to a more changeable situation over time. Their ability to keep their inhabitants and enterprises, to retain their customers and tax-payers, and consequently, maintain a sufficient level of public services and infrastructure, however, has been crucial for their depopulating hinterlands as well.

In Finland also, the general socio-economic inequalities are followed and as well as reinforced by digital gaps – which however small might seem in international comparison, do exist in Finland, and will continue so unless they are attended to in a knowledgeable way. The locations of ICT production and R&D, the availability of physical network infrastructures and related services, as well as other, non-technological components of access all show territorially unequal patterns in Finland. As mentioned above (in 4.2), the vigorous expansion of the telecommunications equipment industry and services was one of the sources of Finland's speedy recovery from its deep recession in the early nineties. An important feature of the IT sector, besides its high capacity of wealth creation, is that its higher-value and skill-intensive activities are much concentrated and clustered in a few

localities.[123] Recently, this has led to a significant increase in spatial divergence in economic development in Finland, too.

These current spatial developments are characteristic to the new, global pattern of restructuring and urbanisation: metropolitan regions "concentrate most of the innovation, the directional activities, cultural amenities, and wealth creation capacity in each country" (Castells and Himanen, 2001:63[124]). Large conurbations are being formed which functionally connect formerly separate urban centres. The most important cause-and-effect chain leading to these disparities is triggered by the favourable employment opportunities offered in, and the consequent migration of the (esp. young and high-skilled) population to, the Helsinki area (Uusimaa) and Southern Finland.

Furthermore, taking a look at the basic 'physical' infrastructure of the I.S., i.e. the network infrastructures and services, a similar spatial pattern of divergence has emerged in Finland to those observable in other countries. However, it makes a difference which sub-sector of telecommunications one considers, and when.

There are no territorial disparities in fixed-line telephony, the whole network is

---

[123] Nokia has research and product development units in the Helsinki metropolitan area (e.g. Espoo), and in Tampere, Jyväskylä, Salo, Turku and Oulu (company website). Oulu, situated more north on the western coast, is the only Nokia-location outside the core region.

[124] See also other works by Castells, e.g. I [1996/2000]: Chapter 6.

digitalised in Finland[125], and ISDN access services are available to nearly all households (ESPON 2002-2004). In general, 'older' ICTs having approached their saturation points in the market, show a spatially more equal picture than newer, more advanced ICTs, such as broadband (BB).[126] An exception from this spatial logic has been observed in mobile telephony, which (as in most of the developed countries) diffused much faster and more pervasively in society than any other ICTs, reaching close to 100 percent in approximately five years.[127]

The diffusion of BB accessibility had a considerable regional variation in 2002, and showed much consistence with general socio-economic indicators (population density, unemployment rates and net migration figures). The territorial pattern in Finland according to a composite 'BB accessibility index' was basically identical with the fine-grained patterns in population density, i.e. urban concentrations (Eskelinen *et al.*, 2003; see Figure 27). The

smaller the scale one observes inequalities at, the more differentiated the picture becomes. There are extensive regions in the North and the East with larger areas lacking sufficient services and / or competition of ISPs[128], resulting in unfavourable monopoly situations and higher prices. There is a similar situation in areas outside municipal centres, where there is a lack of physical access to high speed networks. Surely this is the consequence of market rationales[129].

This is by far not unique in Europe; the situation is rather similar even in densely populated countries. Since technological development does not seem to wait for the un-served areas to catch up, *a new digital gap* has started to take shape due to the spatially differential access to broadband (BB). This is getting increasingly important in terms of competitiveness of companies, consequently, in their location choices, and therefore, for the economic attractiveness of localities and regions. Nevertheless, BB divides are already expected to decrease, for instance, with the development of wireless BB technologies.

The question may occur still, whether BB, or in general, the currently most up-to-date and fastest network technology, is *really* that important. How much of its advantage over lower speed technologies is emphasized by business commercials, and how much of it is really needed in concrete local contexts in peripheral areas? Is there any reasonable hope for those rural and unprofitable regions in Finland (and elsewhere) that they can

---

[125] Technically, the diffusion of broadband is not limited by the capabilities of the basic telecommunications infrastructure: Finland has been among the first countries to digitalise its telecom networks; it had achieved a 100% digitalised network by 1996 already, before for instance Sweden (1997/98), the USA, and Korea (after 2001). (Tuomi 2004: 5-6.)

[126] See 2.1.4.

[127] Reasons behind this include the obviously lower costs of covering the whole country with the network, the high number of competitors in the market, the consequent relative inexpensiveness of mobile phones and subscriptions, as well as the easiness of use of this technology (requiring neither much investment from the households' budget, nor special IT skills by the customers).

[128] ISP: Internet service provider.

[129] See 3.3.4 and the results of ESPON 1.2.2, 2003-2004.

ever, in a self-sustainable way (without long-term public subsidisation) have the same level and quality of network access as available in urban areas?

Broadband has been recently receiving more attention at the European as well as the national level, which is due to various reasons connected to the dynamic and interrelated development of technologies, content and on-line services.[130] Several applications that involve transmission of data in audio and video forms require high-speed connections for not only business but in households, too (Eskelinen *et al.* 2003).

Besides, BB has the advantages of short connection set-up time, and a predictable flat-rate pricing that allows the user to be 'always on'.[131] No wonder that those people in Finland, who started to subscribe to BB in 2003, increased their Internet use significantly (on average, by four hours per week). What is more interesting is that this increase was the most substantial in sparsely populated areas (Tuomi 2004:11). This might indicate that people in Finland do see the potentials of more advanced electronic communication in resolving geographical isolation, and it is very probable that the BB gap will not deepen further. However, the question then follows: how could there be demand for higher levels of services (i.e. BB) in regions where service providers have not yet turned up in great enough numbers to ensure competition and lower prices? Where does this demand come from? Some solutions are proposed in 4.3.2 and 4.3.3.

A synthetic I.S. index was constructed by ESPON 1.2.3 incorporating more elements of access the actual take-up of ICTs, to trace national and NUTS2 regional inequalities across Europe (see Appendix 5B). The map shows that in general, the country effect prevails but besides, the core-periphery pattern of intra-country disparities can be observed in each case, Finland included. "The capital regions and core areas are typically in a better position, whereas the remote and peripheral regions, such as eastern Finland, seem to generally lag behind the national averages" (Frank *et al.*, 2006:114). The authors observe also, that based on this index, regional differences are relatively bigger in Finland than could be expected from its remarkable performance as a country.

The reasons for this are more connected to the permanent *structural and institutional preconditions of the knowledge-based economy* than to the temporary situations in the spatial patterns of network expansion and technological innovation cycles.

Although, the innovation infrastructure itself (universities, national institutions and Centres of Expertise, science parks) has also become rather even regionally in the past one or two decades (as mentioned in 4.2.2), it is *the capacity to utilise this infrastructure* that varies still spatially. This capacity is different among regions according to their industrial structure, private sector R&D activity, as well as according to their individual roles within the national innovation system. Due to the logic of funds allocation by the national innovation system in Finland, the more

---

[130] See e.g. 2.3.2.
[131] See more in 2.1.4.

technologically oriented universities of the four biggest centres (Helsinki, Tampere and Turku in the core region, and Oulu in the north-northwest) can receive more support because they cooperate more with private (IT) enterprises. (Frank *et al.*, 2006).

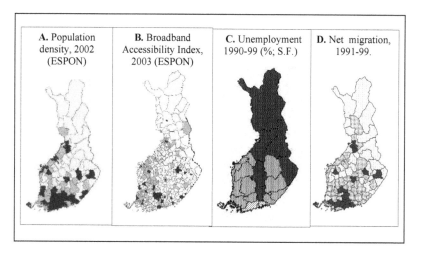

Explanation: **maps A, B** - dark: concentrations of population and BB accessibility; **map C** - dark: higher unemployment rates; **map D** - black: positive net migration, grey: net migration between 0 and -5%, white: outmigration exceeding 5%. (Sources: ESPON 1.2.2; Statistics Finland.)

Figure 27. Spatial inequalities in Finland in terms of population density, broadband infrastructure, unemployment, and net migration

North Karelia (*Pohjois-Karjala*, see Box 7 and Appendix 7), is the easternmost province of Finland. It has been a rural periphery for a long time, with a regional economy depending almost exclusively on forestry, small-scale family agriculture, and some metal and machine industry.

The migration patterns described above (4.3) have been experienced in North Karelia as well. The region can be divided into a distinguished urban centre, the provincial capital of Joensuu and its hinterland made up of some adjacent 'rural core' and an extensive 'rural remote' area.

From the point when regional policy in Finland could no longer support traditional rural manufacturing and public services (as it used to during the high times of the welfare state) North Karelia had to find new resources to restructure its economy. Since the mid-1990s, the Structural Funds and other ways of assistance by the European Union have been of much help in this. (Oksa, 2001).

One major element in the development plans of North Karelia has been for almost a decade, the promotion of a 'regional information society'. As a result, during a sequence of elaborate strategies, concrete programmes and applied projects, North Karelia has successfully combined ICTs and network solutions with some of its traditional sectors and unique resources, in order to increase the competitiveness of its rural economy and generally improve living conditions in its communities.

The first North Karelian I.S. strategy

As the first major step, a document titled *By Joint Work Party to the Information Society - Information Society Strategy and Action of North Karelia 1999-2006* was adopted by the Regional Council as early as in 1999 (see Box 8), also as an integral part of the Provincial Plan and Regional Development Programme 1998-2006 (POKAT). Drafting this document took place in 1997-1998 as part of the NOKIS (North Karelia Towards I.S.) programme, an EU-financed pilot within the Regional Information Society Initiative (RISI) scheme.

The long-term aim of NOKIS was "to make North Karelia a model province where all citizens, enterprises and public organisations can work and act as members of the global Information Society". It put emphasis on the Social Shaping of Technology[132], and interpreted it as a "dialogue between different actors in society; private individuals, different organisations, and technology developers" (Ahonen, 2000:1).

The regional I.S. Strategy and Action had in fact, been launched by the time the revised national I.S. Strategy by Sitra was out. Already in 1999, the Regional Council envisaged a people-centred I.S., with a special accent on spatial inclusiveness, too:

---

[132] See 2.2.2.

North Karelia (*Pohjois-Karjala*) is located in the easternmost corner of Finland, 440 km (within an hour's flight) N-NE from the capital, Helsinki. It is bounded by the Federal Republic of Russia along a 296 km long stretch of the eastern national border. The province has an area of 21,585 square kilometres, 70 per cent of which is covered by forest and 18 per cent (ca. 3,800 km²) by water, as Finland's sixth biggest lake, Pielinen is found here. This leaves some 12 per cent of the area (2,600 km²) suitable for settlements, where the 168,300 North Karelians live (01.2006). The province has a population density less than the national average (17 people / km²), i.e. about 9 inhabitants per square kilometre.

North Karelia is one of the 20 provinces (*maakunta*) of Finland as part of Eastern Finland (*Itä-Suomi*) macro-region (*lääni*). Since 2005, North Karelia has consisted of three districts (*seutukunta*): Pielinen Karelia in the north and Central Karelia in the south with four municipalities (*kunta*) each; and the Joensuu district in the centre, including eight municipalities with the city of Joensuu among them. Joensuu, with a population of over 57,000 people (2004), was but a small town of manufacture and trade till the late-1800s, when it got the rights for commerce and the local sawmills started to prosper. Water traffic was improved by the construction of the Saimaa Canal in 1856, and so trade between the regions of North Karelia, St. Petersburg, and also, Central Europe was made possible. Only more recently, has this small agrarian town grown to become the vital centre of the province. Its population has more than doubled since the 1950s along with the industrialisation and urbanisation of Finland and *the decentralisation of the service sector in the second part of the 20th century*. The establishment of the University of Joensuu in 1969 and its following expansion have been fundamental to the development of the city.

Joensuu is justly referred to as "the forestry capital of Europe", and the region of North Karelia is recognized as the "capital region of European forests"; the region concentrates *forest know-how*, education and research connected to forests and forestry. The University has a separate Faculty of Forestry, the North Karelian 'University of Applied Sciences' (Polytechnic), too, has a strong forestry and wood-industry profile. The European Forest Institute (EFI) and the only Finnish Centre of Expertise in Wood Technology and Forestry are located in Joensuu.

Besides forestry and wood processing industries, *public administration, health and education, healthcare and social work* contribute to the regional economy to a greater extent in North Karelia than in Finland in general (according to their share of the regional and national GDPs).

Life here has always been marked by clean environment and extensive waterways, a peaceful and safe lifestyle and housing close to nature. Despite these precious resources and the recent modernisation and restructuring, the province faces the common problems of peripheries: unemployment, ageing population, and out-migration. North Karelia (as well as the whole macro-region of Eastern Finland), remained an Objective 1 assistance region eligible for the Structural Funds of the EU for the period 2000-2006, and is eligible for further support in the next programming period.

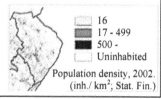

16
17 - 499
500 -
Uninhabited

Population density, 2002.
(inh./ km²; Stat. Fin.)

Box 7. The province of North Karelia. (Sources: Oksa 2001; regional website; interview with Ms. Ahonen, Oct. 2003; website of the Ministry of the Interior, Finland; own illustration)

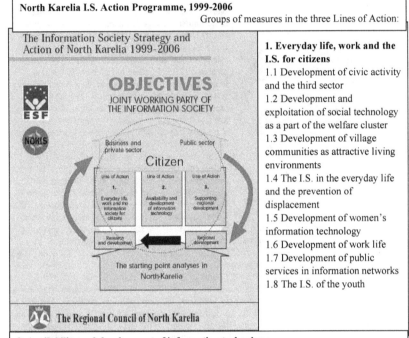

North Karelia I.S. Action Programme, 1999-2006

Groups of measures in the three Lines of Action:

The Information Society Strategy and Action of North Karelia 1999-2006

OBJECTIVES

JOINT WORKING PARTY OF THE INFORMATION SOCIETY

ESF

NOKIS

Business and private sector

Public sector

Citizen

Line of Action 1.

Line of Action 2.

Line of Action 3.

Everyday life, work and the information society for citizens

Availability and development of information technology

Supporting regional development

Research and development

Regional development

The starting point analyses in North-Karelia

The Regional Council of North Karelia

1. Everyday life, work and the I.S. for citizens

1.1 Development of civic activity and the third sector

1.2 Development and exploitation of social technology as a part of the welfare cluster

1.3 Development of village communities as attractive living environments

1.4 The I.S. in the everyday life and the prevention of displacement

1.5 Development of women's information technology

1.6 Development of work life

1.7 Development of public services in information networks

1.8 The I.S. of the youth

2. Availability and development of information technology

2.1 Exploitation of information technology

2.2 Development of ICT, as well as of the technological infrastructure

2.3 Promotion of the availability of teleinformatics

2.4 Content production built around the multimedia

3. Supporting regional development

3.1 Development of the teleinformatics cluster

3.2 Cooperation and development opportunities related to the communication of municipalities and federations of municipalities

3.3 Development of EU-project action

3.4 I.S. projects of the forestry cluster

3.5 Promotion of economic life and employment

3.6 Libraries as centres of information and regional culture

Box 8. The Information Society Strategy and Action of North Karelia 1999-2006. (RCNK, NOKIS, 1999:57; and figure copied from the cover page).

The information society is an entity of interactive communities built by North Karelians, in which information technology must not lead to displacement, but basic services and rights have to be guaranteed everyone.[133]

... (W)e are talking about a society for human beings, which is meeting new challenges and a new kind of action environment caused by technological development. (...)

[Technical infrastructure] ... is a tool for people...

The citizen's information society, however, is not yet here; [it] ...will help people to carry out everyday routines easier and give them opportunities to influence their own life. ... new possibilities ... both for ... industrial and commercial life and regional development.

In carrying out and planning the projects, we must make sure that they are carried out evenly around North Karelia, even in the smallest municipalities. Therefore, knowledge concerning the preparation, application for and funding of the projects and project know-how should be transferred to the whole region of the province. (RCNK, 1999: 5, 34.)

This harmony in approaches was, of course, consciously intended, which is directly and clearly expressed in the first part (titled "the vision of the Information Society and the value choices") of the regional Strategy with concrete references to and quotations from, the national

programme, as well as to the relevant documents issued by the European Union.

Furthermore, the great variety of the partners working together in NOKIS and the democratic representation in the Steering Committee guaranteed political neutrality to the regional I.S. programme, and was an evidence of the fact that there had already been "extensive consensus building on the I.S. in North Karelia" (*ibid.*)

The inclusiveness of participants also ensured that ICTs, as tools for modernisation, were considered in many fields of the region's social and economic life. This can be observed not only in the title, but the structure and content of the Strategy. Since North Karelia's economy is dominated by forest and wood-related industries and research, as well as public services (healthcare and education, especially), in the application phase from 1999, several projects aimed at enhancing the competitiveness and efficiency of these sectors. The *forestry and welfare clusters* in the region have proved to be fertile grounds for I.S. and ICT applications. (See also the groups of measures in Box 7.)

Besides these two areas, the I.S. Strategy of North Karelia defined another line of development: "*the teleinformatics cluster.*" This area of business was then made up of some sixty, rather small enterprises (3-5 people on average) in North Karelia, much concentrated in Joensuu. It was very new to the region, but it was developing rapidly. Over a third of the businesses involved were selling equipment and programmes, another less than third were engaged in software production, and few provided Internet and communication

---

[133] This interpretation echoes for instance, the following definition given in the *Finland's Way to the I.S.* national program: "The information society is a network of interaction connecting people and information systems for people and on people's own terms" (Regional Council of N.K. NOKIS, 1999: 5).

services (RCNK, 1999:47). On the other hand, the conditions in the region (for instance, the high level of education and the existing technological skills) were perceived good, and the advantage from the growth of this cluster (quality job creation, keeping young experts within the province, prospects for cooperation and markets beyond the province and internationally) were elaborated. Their most important features were that they:

• to strengthen programming, communication and the so-called 'neo-media', the line of business that was based on multimedia and Internet;

• to enhance cooperation between the enterprises within the province, and their networking with larger companies from outside North Karelia;

• to give more information to the local IT businesses about public financing opportunities;

• to encourage small enterprises to specialise and become sub-contractors of big IT companies;

• and to achieve a spatially more deconcentrated location of the sector within North Karelia.

These political commitment and visions were followed with much concrete action. Several I.S. pilot projects were funded via another EU initiative, the *Innovative Actions*[134] (I.A.). The first I.A. of Eastern Finland (covering North Karelia and three other provinces: North and South Savo

and Kainuu) was titled *Modern Network Periphery* (MONEP, 2002-2004).

The total budget of this phase was near 3.8 million euros, made up of payments by many different stakeholders following the general principle of additionality. The EU provided over 75% of this from the ERDF (European Regional Development Fund). About 7% of all costs were contributed by the Finnish state; private companies added a substantial 14%, and other public funds gave about 4%.

During the period 2002-2004, twelve pilot projects were funded by the programme across Eastern Finland[135], and three provincial I.S. strategies were

• developed innovative solutions for the *social welfare and health care sectors*, as well as for production and marketing of '*natural products*', paying much attention on the region's characteristics and needs and to complementariness to the Objective 1 programme in Eastern Finland[136];

• generated new forms of cooperation utilising ICTs: created five new operation modes and services and fifteen technological innovations in total; bridged over the traditional barriers between the public, private and civil sectors, combining their different viewpoints and interests by means of, for instance, promoting discussion

---

[134] See more on the Innovative Actions and the Eris@ network in 3.3.2 above.

[135] There was much interest: in total, 48 pilot-project ideas were received and four development organisations applied for funds.
[136] In the selection of pilots, attention was paid to the degree the proposed projects would provide additional value to the current Objective 1 programme in the region. Since the later did not have enough consideration for the health care and welfare sectors, these two were in the focus of MONEP.

between technology developers and potential customers about the opportunities of ICT solutions on the one hand, and the users' concrete needs and wishes;

• resulted in the formation of new enterprises in the region;

• laid much emphasis on monitoring and evaluation of results and impacts, on the continuation of the projects after the programme period, as well the transferability of the results;

• aimed at harmonising I.S. strategies and developments in the four provinces within Eastern Finland via a closer collaboration of the different regional actors;

• were 'internationalised' through their participation in European networks of I.S. expertise;

• and in general, they aimed at overcoming 'social challenges' rather than technical ones: targeted at improving the learning environment and networks for innovations within the region, and integration of the new solutions into people's everyday life.

The managing authority of MONEP was the Regional Council of North Karelia, taking much initiative and having the longest experience in regional I.S. developments. Yet, the Steering Committee was made up of representatives from all four provincial councils, and the Ministry of Interior; as well as expert members from national organisations such as Tekes, and Sitra[137]. MONEP therefore was not the least

a spatially isolated process. Great accent was placed on publicity and dissemination via for instance, the maintenance of a programme web-site reporting on progress and achievements; other printed and digital publications (brochures, a book, a CD-Rom, and articles in regional newspapers and the Eris@ newsletter); and through information events, professional meetings, and press conferences which could draw in further interested partners and participants from the region and beyond.

It is also important to note that on the regional level, too, the focus of projects has obviously shifted towards the creation of a great diversity of relevant content and communication systems, and towards a specifically suitable integration of the human and technological components of knowledge and information networks. This approach indeed, was realised in concrete solutions tailored to the rural-peripheral, sparsely-populated setting of the region (see example actions and projects in Box 9).

The first I.A. of Eastern Finland was followed by a similar programme for the period 2006-2008, with a budget of 3.6 million euros. It concentrates on welfare ICTs both as a source of regional competitiveness and new business opportunities and to improve services for the population.

---

[137] See above in 4.2.2.

Box 9. MONEP 2002-2004 actions in Eastern Finland and example pilot projects

In sum, North Karelia gave a well-timed regional response to the national political developments related to I.S.,[138]

being also aware of international (European) trends in policy and EU funding schemes.

Admittedly, the regional I.S. programme was founded on local initiatives. Since the beginnings (NOKIS), and similarly to the way the national I.S. strategists (e.g. at Sitra) were looking for some successful regional realisation of their aims, North Karelia has been seeking relevant local initiatives within its own territorial-institutional framework. Innovative local applications were sought after especially which could be the realisation of the 'people first' values declared in both the national and regional documents. The following section presents an early and probably, 'trend-setting' example for this situation.

5.2.3 The Learning North Karelia projects

"The basic idea of this project is "learning by doing". The local people working and studying in the project are responsible for the technical building and maintenance of the data system as well as the visual planning and contents. If they don't know or can't solve a problem, they work and study for the answer. One person doesn't know everything but a group can brainstorm anything." (OPPK website)

Although there had been several projects in the region that fruitfully combined technology and rural development objectives before the late 1990s[139], the *Learning North Karelia* community intranet (citizens' network) project (OPPK: *Oppiva Pohjois-Karjala; kansalaisverkko*) launched in 1998 was the initiative that has been able

---

[138] Interview with Ms. Satu Ahonen, Regional Council (October 2003).

[139] E.g. telecottages in the 1980s, and some early forms of local networks (Oksa 2001: 2).

to achieve much success and recognition in Finland and also, internationally.

The OPK project addressed the weaknesses in the region in terms of all components of access to ICTs, information and knowledge, concentrating on the general population and the inclusion of those inhabitants and enterprises living and working in sparse settlements far away from the provincial centre, Joensuu.

In four consequent and overlapping project phases, OPPK had covered the whole province of North Karelia by 2005, starting with the most remote municipalities and finishing up with Joensuu and its immediate surroundings:

- From April 1998 to March 2000, the *Learning Upper North Karelia* project (*Oppiva Ylä-Karjala*) covered the western part of Pielinen Karelia: Valtimo, Nurmes, Juuka.

- From April 2000 to December 2001, the *Learning Hills of Karelia* phase (*Oppiva Vaara-Karjala*) covered the rest of Pielinen Karelia and the eastern part of the Joensuu district: the municipalities of Lieksa, Ilomantsi, and Tuupovaara

- Between 2001 and 2004, the *Learning Central Karelia* project (*Oppiva Keski-Karjala*) aimed at extending the intranet and its services to the southern municipalities of North Karelia: Kesälahti, Kitee, Värtsilä, Tohmajärvi, Rääkkylä, Outokumpu and Polvijärvi. The remaining urban core of Joensuu and its surroundings were also considered, but were found less relevant to the project's mission.

Since its beginnings, OPPK has been built on three major pillars, which in fact, embrace 'access' in its most comprehensive sense. Education and technical counsel service; free 'physical' access points; and the software, content for a community network were provided as part of the scheme. However, the details and the remarkable arrangement and connection of these three pillars into a functioning and *locally fitting construction* were also important factors in success.

1   Educating locals in ICT skills, providing continuous assistance and services to users.

Unemployed locals were trained to be later working in the project itself: they were given jobs consequently in network maintenance and administration and were employed also as trainers and helpers of other residents (future users of the intranet) in the region. This pillar therefore was to enhance 'mental access' – skills and openness for ICTs among the residents of the municipalities. The peer-training practice added considerably to the regional development potentials of the project, as well as to the self-esteem of the local population. It also proved that people accept new technologies and ideas more willingly if they are instructed by someone who is familiar to them, i.e. a neighbour, a kin, a friend from the same village or town – rather than an 'IT professional' assigned from a university or a company.

2   Providing free internet access points. Over a hundred so-called '*nettikioskit* or net-kiosks were established scattered in the region. This was necessary for achieving *inclusiveness* (i.e. 'financial-economic' access) despite the fact that from the late

nineties the number of households having PCs connected to the net was increasing relatively fast in Finland, also in NK. (See photos in Figure 28.)

3   An easy-to-use community intranet (*kansalaisverkko*).

The community network sustains locally and regionally relevant information, interactive services and other useful and interesting substance for the citizens (i.e. elements of content-related access and local utility). The choice of the client programme "First Class" fits in well with the local context, too: it provides a very user-friendly interface (a personalised 'desktop' for each user), a logical, multi-layered and flexibly extendable structure of content, to which all public, private and civil actors are invited to contribute and link up to. The network can be entered also from the World Wide Web, making it possible for the user to stay connected with their home community life while away. As for the physical network, the main server is located in Nurmes, and the households, schools, local authorities and enterprises can link up to it via any type of network technology, narrowband connection is still not an obstacle.

Besides, *the fortunate timing* and "coincidences"; the great variety and number of actors involved in the success of the OYK and its follow-ups are notable. First, the thought of the project occurred in a local working group whose task was to find new uses for the building of a school in Nurmes that had been closed. As the Regional Council had I.S. development among its priorities, it supported the proposal of the local I.S. project. The main funds for the project came from Sitra, yet the local municipalities, the district labour office, and the Regional Council of North Karelia also contributed to it financially. In certain phases, EU funds contributed also (MONEP, 2002-2004).

It was a significant momentum that Sitra showed remarkable interest in this local-regional I.S. experiment. It also co-financed the first evaluation study on it, and commissioned afterwards further reports on its developments (Oksa 2004).[140] The initiator and designer of the project was suggested that he should set up a private enterprise (*Glocal Ltd.*) which would act in the future as advisor and exporter of his special expertise, in order to help further regions in Finland and abroad to achieve similar results. His and his colleagues' special "community network know-how" was soon utilised in the national programme called *Learning Regions* (OSKU: *Oppivat Seutukunnat, 2000-04*) financed and co-ordinated by Sitra, where eight further pilot regions in the country were selected for testing the community network idea more or less keeping its original elements (see Figure 29). Consequently, the key activists in the North Karelian project have become known nation-wide, and their success has attracted international interest, too (e.g. EU organisations promoting I.S. have got interested, and world-famous I.S. theorist,

---

[140] Since 1998, rural researchers Jukka Oksa and Jarno Turunen (Karelian Institute, Joensuu, Finland) have carried out extensive and detailed research on the history, factors of success, and follow-up developments of the Learning Upper Karelia project, and published several articles about their findings in both Finnish and English (see the References).

(Own photos, 2003.)

From the top left corner: access point at Kolinportti roadside service centre (petrol station, café-restaurant, shops, bank, etc.); *nettikiosk* in a small handicrafts shop, by the municipal office and in the library in Valtimo.

Figure 28. Four examples of *nettikioskit* – free internet/intranet access points set up by the Learning Upper Karelia project, 1998-1999

Manuel Castells paid a visit to see the North Karelian practice in 2000.)

The project has also relied much on public-private partnerships, the involvement of local governments, schools, libraries, small businesses, etc. has been vital in terms of *all three pillars*. The number of the active users of the community intranet has been rising fast, and it grew especially dramatically in the first two years, by the end of which 25 per cent of the population of the project area at the time was registered (Oksa – Turunen 2000).

Furthermore, it is important to note that the first phase of the project more-or-less covered the area of the so-called "Pielinen-Karelia" (made up of Nurmes, Lieksa and Valtimo), which is known to have faced most severely, the problems of unemployment, decreasing incomes from forestry and agriculture, the out-migration of the young, and difficulties in sustaining public services and infrastructure (Oksa 2001; see also the tables in Appendices 10 B and C).

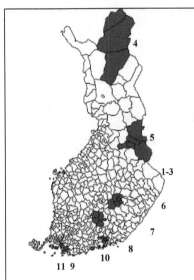

(Based on www.oskut.fi).

Explanation: 1-3.OPPK – North Karelian projects; 4. Northern Lapland (*Pohjois-Lappi*); 5. Kainuu; 6. Pieksämäki district (*PiiSavo project*); 7. Padasjoki district (*ePäijänne*); 8. East Uusimaa (*Kehä 5*); 9. East Turku; 10. Maunula in Helsinki (*Nettimaunula*); 11. Turku archipelago

Figure 29. *Oppiva Seutukunnat* – Learning Regions in Finland

Although the basic telecommunications infrastructure had been a given asset for long, narrowband had remained till very recently the technology the average user (connected at home) can rely on.[141]

---

[141] It is also notable that IT professionals in Joensuu did not see possibilities in co-operating with the Learning Karelia project for the reason that their idea of ICTs and solutions is different: *"...it is quite interesting that if you think about this citizen network – they are very suspicious, these Science Park people about that... They don't understand (it)... I think one reason is*

To sum up, in its local context, the OPPK project was highly relevant; what is more, it targeted exactly those challenges that were mentioned in the regional I.S. strategy documents and among the priorities of the national policy, too.

5.3 Subnational developments in the Hungarian I.S. [142]

5.3.1 General and ICT-related inequalities in Hungary since the beginnings of transition

General spatial inequalities

As illustrated also in the Finnish example, the degree of *inequalities in subnational territorial development* is always determined on the one hand, by the structure of the economy and the spontaneous market processes, and on the other hand, by the objectives and actual practices of the national economic and regional policies (Kiss J., 2003). In pre-transition Hungary (more precisely, from the 1960s), redistributive policies achieved a relatively lower level of inequalities within Hungary than what the situation was in the

---

that it's not invented there ... well, that's why they don't believe that's real business..." (quoted from project manager Mr. Koskikallio, 2003).

[142] This chapter is partially based on the author's paper for the 43rd ERSA Congress, (Jyväskylä, 27-30 August 2003), and is in part outcome of research being carried out for the ESPON 1.2.2. project. (see References).

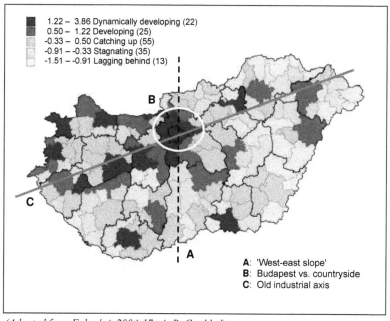

(Adapted from Faluvégi, 2004:17; A, B, C added).

Figure 30. Macro- and subregional socio-economic inequalities in Hungary, 2002

West. An important way to achieve this was the deliberate industrialisation of several, traditionally agrarian, towns in the countryside: state industrial investments targeted a selection of these, and resulted in their catching up to the rest of the country and in absolute terms, in significant modernisation of their local economies and employment structures. This speeded up out-migration for jobs from the smaller settlements within these regions. Since it was definitely not among the political priorities to prevent this (but quite the contrary), their physical and institutional infrastructures eroded fast, with the living standards and

their population. (Perczel, 2003, Enyedi, 1996).

Then, spatial inequalities in Hungary were growing fast with political and economic transition from 1989/90, and their pattern also changed. As soon as market forces had been let loose, many municipalities and regions that enjoyed relative prosperity under Socialism suddenly faced depression, and the living standards in bigger urban centres and small villages polarised further.

147

On the macro-regional scale, a 'west-east slope' in economic well-being and average incomes appeared in Hungary (Figure 30, A). A reason behind was that foreign direct investment (one of the most crucial 'dynamic' factors) particularly in and around Budapest and in the north-western regions, did not cross the line of the Danube for a long time, and therefore, in the 1990s, Eastern Hungary benefited from it only to a limited extent. Another major distinction in spatial development has existed for long between the capital city (Budapest) and its region versus the 'countryside'; the divergence of which increased further after 1990 (Fig. 30, B). In addition to these two features, at a lower, sub-regional level, a less straightforward pattern of inequalities have emerged in Hungary, though these rather blur than overwrite the above-mentioned major macro-regional tendencies. (Faluvégi 2004; Nemes-N., 1995, 1998a)

The map in Figure 30 shows this fragmentation after twelve years of transition: 150 statistical sub-regions of Hungary (each made up of several municipalities) were classified into five categories according to a complex development index (Faluvégi, 2004:10-15).[143] This fragmented spatial structure has emerged due to local-regional combinations of negative and positive factors alike. On the one hand, structural crises selectively hit these regions and their included municipalities: affected those especially, which had earlier specialised in the traditional branches of manufacturing (i.e. in particular, the eastern regions of the old industrial axis stretching from Central Transdanubia to the north-easternmost corner of Hungary, Fig. 30, C) or had only agriculture as the basis of their economies (most of rural Eastern Hungary and the SW region, S. Transdanubia). On the other hand, capitalisation on local, especially, human resources contributed to the success of some sub-regions and municipalities in Central and W-NW Hungary, and also within the otherwise less developed regions. "After 1990 villages entered 'the market of settlements'. Their position, their pathway was determined by their geographic location and transport links, natural and environmental conditions, labour-market status, the condition of the local society and their purchasing power among several other factors" (Beluszky & Sikos, 2007).

Along with political transition, administration of the country was decentralised, and local self-government replaced the socialist 'district.' Many local governments have gained the ownership of land, businesses and property from which income could be obtained, and they were given the right to decide on their own budgets. Besides, local governments also were given a lot more *responsibilities* than socialist districts had ever held before: greater roles in education, health care, housing, and public works. However, typically, local tax revenues and additional income gained from own assets cannot cover the increased expenses. This has been certainly the case with most of the small rural

---

[143] The 'complex development' indicator was created via factor analysis; the factor selected in the end covers over twenty independent variables on socio-economic development. Other similar classifications of sub-regions have been calculated and mapped by the Central Statistical Office (www.ksh.hu), too.

communities in problematic regions, where due to the deteriorated state of infrastructure and the low economic basis for revenues (aging population and little entrepreneur-ship), the provision of the very basic functions leave little budget for the governments to spend on social services for their populations, or support local economic development programmes. In concrete figures, from a relatively recent survey: 98% of all villages have no nursery school, 45% lack a kindergarten, 55% an elementary school, 56% a police presence, 69% a veterinary surgeon, 42% a district nurse, 75% a pharmacy, 60% a post office and 61% a club for the elderly (Halloran – Calderón V., 2005). Over a thousand rural municipalities (32% of all villages) have less than 500 inhabitants; and besides missing these institutions in place, access to them in other settlements nearby is limited by a poor (and still, deteriorating) public transport system.

Nonetheless, these difficulties of adaptation to the changed social-economic and political environment have been to some extent counterbalanced by new *possibilities* (offered by the same transformational processes) which could facilitate local growth and improved competitiveness. As a result of what Faluvégi and other authors referred to as "new active components" or 'dynamic factors', the development – and deployment – of the information technologies, the expanding transport networks, and the increasing role of services, as well as the practice of more efficient human resource management, considerable changes were expected in the early 2000s in the socio-economic spatial structure (2004:4). The latter aspect (the promotion of

human capital) has been considered as a key task in rural-peripheral areas: their population is lacking certain levels and types of education and skills, and therefore, represents only a potential labour resource.

Two logical questions arise from the above: how these continuities (legacies, difficulties) and new development potentials are reflected by the spatial inequalities in I.S. development in Hungary in / after transition; and how much ICTs could contribute, as new 'active components' to levelling out the disparities across the country? (Or: have they helped, at all, in decreasing the inequalities?) In short, similarly to the Finnish case: it is essential to understand whether *the diffusion of different information and communication technologies* can be regarded as a new symptom of, as well as a new factor in, spatial convergence or divergence in Hungary.

ICT-diffusion in Hungary

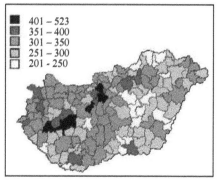

(Source: CSO/KSH, Hungary.)

Figure 31. Number of telephone main lines per 1,000 inhabitants in Hungary (150 sub-regions), 2004

Just as international organisations have tried to benchmark the development of the I.S. on different territorial scales, and most recently on the sub-national scale, similar ventures are being currently undertaken by Hungarian regional scientists, geographers and experts of various other fields, as well as by planning institutions. The question, what indicators are available and can be used to measure informational development on the sub-national level, has always been a central one. Learning about the spatial variation in these factors separately may significantly contribute to our understanding of why and to what extent regional inequalities in I.S. development resemble or deviate from the already existing spatial patterns in economic growth.

The overview of the changes in the telecommunications sector and of the national I.S. political intentions and aspirations (4.3) suggest that also in Hungary, the emergence of ICTs and related services has been one of the most visible dynamic factors in the transformation of the economy and everyday life in general. In the following I give a few illustrations of their *spatial* diffusion patterns. Because of the scarcity of data, only three technological indicators are included, representing different 'depths' of access, and applied to different regional scales. The diffusion of fixed telephone main lines (Figure 31) and the proportion of ISDN lines to 1000 main lines (Figure 32) are indicative of 'realised', actual physical access (show the spatial diffusion of usage, subscriptions – inclusive of 'financial access', too). The areas covered by ADSL services illustrate only potential physical access (the roll-out) of a more advanced,

broadband technology, by a single (though major) service provider in Hungary. I consider the following points to be the most important observations:

The spatial diffusion of fixed main lines and ISDN all indicate the traditional west-east and Budapest vs. countryside divisions in Hungary, which were generally present in the 1990s according to several socio-economic indicators (such as GDP per capita, taxable income levels, FDI). Most probably however, the access to ISDN in reality showed a more detailed pattern, with higher concentrations of ISDN lines in major urban localities.

The diffusion of ISDN, although the scale of the maps below does not allow differentiation *within* counties), followed a typical course of the time: starting in the capital and its region, then continuing in most of the western part of the country, leaving much of the eastern area relatively underdeveloped. It is also visible in the maps and diagrams of Figure 32 that after a certain length of time, regions outside Budapest started to catch up to each other (and thus differences decreased *within* the countryside, see the diagrams), while the level of ISDN penetration in them never reached that of the capital. The reason for this is very likely to be the emergence of alternative, and more advanced technologies, namely broadband applications (Internet via cable TV and ADSL; see above in 4.3).

As regards ADSL infrastructure and service provision, map 33/A illustrates the territorial differences of accessibility by potential subscribers: it does not indicate real diffusion (unlike subscription data would be,

150

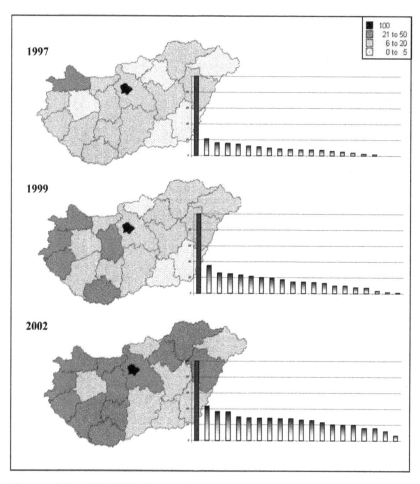

(Source of data: CSO / KSH, Hungary.)

Figure 32. ISDN lines per 1000 inhabitants in the 20 county-level regional units in Hungary, relative to Budapest (Bp.= 100).

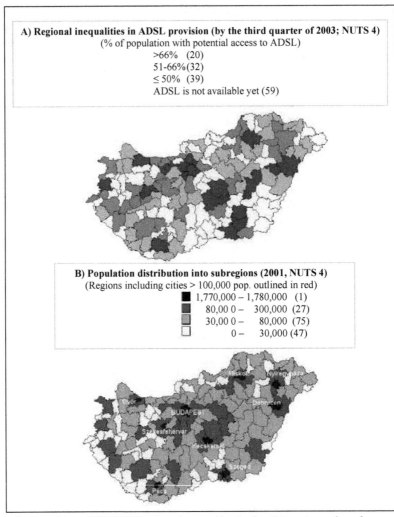

A) Regional inequalities in ADSL provision (by the third quarter of 2003; NUTS 4)
(% of population with potential access to ADSL)
>66% (20)
51-66%(32)
≤ 50% (39)
ADSL is not available yet (59)

B) Population distribution into subregions (2001, NUTS 4)
(Regions including cities > 100,000 pop. outlined in red)
1,770,000 – 1,780,000 (1)
80,00 0 –   300,000 (27)
30,00 0 –   80,000 (75)
0 –   30,000 (47)

(Source of data: CSO / KSH and service provider Axelero Internet, member of the Matáv Group.)

Figure 33. Contrasting spatial variation in population and ADSL coverage of the 150 sub-regions in Hungary, 2003.

if they were available). Still, it was linked to spatial patterns of demand *assumed* or even *observed* by the service provider using direct market surveys, or available regional socio-economic data. (Nevertheless, it is questionable whether supply and demand are always well matched.)

Consequently, the territorial pattern of this 'potential physical access' to Internet via ADSL was fine-grained in 2003. The traditional east-west slope was not very significant any more. Compared to the spatial distribution of population in Hungary (33/B), it becomes obvious that the key guideline for the Internet provider is population density, i.e. the perceived size of the market. Also, densely populated regions are generally more urbanised and so they have more diverse economic bases with a higher share of services and business activities which are considered major consumers of ICTs.[144] (See also Figure 34).

It is easy to predict in which regions *Axelero* would invest and provide its different levels of broadband services in the future, following concentrations of population which are assumed to secure profit. The only reason for developments to

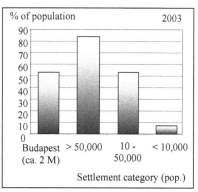

(Source of data: Axelero website.)

Figure 34. ADSL provision in settlement categories (pop. size) in Hungary, late-2003; by Axelero Internet.

happen otherwise (i.e. sparsely populated, poorer regions having access first) could be Universal Service Obligation extended to broadband. This is, however, very unlikely in Hungary in the foreseeable future since that there is no such case in more advanced EU member states either (see 3.3.1 and 3.3.4; also BT, 2007). A frequent argument against the inclusion of BB within the scope of USO is the claim that for enhancing e-inclusion, besides 'connectivity' (physical-financial access), societies have to concentrate more on improving 'content' and 'capability' (mental access). Besides the programmes introduced by the national government in Hungary (4.3), there has been many initiatives from below (by local and regional actors) targeting these three C's. The most prominent of these, I think, is the telecottage movement.

---

[144] Note the exception of the group of sub-regions in Békés County (in the south-easternmost corner of Hungary). The total absence of ADSL here is due to the fact that the map is based on Axelero / Matáv Group data and in early 2003, Békés was the only county in Hungary that belonged altogether to another service provider. Hungarotel owned the concession rights here as a minor fixed line competitor of the incumbent Matáv, but in fact, it was only in April 2003 when first, in some parts of the two biggest towns (Békéscsaba, Orosháza) ADSL was made available by Hungarotel. This company, too, chose the areas which they considered the most surely profitable, to test the new ICT.

5.3.2 A bottom-up initiative: the telecottages (1994 -)

Early developments: Csákberényi Teleház setting an example

As already mentioned, one of the gravest legacies of the Socialist era in rural-peripheral areas was concerning infrastructure, this meant serious problems with insufficient sewage systems, the 'standard' of dirt roads, and a *poorly developed telecommunications network*. In 1990, only about 9 per cent of the population had fixed telephone lines installed at home, the majority of which were concentrated in the capital and the bigger cities (HÍF). Many villages had just one public telephone, or even no connection at all but the one in the neighbouring municipality. As mentioned in 4.3.2 above, the urgency of the situation was recognised by the state soon, which, when privatising the sector, obliged the national telecommunications company to improve the inclusiveness of its services (i.e. to impose universal service obligation in turn for granted monopoly). Therefore, fixed line telephony diffused remarkably fast, especially from the mid-nineties. This also contributed to the environment encouraging the creation of the first telecottages (Hungarian 'telecentres'), adding to the economic necessities and opportunities outlined above.

The idea of the 'multipurpose telecentre' was not altogether new in Europe in the 1990s; it is said to have been 'invented' in Sweden a decade earlier (see Box 10 below). Yet, since the essence of telecentres is that they "can be used for any

purpose by anyone, ... according to demand" (Németh, E., 1997), it is no wonder that they have spread since in many developed and developing countries, and have taken up various 'national shapes', incorporating various levels of ICTs.

The telecottages in Hungary are adopted–adapted variants of especially this Nordic 'innovation prototype'. Hungarian librarians collected and translated accounts on the first Swedish example, its transfer into Finland, and also some similar cases from other Western European countries. In 1992, they published this information in a booklet and circulated it within their national library network as a recommended solution for small village libraries in Hungary to sustain their services in the difficult economic situation. Soon a so-called 'telecorner' was set up in Nagymágocs (Csongrád County, Southeast Hungary), an agriculture-based municipality of 3,500 inhabitants, yet this attempt failed within the same year. According to some accounts, there was a problem with the staff, and another reason could be that it had only a single purpose, the modernisation and extension of the local library services (ITU 2001). However, another telecottage was founded in 1994, in *Csákberény*, a small hillside community in mid-western Hungary (Fejér County; pop. 1,300). It was born in the same year when the village got its first fixed telephone line (see Box 11). '*Csákberényi Teleház*' proved to be much more permanent than Nagymágocs 'telecorner'; it has been functioning for over twelve years.

The Swedish **Härjedalens Telestuga** in Vemdalen (a village 450 km north of Stockholm) is known as the ancestor of all telehouse initiatives in Europe. It was founded by a much-travelled Danish man, the interpreter and translator Henning Albrechtsen, who settled down in this small village when his retirement was approaching. The region of Härjedalen was facing serious problems: due to its extremely low population density (1 inh. / km²), and poor connections and accessibility it was losing especially the young and active segments of its population, as well as its local businesses.

(S.: www.harjedalen.se, edited by S.N.)

Albrechtsen got the idea of opening an 'everyone's office' from a seminar presentation on rural development in 1985 (delivered by the Danish Jan Michel), and established the *telestuga* in Härjedalen after a few months (13th Sept. 1985) equipped with 19 personal computers, a fax machine and other office tools, as well as with three trained staff. Albrechtsen himself could take advantage of this facility in his work as a translator, while he also gave others the opportunity to do distance work (or 'telework'). The small local factories could establish connections with businesses further away, and soon received orders, could fully use their capacities again, and could even hire more employees – and the regional economy started to grow. The initial investment of 1 million Swedish *krona* (ca. USD 170,000) was offered as contributions from the state, the incumbent telecommunications company, the local government, however, the *telestuga* became self-sustaining very soon.

In the early 1980s, there had already been similar attempts in other countries (e.g. telework centres in France and Great Britain) but those were much less focussing on their communities than Albrechtsen's telecottage.

(Based on: interview with Mr Gáspár, 2003; Andrew Bibby, 1995; Global Ideas Bank; Hautaviita, 2000)

Box 10. The story of 'the very first' telecottage, *Härjedalens Telestuga* in the 1980s

About four years after the political and economic transition began in Hungary, on 14 July 1994, *Mr. Mátyás Gáspár*, a college professor in Budapest (teaching public and community management, as well as community informatics) founded **Csákberényi Teleház** in his second-home village located in Fejér County, Central Transdanubia.

A short time before this, Mr Gáspár had come across a pamphlet about international examples of rural telecentres, compiled and translated by a librarian and disseminated in the national library network. Then, "the idea had been nursed for two years in the minds of some local residents of Csákberény: the public administration manager, the mayor, and some other inhabitants were considering launching a local community-development programme" (Gáspár, interview, 2003). For the purpose of its management, they needed a separate office, a house which had many essential tools in one place: a computer, photo copying and fax machines, other office equipment for different tasks. It also had to provide public space, a shared room for the local community.

Since, Mr. Gáspár has been managing the *Teleház* together with his wife, Mária Takáts. They were also the ones to initiate the establishment of the civil organisation called *Hungarian Telecottage Association* (HTA), which Mr Gáspár served as President for a decade (1994-2004).

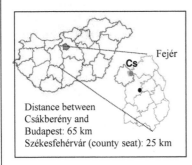

Distance between Csákberény and Budapest: 65 km
Székesfehérvár (county seat): 25 km

The building converted to fit the purpose is in fact, a small traditional Hungarian village house, located in the village centre close to the primary school, the post office, and the church.

Box 11. The story behind the establishment of Csákberényi Teleház: the 'Reference Telecottage'

156

Although, *Csákberényi Teleház* was the outcome of a local, bottom-up initiative in 1994, it did gain support from the Ministry of Welfare, too. This indicated some early interest on the part of the national government despite the fact that at this time, telecottages were not regarded by higher politics as an innovation to include in the national development plan.

Nevertheless, the founders of the first successful telecottage had another ambitious plan in mind, by which they also hoped to draw the attention and the support of national and international authorities and organisations. They decided to share their experiences and their expertise in telecottage-production with actors in other rural municipalities, and spread the use of this new tool in community development throughout the country and even beyond Hungary, across the CEE region. This could have not taken place without new participants, a heavy reliance on networking and the ICTs themselves, and the national 'institutionalisation' of the project. After the first telecottage proved functional and sustainable, a series of processes was set in motion, which has ultimately led to the highest number of telecentres per population in the world.

In 1995, the *Hungarian Telecottage Association (HTA)* was established as a civil organisation under the leadership of the telecentre manager in Csákberény (Mr Gáspár) with the aim of disseminating knowledge on telecottages in the country. The year 1996 meant a major turning point: the 'Network for Democracy Program' (DemNet) was launched to support civil society organisations financed by *USAID through United Way International.* It helped establishing over 30 new telecentres in Hungary in 1997-98. Some municipalities could also draw support from *EU pre-accession funds* for their telecottage development. In late 1997, the *Hungarian Government* finally made its move towards the telecottages. On the first Hungarian Telecottage Symposium, the *National Telecottage Programme (NTP)* was announced in 1998. Along with the organiser HTA, representatives of several ministries, public and private organisations participated in the meeting, which gained excellent publicity in the press. The Government offered HUF 100,000,000 (445,000 ECU) from the state budget, which complemented with additional available resources, was calculated to be enough for developing about 150 new telecottages. The Association set the rules and conditions for the newly established telecottages, making sure that the original idea and 'spirit' would be preserved and that the telecottages would be sustainable on the long run. In the late 1990s, optimistic prognoses were made for the future about the increase in the number of telecentres in the country (see in Box 12).

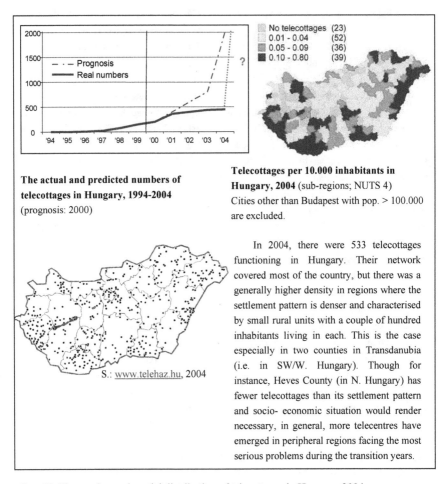

The actual and predicted numbers of telecottages in Hungary, 1994-2004 (prognosis: 2000)

Telecottages per 10.000 inhabitants in Hungary, 2004 (sub-regions; NUTS 4) Cities other than Budapest with pop. > 100.000 are excluded.

In 2004, there were 533 telecottages functioning in Hungary. Their network covered most of the country, but there was a generally higher density in regions where the settlement pattern is denser and characterised by small rural units with a couple of hundred inhabitants living in each. This is the case especially in two counties in Transdanubia (i.e. in SW/W. Hungary). Though for instance, Heves County (in N. Hungary) has fewer telecottages than its settlement pattern and socio- economic situation would render necessary, in general, more telecentres have emerged in peripheral regions facing the most serious problems during the transition years.

Box 12. The number and spatial distribution of telecottages in Hungary, 2004.

The use of telecottages: technology, information, community and learning

The HTA defines the mission of telecottages in the Hungarian context as an integral part of the 'intelligent locality' concept (Figure 35):

A telecottage is a community and service organization that ensures **access to information and communications tools, information and services**, provides users **professional and trained help** and addresses **additional local community needs**."

(It) "can operate in many types of institutions and legal entities (independent institution, library, community house, school, post office), and it is not classifiable in a single service branch or economic sector, but in its own **hybrid organization and organizational cooperation**, i.e. usually owned by a civil organization, hosted in the local government, and operated by a private company..."

(Gáspár in Telefalu, my emphases and translation.)

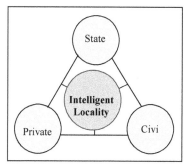

(Adapted from Nagyné T. in Bihari, 1999:45.)

Figure 35. Users, interests and partners in the telecottage: the idea of an intelligent locality

Telecottages generally, can play an important role in relieving all three limitations in 'access' to knowledge and resources in rural, peripheral regions in Hungary: the lack of 'hardware', the problems with ICT skills and knowledge, as well as the motivation barriers. Nevertheless, the assortments of services they provide, and their 'accommodators' (host and operator) determine how they can achieve all or parts of these tasks. These, on the other hand, are just as diverse as the villages and communities they serve across the country (see also the detailed account on the SGP telecentres below). Some of them are housed in separate, purpose-built 'cottages', while many of them occupy a room in the local administration building or the library (Murray, 2001, Gáspár, 2003). Relatively few of them are truly multi-purpose community spaces with the newest technology. Still, in general, they are able to provide *access to ICT, information and knowledge* as well as new and popular *community space* for the residents and enterprises in their neighbourhood:

• ICTs and simple office services

As mentioned also in 4.3.2, in 2003 Internet in households was still little diffused in Hungary (8 % of the population), yet about 15-17% actually *used* the Internet (HÍF, BellResearch) dominantly at the workplace, in schools, and public facilities, such as telecottages and libraries. This indicates a substantial demand for public (physical / financial) access points. Figure 36 shows that in telecottages, connection to the Internet (surfing, looking for information), office facilities and e-mail were among the most popular service- categories in the late 1990s

159

according to the proportion of visitors using them.

- Information and training centres

Many telecottages have come up with more creative 'information products' and more complex functions to stay useful and keep up with changing social and technological conditions. The profile of the most successful examples includes locally and regionally relevant information and knowledge-intensive, specialised services that support entrepreneurship and rural development projects.

SERVICE CATEGORY	USERS
	% of all visitors
1 Office services	
(Photo-copying, fax, etc.)	**85**
2 Provision of community space	**75**
3 Access to Internet	**61**
4 Universal information services	**57**
5 Computer games	**51**
6 Counselling	**50**
7 E-mail	**44**

(Based on Molnár, 2000.)

Figure 36. The most popular services by telecottages.

Rural entrepreneurs face several problems including the lack of information, their perceived and actual isolation, and poor infrastructure being the most crucial ones. Therefore, inexpensive office space and equipment, Internet services, consulting, forums and training, new ways of marketing and networking with other SMEs in and beyond their region mean a huge advantage to them (Beaton, 2002). An increasing number of telecottages has recognised the significance of this, especially in connection with village tourism, organic farming, agro-market-information, and telework.

Institutionalised in the framework of the NTP, many telecottages took up the role of EU-related information centres (the *Csákberény 'Referencia Teleház'* was among the first to do so opening a so-called European Information Point in 2003). Orientation about the LEADER+ programme for rural development has recently become almost a standard item included in telecottage websites. Many of the telecentres assist in applications for funding, provide training in project management and initiate development projects themselves.

These activities have especially been important for the fact that on the sub-national level, the whole idea of communities and regions being actively responsible for their own future and sustainability still needs to be implanted into the ways social actors in Hungary think about their individual and community lives. The additionality principle in funding, applying for aimed grants, drawing up local and regional development strategies, co-operating across sectors and geographical boundaries, coming up to fixed standards and participating in monitoring activities, etc. are all present in the NTP. Making people learn these through practice on the local level in order to realise their local interests and ambitions had been a way of preparing society for the EU regime. This is indeed, vital in the case of regions that go through restructuring and need a diversification of their economies.

It is obvious from Figure 36 that besides technology and information services, telecottages have been popular also for their

160

community space function, their good atmosphere and interesting cultural programmes. It is rather indicative that 62 per cent of telecottage visitors claimed in 2000 that the life of their communities has changed positively since their telecentres were set up. It is true, that this improvement had been due partly to the fact that Hungarian telecottages are not only public access points, but *community* access points, and that they often fulfil tasks that make up for missing public services (Molnár 2000). The community space function may be realised through informational activities such as editing locally relevant digital and printed newspapers, radio programmes, to housing social events, organising fairs, meetings of civil organisations, providing room for different training and leisure activities for children and the elderly. So, telecottages can have a significant associational power.

Besides, the responsibilities taken up by individual telecentres may be basically anything to meet emergent local need. It is included clearly in the HTA Statutes that telecentres, if necessary, should assist municipal governments in the provision of public services under individual contracts. This has been especially important in the smallest villages where the relevant institutions are missing or forced to work in very difficult circumstances (see also 5.3.1). A *teleház* therefore, can function as a post office, or even, some sort of a health and family centre, can arrange the transport of children to distant schools, or act as a tax advisory or unemployment office. Telecottages often provide room for and

cooperate with the 'village caretaker' (*falugondnok*) in these functions.[145]

Internal and external exchange of knowledge, 'export' of expertise

The telecottages have acquired immense experience in matching ICTs with community development and in practical organisational issues. Best practices are circulated in the Hungarian network (largely supported by ICTs), and are published and shared widely, resulting in synergies, increased tacit and explicit knowledge stock, new associations, and encouraging even the physical mobility of the actors in forms of participation in seminars, training sessions, cultural exchanges. From 2004, most of the telecottages were included in the eHungary programme of the Government (see about *KözHáló* in 4.3). This was a much debated[146] but eventually, a practical solution for at least two reasons. It helped the 'eHungaricised'

---

[145] The 'village-caretaker' concept was also the result of a civil initiative in the early nineties, and had developed into a network of undertakers working in over 820 small villages across the country by 2005, institutionalised and funded early by the Ministry of Social Affairs in 1991. The network is administered by a national association (*Magyar Tanya- és Falugondnoki Szövetség* since 2000) and several regional civil organisations.

[146] Some telecottages chose not to be part of the *KözHáló* public network for various reasons such as distrust, concerns about the conditions they needed to fulfil, or wanting to stay independent. During the interview with the head of the Association in late 2003, he said, however, that one of the weaknesses of the telecottage movement was its being little standardised and very heterogeneous, which limited their ability to become a potential partner in providing public services across the country.

telecottages to up-grade their technological standards (while they could continue their other cultural and social functions). In turn, newly established eHungary access points could get training and assistance (e.g. through the *telementor* network) from the Telecottage Association to develop towards becoming a telecottage in their location.

Also, already since 1998, building on their know-how experience, the International Telecommunication Union (ITU), in cooperation with the HTA and the International Association of Teleservice Centres have organised several conferences for a broader geographical dissemination of this special know-how.

Naturally, through existing cultural links, and having societal features rooted in shared historical experience, the neighbouring countries of Hungary (especially Serbia and Romania) have been the first to be interested in telecottage practices. There are examples of direct cross-border networking between Hungarian telecottages and others in for instance, Voivodina and Transylvania. In 2004, Mr Gáspár gave up his active presidency of the HTA to found the European Union of Telecottage Association (EUTA) to provide these accomplishments a greater scope and publicity, and some presence on the international political scene: it cooperates with the International Association of Community TeleService Centers and the WSIS (see 3.2). EUTA is an international civil organisation including seven member

associations[147], and the experience of some 1,000 telecentres (2007).

5.3.3 A study on the Southern Great Plain Telecottage Region, Hungary

As the number of telecottages was approaching 200 in Hungary, it was practical for the national association to set up seven regional divisions with representatives in the HTA board. However, the telecentres in the Southern Great Plain had already established their separate civil organisation 'from below' (see Box 13 about the region, and Figures 30-33 in 5.3.1 concerning its position in the country).

The SGP Telecottage Association (*Dél-alföldi Teleházak Egyesülete, DTE*) was founded in 1999 by 21 telecottages to make it easier for them to engage in partnerships with other regional actors: telecommunications and other companies, non-profit organisations, as well as the Regional Development Agency and the county governments. The Association aims at increasing the number of and the knowledge about, the telecottages in the region; and at integrating their activities with other (regional and national) development plans and programmes. They have been successful in achieving much along these goals:

• By 2004, the number of telecottages had nearly quadrupled (to 73).

• The SGP Telecottage Region had participated in several fruitful partnerships with other NGOs, and some ministries,

---

[147] Hungary, Russia, Bosnia and Herzegovina, Bulgaria, Slovakia, Serbia and Montenegro, and Estonia (in 2007).

regional employment centres, etc. for example:

- to further educate and place young unemployed people into jobs in telecottages (distance work and '*telementor*' projects),
- to train telecottage staff in environmental issues and sustainable development (2005),
- for an efficient distribution of welfare services by means of ICTs in the southern part of Csongrád County (2004),
- and to train interested e-Hungary points to become more like a *teleház*, a *community access point* integrated into their local social and institutional contexts (2007).

The SGP Telecottage Region is particularly advanced in innovative information and communication services. For instance, their on-line search-engine helps in finding adequate project partners and sponsors, thus encouraging joint applications for funding and collaboration in the region. Also, the telecottage known as the official media centre of the HTA is located here (*7Határ Studio / Teleház* in Mártély): it has taken up a central role in dissemination and documentation of successful telecottage practices in the SGP, and in the promotion of regional identity and cultural resources. The regional association has been also more active than other regions in strengthening links across the national border both towards Serbia and Romania by organising conferences, mutual visits, and training with the foreign partners.

This seems to be an interesting incidence of *regionalism* in comparison with the top-down 'regionalisation' of the HTA organisation. The efforts of the SGP Telecottage Region indicate a tendency which complements the still rather centralised institutional system of regional policy in Hungary.[148]

A logical question is whether networking among the individual telecottages is particularly intensive within this special regional context. This assumption is encouraged by the facts that telecentres are equipped with the tools and experience necessary for cost and time-efficient communication, and that most of them have learnt their 'trade' from each other (see Figure 38 for the spatial clusters of telecentres according to their birth-years, for instance). Below, I briefly review some of the most important results of my survey-based research carried out in 2005 which focussed on telecottages in the SGP Region. I aimed especially at understanding *how their sustainability, managing-operating body, their ICT equipment and service-profiles, and their networking activities are related to*

---

[148] In Hungary, SGP and the other six *planning and statistical regions* have development councils and agencies, but no governments and administrative powers. The Act on Regional Development (1996, 1999) introduced the objectives and the institutional system of regional policy in Hungary. Following the latest amendment (2006), there are 5 sub-national levels. The macro-regions (3; NUTS 1), planning and statistical regions (7; NUTS 2), and the sub-regions (168; LAU 1 / NUTS 4) are *not* public administration units. Counties and the capital (20; NUTS 3) and the municipalities (3152; LAU 2 / NUTS 5) are the spatial units of traditional public administration with local self-governments since 1990 (CSO/KSH, Hungary).

163

Area: 18,339 km^2 (20% of the total national territory.)
Population: 1.3 million
Pop. density: 73 inhabitants per km^2

A distinctive *settlement structure:* big cities (the three county seats, among them the university city and regional centre, Szeged), rural towns, large villages and many scattered farmsteads. So, besides a higher-than-average rate of urban population (65.6%) and 180-200,000 people (44% of the rural pop.) living on distant farms.

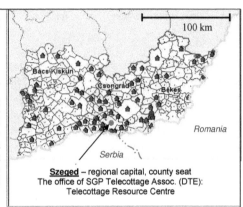

Szeged – regional capital, county seat
The office of SGP Telecottage Assoc. (DTE):
Telecottage Resource Centre

Aging demographic structure and the out-migration of the young is a problem in most of the region.

Accessibility is relatively better in the north-western part of the region, however, the M5 highway had not reached Szeged before 2005. Most of the municipalities in Békés County and along the borders have rather poor accessibility on road to the rest of the country via M5, as well as to the county seats or the sub-regional centres within the SGP Region.

Industrial production rates are relatively low partly for the inherited significance of the food and textile branches and partly for the lack of investments and scarce foreign capital. The region is rich in natural and cultural resources for high quality agricultural production (not only of the popular 'hungarica', such as *paprika*), eco- and cultural tourism (nature reserves, spas, folk art and traditions); however, much investment is still needed into the modernisation of these sectors. The SGP is second in the country after Central Hungary considering tertiary educational and research institutions, and the size of its human capital; however many of these activities are under-resourced and much of the innovation network is concentrated in Szeged.

(SGP Regional Development Agency, 2003; KSH/CSO Hungary)

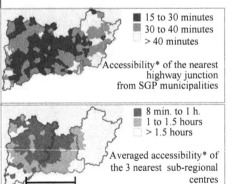

■ 15 to 30 minutes
■ 30 to 40 minutes
□ > 40 minutes

Accessibility* of the nearest highway junction from SGP municipalities

■ 8 min. to 1 h.
■ 1 to 1.5 hours
□ > 1.5 hours

Averaged accessibility* of the 3 nearest sub-regional centres

* Duration of travel, 2001

Box 13. The Southern Great Plain Region, Hungary.

each other (see the use of ICTs in this data collection and other information about the survey in Appendix 8.)

One of the major findings is that relatively few of the SGP telecentres are truly multi-purpose community spaces, and / or equipped with the latest technology. Often, they specialise in simpler office services and have just narrowband connections, a few PCs, and rather limited opening hours. Some of these, however, can boast with tens of civil organisations cooperating with them in organising cultural and other local events, activities. At the other end of the scale there are telecentres 'armed' with the latest arsenal of networked computers and other digital tools, and fast Internet (e.g. some of the libraries which joined also the e-Hungary programme). Not all of them can offer technological expertise, and many of these seemed less active on the socio-cultural side. They have diverse perspectives on their future sustainability, too (Figure 37). My interviews and observations also confirmed that the telecottage scene in the SGP region

is rather heterogeneous. Based on the questionnaires filled in by the 29 respondents (40% of telecottages in the region), three basic types – or survival strategies – can be outlined.

First, many telecentres have sought the support of their *municipality*; these are owned partly or completely by their local governments and housed in the library, the village school or located in the municipal office itself. Their existence and the employment of at least one staff is more-or-less secured (see the information on staff in Table 6). However, there are some risks. These telecentres are usually more dependent on local political developments (i.e. elections every four years, which, in Hungary a genuine factor of uncertainty). Also, their locale (e.g. a 'silent' library or a too 'formal' office within another institution) may limit their community-space function.

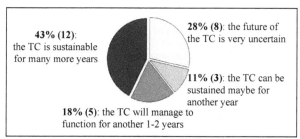

43% (12): the TC is sustainable for many more years

28% (8): the future of the TC is very uncertain

11% (3): the TC can be sustained maybe for another year

18% (5): the TC will manage to function for another 1-2 years

(29-1 telecottages: one TC completed the questionnaire only partially) *Survey: 09-10. 2005.*

Figure 37. Respondent telecottages in the SGP region about their visions of their future sustainability

Table 6. The distribution of respondent SGP telecentres (29) according to the number and type of employee and the managing-operating organisation.

Staff / managing-operating org.	Local gov. (or local gov. + civil org.)	Private enterprise	Civil organisation	*In total*
Volunteer(s)	0	0	3 (19%)	*3 (10%)*
1-2 part-time staff	2 (17%)	0	2 (12%)	*4 (14%)*
1 full-time (and maybe 1-2 part-time) staff	8 (67%)	0	7 (44%)	*15 (52%)*
More than 1 full-time employees	2 (17%)	1 (100%)	4 (25%)	*7 (24%)*
In total	*12*	*1*	*16*	*29*

(%: managing-operating organisation type = 100%) *Survey: 09-10. 2005*

Table 7. The distribution of respondent SGP telecentres (29) according to the level of ICT equipment and the managing-operating organisation. *Survey: Sept.-Oct. 2005.*

ICTs / managing-operating or	Local gov. (or local gov. + civil org.)	Private enterprise	Civil organisation	*In total*
Low level	4 (33%)	0	4 (25%)	8 (28%)
Medium level	7 (58%)	0	7 (44%)	14 (48%)
High level	1 (8%)	1	5 (31%)	7 (24%)
In total	*12*	*1*	*16*	*29*

(*Based on the number of PCs with Internet connection, bandwidth of Internet connection; %: managing-operating organisation type = 100%)

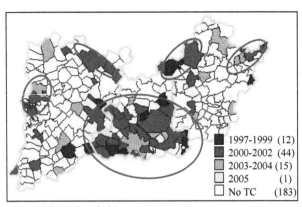

Survey: Sept.-Oct. 2005.

Figure 38. The distribution of the 72 telecottages included in the survey according to their years of opening in SGP municipalities.

166

Table 8. The distribution of respondent SGP telecentres (29-1)* according to their visions of their sustainability and their connectedness**.

Survey: Sept.-Oct. 2005.

Sustainability / connectedness	No connections	Low connectedness	Medium connectedness	High connectedness	In total
Very uncertain	5 (41%)	2 (18%)	1 (50%)	0	8 (28%)
Maybe for a year	1 (8%)	2 (18%)	0	0	3 (11%)
1-2 years for sure	2 (17%)	0	1 (50%)	2 (66%)	5 (18%)
On the long run	4 (33%)	7 (64%)	0	1 (33%)	12 (43%)
In total	12	11	2	3	28

Notes:

*One TC completed the questionnaire only partially; %: all in the class of popularity /column/ = 100%)

**Connectedness:* measured by the number of references to the TC by other (respondent) SGP telecottages.

No connections: not mentioned by any of the other TCs in the region

Low connectedness: mentioned by 1-2 other TCs in the region.

Medium connectedness: mentioned by 3-4 other TCs in the region.

High connectedness: mentioned by 5 or more other TCs in the region.

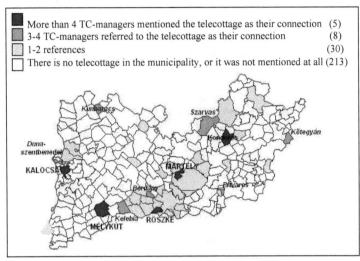

More than 4 TC-managers mentioned the telecottage as their connection	(5)
3-4 TC-managers referred to the telecottage as their connection	(8)
1-2 references	(30)
There is no telecottage in the municipality, or it was not mentioned at all	(213)

(Note: including all references, i.e. also the 25 TCs in the SGP region which were mentioned but which themselves did not respond). *Survey: Sept.-Oct. 2005.*

Figure 39. The distribution of SGP telecottages mentioned by respondent telecottages according to the frequency of reference

Second, a number of telecottages organize themselves around *local-regional civil society groups*. They are usually very lively and popular, and are engaged in diverse cultural and other local activities. Their ICT infrastructure varies from very poor to modern, and in fact (based on the small survey, had slightly better technology in general, than the telecottages owned partly or completely by the local government; see Table 7). Third of them however, have to rely on volunteer and part-time labour. Their sustenance depends on foundations such as the National Civil Fund, from which support has been more and more difficult to obtain; but they increasingly use the opportunities provided by the EU. Civil telecottages are still the most common (e.g. two-thirds of all telecottages) in the SGP region, and I had the impression several times that their managers (often doing volunteer work) are among the more optimistic and enthusiastic ones, too.

The third strategy is to start a locally or regionally relevant, information-intensive business, focusing on a set of services (counselling, media, training, etc.). They naturally have permanent staff and a competitive level of ICTs. Their sustainability depends on the enterprise and its ability to fill a niche in their respective areas, yet there is a risk of their becoming purely profit-oriented, and attracting only a selected segment of the local society (the one private telecentre in the region which responded in the survey do not belong to this later category; the others are closer to a well-equipped internet café or shop with office services).

(Own photos, 2004/2005).

1. Telecottage combined with the village library, cultural centre, and the club for the elderly in Kamut (civil org.); 2. telecottage in the municipal library and cultural centre in Algyő (local gov.); 3. telecottage specialised in EU information for farmers in Ruzsa (civil association supported by the local government), and 4. a very active telecottage on the Serbian border in Röszke (civil organisation with the local gov. and cable TV company among the members, building provided in school-yard by the local gov.). In the centre: a lonely farmstead near Ruzsa, Csongrád County.

Figure 40. Telecottages in the Southern Great Plain Region.

Many positive and fewer negative examples can be found for all three kinds. Of course, most of the telecottages are hybrids (e.g. public-civil) or transforming from one to the other to keep the telecottage relevant amidst the changing circumstances and the arising new opportunities. Continuity is a very important factor in sustainability, especially in terms of the human element and local embeddedness. This is observable for instance in the problems caused by frequently changing staff and managers, which most often has

been the outcome of the lack of money, and in fewer cases, of political and other personal conflicts.

Information from the survey and the interviews also suggested that those telecottages which have managed to keep up their work in their municipalities for a longer time (more than 4 years), and have established a distinctive profile for themselves, specialized in something are also the ones which network with more telecottages in the region and beyond, even across the national border. They have earned

Kondoros: telecottage by a civil organisation

(Own photos, 2005).

Figure 41. Inside and outside the telecottage in Kondoros, Békés County, SGP Region

a good reputation, much respect, and many friends within the national organisation; and several younger telecentres have relied on them for advice, technical help, and cooperation. These few important 'nodes' in the region have a significant associational power both bonding within their own village or small town, and bridging their localities via other telecottages to neighbouring and more distant regions (see Figure 38). It is important to note that their managing-operating organisation is dominantly civil or hybrid: working in close cooperation with other private and public entities, and are supported by the local government in form of a salary or a building (e.g. in Röszke).

(Sources: own photos from 2004; photos from 2006 provided by 7Határ, Ltd.; Telecottage local radio website)

From top left to bottom right: Mártély, Fő utca (main street) where the telecottage is located (2004); local youth learning to make film with the help of the telecottage (2006); the manager (2004-), and the founders of the telecottage (and Studio Kft.) in front of the *Teleház* created in an old traditional village (2004); three photos of the studio and the common room of the telecottage (2006); Studio Kft interviewing Mr Gáspár, HTA head in Budapest (2004); picture from the website giving access to the local Szóbeszed (~ 'tittle-tattle') radio produced in the telecottage with daily live broadcasting.

Figure 42. *7Határ Teleház and Studio Ltd.* in Mártély, Csongrád County

Kondoros *teleház* (Figure 40) cooperates with over a dozen civil groups, and although does not own the latest technology, it offers social space made attractively furnished with local cultural treasures. Among the major nodes that were detected by the survey, the telecottage in Mártély is the only to be owned by a private company; however, it also fulfils many civil functions.

The survey found only a looser set of relationships horizontally, and a few important and popular telecottages as major nodes of information and knowledge flows instead of a strong and inclusive network of telecentres across the region. However, it seems based on the above, that the viability of telecottages is linked with their ability to cooperate with a diversity of partners within and outside their localities. The frequency of (net)working with other telecentres in and beyond their region is also connected to their longer term sustainability. This last observation is most likely to be supported by the last case study in this dissertation, since one of the actors involved in it is Mártély *7határ Teleház*, the multimedia telecottage (see photos in Figure 41 above).

5.4 Cooperation across space and cultures for a local solution [149]

> "Tell me and I'll forget. Show me and I'll remember. Involve me and I'll understand."
> Confucius

5.4.1 Introduction: research ideals and approaches

The following study is an extension of the previous sections in terms of its subject, as well as considering the shift in epistemological stance, methodology and style. It reports on *the birth and evolution of cooperation between the Finnish and Hungarian local actors which are introduced above;* their joint planning of an innovative ICT application for the development of a set of rural municipalities in Hungary. It brings together on the one hand, the international / European dimensions of I.S. policies and values (Chapter 3), and on the other hand, local-regional development (5.2 and 5.3) that comes from practices that have emerged in two distinct national contexts (Chapter 4).

In fact, this last case study is an actual spin-off from *doing* research presented in 5.2-3. My work related to the bottom-up and civil involvement in developing I.S. was first characterised with a still more or less detached stance from the cases, and it was learning about the specific development projects in the two countries separately. Meanwhile, gradually, I was personally drawn closer to the objects of my

---

[149] This section is a revised version of the studies published in Finnish (*Maaseudun Uusi Aika*, 2006/3), and in Hungarian (ISTRI: *Kutatási Jelentés* 2005).

research, to the point when I found myself connecting them.

As indicated in 5.2-3 above, North Karelia and the rural settlements in the Hungarian countryside (including those in the Southern Great Plain) show similar *symptoms, i.e. of rurality and under-development*, and a particular relationship between people and technological innovation. Consequently, the objectives and the tools of the Finnish and Hungarian solutions show a lot of *similarities*, too.

Already while working on the North Karelian and SGP studies separately, interesting analogies and even some concrete linkages emerged between the two; there were some recurring stories which could not be a total coincidence. So, I put aside the data tables and maps for a time, and drew a blank sheet (or rather, opened a new .doc file, to be more authentic here.) I decided that I should give testimony to networks that have been at work; the information and communication webs of people and technology which somewhere and at different times have connected even the developments in Finland and Hungary.

Furthermore, as this last case study shows, the spatial-economic settings of the two cases introduced in the above, are relevant also as the *origins of the different experiences* of the cooperating partners. Again, spatial-cultural (geographical) contexts do matter.

The similarities and especially, the differences come out more visibly when the two contexts meet in some way. They were given the possibility to come together directly by my field work in both regions. However, their cooperation was an outcome

of several more, both human (social) and technological factors: the former especially, motivated, the later mainly facilitated it.

I am able to write this account on the evolution of such networks after having acknowledged that I am a part of them - both in a technological and a social / human way. As a researcher in social sciences I have experienced that as soon as I leave my desk – or to be more accurate, already the instant I open a chat session or send e-mails out, I myself have an impact on the researched. Providing I am conscious of and responsible for this effect (which I hope and believe, I am) – I have an active role, function and position in the networks I study. Hence is this study also an experiment for me with a new approach, methods and ways of presenting my ideas.

Initially, the closest definition of my doings while connecting people and ideas was *participant observation* of processes using ethnographic methods. These represent a humanistic, interpretative manner instead of a positivist stance. Rather than testing hypotheses, participant observation and ethnographic research *examine few examples* or just one case, and place emphasis on *exploring the characters of individual social phenomena*. They typically use *unstructured data*, and *explicitly interpret them* in terms of the meanings and functions of human actions, presenting results primarily by means of *verbal description and justification*. (Denzin – Lincoln, 248-9.)

The most recent phase of my involvement with the Finnish and Hungarian local ICT-developers' work resembles to an embryonic form of *participatory action* research (PAR), as it matches the following of its main aspects. It is *aware of its intervention* in the context that it is working within. It "sets out to explicitly study something in order to change and improve it", yet it may (as in my case) also be *motivated by the experience of some successful solution*, provoking a desire to reproduce or extend that practice. PAR has a double aim: 1) "to *produce knowledge and action directly useful* to a group of people"; and 2) "to *empower* people at a second and deeper level through the process of constructing and using their own knowledge" (e.g. consciousness-raising; Denzin and Lincoln, 327-28). Finally, PAR "is *active co-research*, by and for those to be helped", "*action which is researched, changed and re-researched*, within the research process by participants" – and not just research that we hope will be pursued by action (Wadsworth 1998, my italics).

This last instance is particularly true to the case in focus here because even in the course of its first planning phase, strategies and priorities of the joint project were several times re-considered by the partners while their knowledge was expanding and the circumstances were changing.

Finally, I am able to give an insight of I.S. at work because I have had the possibility to meet and get inspired by, a range of interesting and committed people in both Finland and Hungary. I try and mention most of them in the following pages, also in acknowledgement of, and encouragement to their work and in appreciation of the assistance they have given me.

5.4.3 The story of cooperation

Mártély "meeting" Nurmes, and Nurmes seeing Mártély

As I mentioned in 5.1, the interviews with the intranet-developers and the telecottage activists in 2003-04 were all rather unstructured, and the way of selecting the targets was basically a snow-ball method, while following the lines of the stories I heard. In Finland, I started by consulting researchers who knew a lot about the *kansalaisverkko* development and its general background, and who could direct me to people at the Regional Council and in the *Oppiva Pohjois Karjala* projects. Therefore, very soon I could meet some key personalities of both national-regional and local significance. They shared with me their, at many points interconnected, stories and their more general ideas concerning people and technology in the Finnish countryside. Besides, occasionally they asked me whether I knew of any comparable initiatives from my native country. In response, I told them what I then knew about the Hungarian-style telecentres.

I had truly a positive experience in Finland, therefore I was encouraged to follow the same technique and find the main figures of the *teleház* movement in Hungary. I had known about the existence of telecottages for years, and had visited one of them about seven years before. Emboldened after some consultation with sociologists working on the I.S. field in Budapest, I began my search by sending an e-mail straight to the founder of the first *teleház* and leader of the Association, explained him about my interest, and asked him for an interview. I was very pleased by his prompt reply, and also because the meeting turned out to be an exciting discussion rather than a one-sided interrogation. Soon I got the privilege of participating in official meetings of the telecottage organisation, to be present even when important decisions were negotiated. Besides, Mr Gáspár invited me to another, less official meeting where I could have a lot of informal and more relaxed conversation with telecottage activists and supportive mayors from all over Hungary.

This occasion was in fact, a 'post-new-years' party' held in January 2004, but convened also to talk about the future of the movement. It was hosted by the tiny south-western village of Alsómocsolád (358 inhabitants, 2004) the mayor of which is a prominent supporter of the movement. He and the local teleház-manager seemed to know and even be friends with several other activists from the whole country. Two telecottagers, *Árpád Csernai* and *Anita Hegedűs* from Mártély in the Southern Great Plain Region, were also among those who heartily accepted the invitation, despite the long drive amidst snowdrifts. They showed much interest in my work and life in Finland, this "little-known country in the distant north". Soon, after the more serious part of the meeting had been concluded, and at just about the time when the atmosphere started to get quite casual, they appeared with a camera and a dictaphone. I realised that I had been picked as a fresh 'topic' by two professional journalists. The interview was soon after published in one of the electronic forums they edit and manage, *Teleház Magazin* (see the link in the References), with the title referring to Finland as *"The land of virtual telecottages."*

The party over, I needed to return to the capital city, which was quite a challenge after midnight from this tiny back-of-beyond place. The drive home was long enough on the icy roads for some more friendly chat. So, I could found out more about the special orientation of their teleház in Mártély, i.e. that it is also the official media centre of the Hungarian Telecottage Association, and that Árpád had been for years one of the seven regional representatives of the HTA board (naturally, of the SGP). What is more, I was offered the unique opportunity to join their film-making team in their tour around telecottages later that month, when I could conduct some interviews myself as well as could get access to their recorded material.

The documentary tour included several telecentres in the SGP region, and also reached across the southern border to some *teledomovi* in Voivodina, Serbia (where Árpád was originally from). During these days I was also telling the Mártély telecottagers about my work, and the North Karelian community intranet and its Nurmes-based inventor. Then already, I sensed their *interest and openness* from the questions they put to me. Soon after I returned to Finland, at their request, I connected them to Mr Koskikallio via e-mails and chat sessions.

Mártélyi Teleház *saw a possibility to extend the life-span and modernize the activities of their telecottage* preparing it for the times when people even in rural Hungary can have fast internet connections in their homes. Furthermore, they

175

recognised the strengths of the intranet as a tool to modernise and integrate their already working platforms – the local and regional portals, the on-line magazine they edit, the local radio they operate, and the documentary movies they make and publish, for instance. They also considered a possible documentary tour to North Karelia as a way to obtain new filming material, which, Mártély telecottage being a private enterprise, was an important motivating factor, too.

Similarly, the Finnish partner *saw a business opportunity and an interesting challenge* in cooperating with Mártély, and was also convinced of the appropriateness of the *timing for introducing the community intranet concept in Hungary.* Certainly, the shared problems of rurality and the basic common approach in solving them (i.e. the ICT-orientation; dealing with all levels of access simultaneously, and tailoring the solutions to local community needs, etc.) provided a solid ground for co-operation.

The initial joint plans

During the different phases of planning the hybrid application, communication has been dominated by e-mails and chat sessions, sometimes having both, or rather all three, cooperating partners on-line simultaneously (since I increasingly considered myself as a partner, too). This is not surprising considering that I myself was living in Joensuu, the urban centre of North Karelia, the intranet-innovator was working in the distant municipality of Nurmes, and Mártély is situated some 2000 km away from both of these places. It is therefore no

wonder that *the personal technical skills and the easy physical access to ICTs have been a crucial condition to all parties involved.*

Several interesting issues have come up; some were related more to ICTs (see Box 14); while some – even more intricate ones – were concerning national and local policy and political issues and mismatches of different nature: financial asymmetries, unfamiliarity with each other's ways of thinking, the different cultural settings, bureaucracies and mentalities. Yet probably the greatest problem for me, and I assume, for the whole cooperation, was a more straightforward one: *the lack of a common language* (in its literal meaning), *and hence an over-dependence on my person as a mediator.*

The peak of the cooperation was in the summer of 2004 when the Finnish partner travelled to Hungary (for an international conference organised by Eris@ in Budapest; see 3.3.1). After the event, and then a short meeting with the head of HTA, Mr Koskikallio visited Mártély and its neighbourhood for a couple of days, where he could meet the local partners face-to-face and experience some of the good and the not so good sides of the 'rural Hungarian realities'. These later aspects however, were not discouraging the least, rather the opposite: there were problems to solve, an interesting challenge. A concrete project plan was drafted within a few weeks including a visit and training seminar in Finland. The types and the combination of network infrastructure were considered which could be the most suitable for the region's settlement pattern and social composition; the means of setting up the

The initial idea of the hybrid solution was a simple one:

1. Using the already existing ICT- and knowledge-assets of Mártély Teleház, similar training seminars can be organised first with the involvement of Finnish expertise, later through local teachers.
2. Additional free intranet-points could be set up using older PCs in and around the village.
3. The software licence used by the NK *kansalaisverkko* (after translating it into Hungarian), the network-maintenance and management services by Glocal Ltd. and the server machine located in Nurmes can be hired by the local community for a rather low yearly charge per user.
4. The content of the community intranet should be then shaped locally with the involvement of all sectors, in which the experiences of the Finnish partner can be used, too.

Having these so established, the issue of the locally used network technology rose: what is the best choice in the case of this community for the provision of data flow at a sufficient speed/quality, at a reasonable cost?

Are there *local Internet-providers* to make a partnership with? Should there be *a single network solution, or rather a combination* of the most suitable ones? Should Mártély wait for the *national intervention*, i.e. ADSL to reach every single locality in the country within 1-2 (?) years, or rather take measures on its own in advance to gain some competitive advantage in time as compared to other localities in the region?

What is sufficient speed of Internet access in the case of a community which is just learning to use ICTs and an intranet to access regional services, information and realise their individual and common goals? Should a fixed telephone line and modem based solution be enough, or would it mean very soon a drawback as it will found the grounds of a new digital gap, that is the 'broadband gap' between Mártély and other settlements? Maybe xDSL-based or other forms of broadband is a necessity only in 'hot spots' of the village, like the Teleház, the free Internet kiosks, the school, the local authorities, and the *Civil Ház* (a centre for the local civil society), while household terminals could connect up to the local server(s) with their telephone lines.

Cable TV, on the other hand seems to be a perfect solution in the case of Mártély, and it does indeed allow for faster data flow: the *Teleház* managers understand that *local people* are much more willing to support the installation of cable TV, and in the more compactly settled (old and new) parts of Mártély it is a feasible technology. The village is expected to have its sewage system constructed in the very near future, why not use the ditches at the same time to lay these cables? Would that be a technologically sound solution, though? (Or should there be separate ditches dug for the cables?) Still, in the later case it would *save some costs* (reducing engineering costs) if the two constructions happen simultaneously. How about the households/farms situated in a scattered way in the *outlying area*? For them, microwave technology could be the network technology that makes sense. ...

Box 14. Planning the community intranet in Mártély: questions related (not only) to network infrastructure.

intranet kiosks in Mártély and its sparsely populated outlying areas were discussed, and the initial terms of the contract between Glocal Ltd. and Mártély 7Határ Teleház and Studió Ltd. were established.

To be able to get the project actually started, the telecottagers began fund-hunting with the jointly prepared documents in their locality (yet with little hope for more than moral support from their community), as well as by responding to national tenders that matched any components of the project: developing the technological infrastructure, training, or introducing 'e-governance'. They kept on trying during the next ten months or so. The lack of capital in Mártély to cover the 'own share' of the total budget was a crucial problem, but it was overcome by different combinations of resources from local enterprises, including 7Határ Studió itself, and some support from the local government. However, their applications failed one after the other, and the partners had some lengthy pauses in their interaction, due to being busy with other projects and losing hope.

The last attempt at getting funding was made in early 2006, this time, from the European Union. In fact, it was I who had come across the tender on-line on a computer in Mártély telecottage, a few days before my return to Finland. The partner in Nurmes was informed in an e-mail right away, and communication gained some impetus again. In Finland, we drafted an improved project proposal with Mr Koskikallio, communicating via the Internet with Mártély as well as a third, French

partner (see excerpts from the project proposal in Box 15).

This time, the community intranet project plan was adjusted to fit the European Union's town-twinning initiative. The participation of Nurmes in Finland, Mártély and its neighbourhood in Hungary, and Privas, a small town in Rhône-Alps region in France meant that municipalities from three EU member states of different age (and therefore, different experience of the European regime and identity) were drawn together. Mártély had much fewer residents (1,300) than the other two municipalities (towns of ca. 9,000 and 10,000 people), but it was seen as a potential node that would bring into the project some other villages near it with telecentres (which, based on the survey I report on in 5.3.3, was a rational anticipation).

It is obvious, that the technologies to be used and the emphases of the initial project idea had to be slightly updated and adjusted to the requirements of the funding organisation (the Directorate General Education and Culture of the European Commission). First of all, this time more significant financial commitment was required on the part of the three municipal governments. Second, the production of content was more emphasized than the actual technological solutions. The ultimate aim was to generate discussions and learning between these actors in the three municipalities about local identity, 'Europeanness', and networking; in this, the intranet was the innovative tool besides other, traditional practices in town-twinning. Beyond their local tasks each partner had to fulfil, a very fitting division of labour among

'Promotion of active European citizenship' – Support to town twinning actions: Conferences, training seminars and information campaigns
"To involve citizens closely in reflection and discussion on the construction of the European Union; To intensify links and exchanges between citizens from the countries participating in the programme; To promote and disseminate the values and objectives of the European Union... "

"The general aim of the project is *to strengthen and consolidate the cooperation between three municipalities / regions in three different member states of the European Union.* This we wish to achieve with the help of *new information and communication technologies that suit the purposes of the town-twinning movement in Europe.* This relatively micro-scale experiment, if successful could serve as a best-practice model for other municipalities in Europe.

In spite of the many differences between our regions, we do face very similar kinds of challenges in the near future. We all are rather remote/peripheral regions with many common problems - and we all share the common strong belief in future. We are also convinced that with our common efforts for a better future, we are able to give our modest contribution in coming up to the new challenges the whole EU is facing at present.

In the present situation, it is very important to create new *cost-effective means*, media and channels for inclusive cross-cultural dialogue between geographically distant communities. This can bring the (local, national and trans-national) decision processes nearer to "grass-roots level citizens".

The main aim of the project is to create *a new tool* for cooperation between regions, and European citizens *which complements traditional ways* of communication. During the project we will create a common Intranet-system for the three participating municipalities, and with the help of common meetings and seminars we will teach and train the ways to utilize this new media for deepening communication and cooperation between them, and their citizens. The aim is to create a **"virtual agora"** open to every citizen in these municipalities. With the active participation of these citizens the shape, looks, content of this virtual agora will be shaped according to the users' tastes and needs.

With the Virtual Agora project...

o ...we want to create a functioning model for the new kind of international cooperation between regions. We can create a ground for cooperation between different sectors and actors (schools, cultural organisations, local administration, different social, age and interest groups, etc.) During the project we will recruit and educate officials and members of different civic organisations to utilize the possibilities of the Intranet-system, so that the maximum benefit can be achieved.

o ...we want to prove that the diversity of localities across Europe is a *strength* rather than causing inefficiencies and conflicts: if the right means and channels of communication are implemented, the people are able to find a common voice and work fruitfully together.

o ...we wish to spread our knowledge and experience to other regions with similar kind of problems and challenges. We also hope that working together we could further develop our model and make it even more effective. Our aim is to document both the pros and cons of our experiment. We really hope that this documentation can create a good "best practice" to adopt and adapt by other municipalities/regions. We are also prepared to give a detailed and interesting account of the main phases of the project in the form of a documentary movie (the Hungarian partner is responsible for that part of the dissemination work). We are also prepared to invite representatives from our neighbouring municipalities to the project conferences and training sessions. That is an important part of the dissemination process of our experiences.

Box 15. Excerpts from the project proposal 'Virtual Agora', 2005 (Source: documents from Glocal Ltd.)

the partners was defined. In short, Nurmes was responsible for the *ICT infrastructure* supporting the intranet, further adjusting the system to the needs of the virtual agora, and was put in charge of the related *technological training* and maintenance. Mártély was to *document and disseminate* the achievements of the project as a good practice (via EUTA, for instance) and ensure innovative *convergence of different media via the Internet*; and the French partner was given the task of *developing content around the theme of local and European identities.*

Unfortunately, in early 2006, this application sent in the first round was turned down. What is more, the publication of the decision on the EU website, was late (which fault was admitted also by the responsible authorities), so much that it was several days *after* the final deadline set for the second round of applications. Having missed the last opportunity that year, all partners gave up, and stopped planning altogether. Mártély was little willing to start negotiations about related financial issues with their local government (local elections were during the autumn of 2006). Glocal Ltd. started focussing more on the developing countries in marketing their intranet idea, sensing that 2006 was probably the last year when it could still hold some relevance in Eastern-Central Europe.

5.5 Summary

5.5.1 Summary in terms of digital divides and inequalities in access

a) *"Are the long-standing centre-periphery relations, the urban-rural divides reproduced in course of the diffusion of ICTs and their valuable applications?"*

In general, regions with a lower density of population and enterprises in Finland lag behind the national averages concerning especially the availability and diffusion of higher-tier ICT infrastructures, and applications for growth-oriented strategic economic activities. The location of the IT industrial cluster and R&D activities, the spatial patterns in ICT roll-out and investments by network service providers favour the core areas and urban centres in Finland as opposed to the areas in semi-peripheries and distant rural regions. Besides, general social and economic inequalities that relate to the levels of I.S. readiness (mental access), intensity (usage) and impact (content, utility) variables show a similar territorial pattern (however, not as divergent as in the case of, for instance Hungary.)

Although the networking institutions of the Finnish innovation system have several benefits to the overall national performance, and have achieved in some ways a relatively even web of institutions across the land (e.g. universities and science parks), they are less efficient in addressing the problem of distant rural regions and semi-peripheral areas. Some negative bias is built into the logic of R&D funding towards regions with less IT-oriented and more traditional economic profiles: for the sake of national efficiency and growth, state endowments concentrate more on those sectors and regions where private funds are already significant and increasing.

In the case of Hungary, a series of evidence is given above to show how old spatial structures are being reproduced in the diffusion of ICTs (despite the fact that the indicators used do not show the demand side). It is observable nevertheless, that in recent years the macro-regional differences have decreased while the finer grained spatial inequalities between urban and rural municipalities and sub-regions have become more prominent – for the same reasons as explained above in relation to Finland (and internationally: see 3.3.4).

5.5.2 Summary in terms of different spatial and political scales

b) "What interactions have been in the Finnish and Hungarian local cases between the bottom-up initiatives and the top-down policies of the national actors?"

In terms of spatial and regional development in the 'information age', even in a highly equal society as Finland, peripheral and rural areas deserve some special care. Yet this does not necessary have to be in the form of direct subsidies for ICT infrastructure – which, as a matter of fact, is an alien idea to current global (and European) trends in flexible restructuring and political processes. Although in their case, physical access to the networks can be

achieved at generally lower standards than in urban areas, they are not doomed to be losers.

In Finland, appropriate and original responses have been given to these challenges by *local and regional initiatives*, such as the North Karelian I.S. strategy, its extension to the region of Eastern Finland, and one of its local 'offsprings', the Learning N. Karelia community intranet. These, on the other hand were well-received and helpfully reacted to by the national authorities.[150] In my view, this *complementariness* has been due to the coexistence of a clear national commitment, of the Finnish 'cluster policy', the public-private partnerships between administration, research and business, the favourable national and European funding possibilities, the creativity of some individuals and their ability to trust in their regional and national governments and their bureaucratic procedures.

All these make Finland obviously more successful in developing an inclusive I.S. than most of the other European states, more-than-basic infrastructure is available across the whole national territory and content-development has been promoted in a conscious way both from top-down, and bottom-up.

As regards the Hungarian cases, again, a slower *evolution* of cooperation can be traced from the mid-nineties between the state and the 'grass-roots' in terms of I.S. development (and in general). The first telecottages were created by local individuals for their communities to be that

---

[150] See also the relevant conclusion (answer to the question 'c') in 4.4.

181

'new active component' or 'dynamic factor' offered by the emerging information age, which pulls their villages out from their distressed situations. Besides, they tried to provide for missing public *services and infrastructure, those which the state could not supply*. Initially, much effort from below was necessary, to raise public awareness and recognition by the Government of their achievements. This caused a delay of some 4-5 years in truly harnessing the potential in these local institutions (which is a considerable length of time considering the technological nature of these innovations). Finally, in the late nineties, the cooperation between the civil and private sectors, some help from the State, as well as to a rather significant sum of foreign donation could allow telecottages to start mushrooming throughout Hungary. The Government's ambition to comply with the European guidelines concerning PIAPs gave an extra impetus to work together with the civil movement, acknowledge and relying on their accumulated know-how about efficiently integrating ICTs in the life of rural communities.

5.5.3 Summary in terms of socio-technological networks

c) *"How can these actors handle the task of improving access to ICTs and utilise their benefits for local / regional development?"*

The 'three pillars' of the Finnish community intranet project and the mission of the Hungarian telecottages have a lot in common on the subject of this question:

1   They use both the modern technologies and the real (*teleház*) or virtual (*kansalaisverkko*) community spaces, as one another's 'hook', or motivation. On the one hand, they attract people with technologies to participate in the community and connect to resources outside it. On the other hand, they manage to draw people closer to these technologies by satisfying them in their needs for self-expression, socialisation, and exchange of ideas, learning, leisure and entertainment.

2   Therefore, in their respective cultural settings and technological circumstances, both 'projects' have a great potential in raising trust in their communities in ICTs, in services, and last but not least, their institutions. Trust – and social capital – is both an important condition for and product of, their networking.

3   Also as a consequence (of no. 1), tool and the purposes invisibly merge; and usage is increasing both quantitatively and qualitatively. The latter is visible in the achievements of both the intranet and the telecottages, in the creation of locally and regionally relevant content as well as in intensive networking.

4   Networking is innate to both innovations. This is not merely the direct outcome of employing ICTs in their practices, though they help as a (relatively inexpensive and to their geographical conditions, well-suited) tool. The fact that both 'projects' had to recruit and keep up the interest of different local (i.e. public, private and civil) parties, regional actors, and national stake-holders is one of the reasons for their tendency to connect actors

horizontally and vertically. Also, their 'learning by doing' practices make them open to external information and actors. Their eagerness to share their success – out of pride and / or for profit (for the survival and up-grading of their innovation) – encourages them to join already existing networks (the Karelian project becoming a member of Eris@), or create and extend their own (HTA, SGP Telecottage Region, EUTA in the Hungarian example). Also, their 'learning by doing' practices make them open to external information and actors.

5   The example of Nurmes and Mártély trying to work together shows this

latter instance clearly; and the fact that they could not achieve their goal does not mean that other similar efforts could not be successful. However, some of the asymmetries which caused a problem in their cooperation could be attributed to the fact that these two partners had not shared a single network of local I.S. innovations. More concretely, for instance, Mártély Teleház had not been aware of the existence of the European IANIS / Eris@ or RISI initiatives, and the opportunities these could have offered, while the Finnish project leader could not entirely understand the actual scope of the telecottage movement.

6. Conclusions

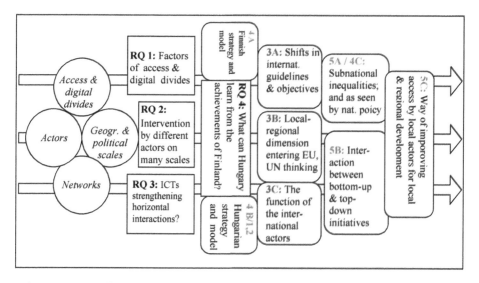

Figure 43. Unraveling the main and sub-research questions organised along the main concepts of access, actors and scales, and networks.

6.1 Answers to the main research questions

As I indicate in Figure 43 above (expanded from Figure 5), the questions I answer at the end of each empirical chapter serve to find answers to the four initial main research questions (RQs). The first three RQs take access, scales / actors, and network as their respective foci of perspective, and the combination of the findings from Chapter 3 (international cases), Chapter 4 (the national case studies) and Chapter 5 (investigations on the sub-national level) help answering their interrogatives. Finding the answer to RQ 4 on the other hand, is less straightforward in this regard. Though it is concerned with I.S. development by national actors, and

therefore relies mostly on sub-questions 4A and 4B, it incorporates a lot of other issues, too.

RQ1 *What are the factors behind the differentiation in access, the emergence of digital divides concerning the rural peripheries of developed countries?*

Access is a rich concept in the interpretation put forward in this dissertation. It is proposed that access needs to be understood as a *combination* of physical-infrastructural, financial-economic, and educational-cultural (mental), as well as content related elements. These are the general aspects of an individual's (or a household's, a business's) access to information, knowledge, communication,

185

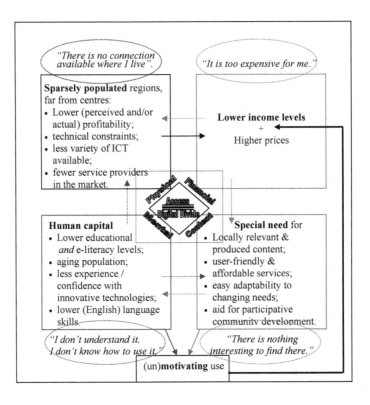

Figure 44. Conclusions from the case studies: problems with access to ICTs in rural-peripheral areas and small rural communities. (Arrows indicate influence.)

and learning; and ultimately, to the benefits of the emerging I.S. In the empirical studies above, much evidence is found for the emergence of urban-rural (centre-periphery) digital divides of different extent in the countries of Europe, and more specifically, within Finland and Hungary.

The growing concern with spatial developments on the UN and EU agendas, the results from the surveys with national public and private actors, as well as my interviews and personal observations about local and regional initiatives in the past one

and a half decades, verify the preliminary assumption that *rural-peripheral regions and communities are in a distinguished and vulnerable position in emerging information societies*. Figure 44 below gives an overview of the main factors identified (expanded from Figure 2).

The first observation is that rural-peripheral areas in Finland and Hungary (and in other European countries in general), have been less attractive for telecom infrastructure investments, and are usually the regions where the state-of-the-art ICTs become potentially available only with a considerable delay relative to core regions and urban centres. The only exception to this has been the spatial diffusion of the use of mobile telephones. There is strong evidence that telecommunications companies (esp. those which construct the network infrastructure) go first to places dense with population, businesses and other information-intensive activities (education, research, administration) to ensure their profit; and so rural areas are supplied with these technologies only subsequently, if at all.

Second, households in rural-peripheral regions do not represent an affluent and motivated demand for higher-level telecommunications services; and this is because they have generally lower income levels and a more aging demographic structure. This weak (actual and perceived) demand results also in low levels of competition between service providers in these regions, which in turn, leads to higher prices. This was the situation in North Karelia in the late-nineties, and is definitely valid to the small village communities in Hungary. Consequently, even if connections are in place technically, without intervention (special motivating programmes and subsidies) the numbers of subscriptions for Internet will stay low in these regions.

In this regard, advanced information societies have achieved relatively more, partly because the diffusion of ICTs have been going on for a longer period of time making society more responsive and technological adoption cycles more rapid (as the case of the Nordic countries shows). However, even in Finland, territorial disparities, the urban-rural digital divides do exist.

A third and very important claim is that being motivated to use Internet (or even subscribe for it at home) is a crucial factor in the cost vs. benefit dilemma (i.e. the choice influenced by tariffs and income levels is a value-based decision). Inherent to the demand side, motivation comes from the group of features I summed up in the notion of 'mental access'. Several of the cases presented in this dissertation underline that these include not only the basic and more specific ICT-skills (e-literacy), but the more general affinity and some attitudinal features (openness, curiosity) towards technological innovations, and importantly, towards foreign languages (especially English).

Further motivation elements, which are closer to the supply side, include aspects such as the user-friendliness of ICTs and the richness and relevance to the actual needs, of the provided services and on-line content. Of course, inter-linkages exist here as well. The perception of the benefits from usage depends also on the potential user's mind-frame, i.e. both skills and attitudes. Also, more sophisticated and higher-value content necessitates more skills on the user's side; and better-skilled users are able to modify and create content (e.g. websites, blogs, etc.) themselves for their own or their communities' purposes. On the other hand, the availability of a diverse and useful content contributes to the improvement of e-literacy among the population. Evidence for this is provided in this dissertation in the example of the continuously expanding and diversifying list of telecottage functions on the one hand, and by the fact that the general users of the intranet in North Karelia have gradually grown more-or-less over-skilled compared to the relative simplicity of the original intranet content.

Peripheral regions and small rural communities meet challenges in all the mentioned regards. The fact (and the consequences) of the out-migration of the young and the higher-skilled poses a major problem to both Eastern Finland and the villages in the Hungarian peripheries. Having to support an already very dispersed and sparse population, infrastructures are increasingly difficult to keep up in rural Finland; and with the political-economic transition, many of the small local governments have had to face financial crisis in Hungary, where schools and other basic services had to be 'rationalised' over a short period of time. The amenities that keep the active-age population in place and encourage local entrepreneurship, the services that support the improvement of all kinds of (financial, human and social) capital, also include telecommunication and information infrastructures; hence the vicious circle of missing access components is established in these regions.

The digital divide(s) between centres and peripheries, between rural communities and towns exist because of the mentioned causes and their mutually reinforcing mechanisms. Intervention is necessary in the affected regions of Finland and Hungary. The next logical question concerns on what level and what kind of intervention is required in these mechanisms in order to ignite positive tendencies.

RQ 2 What are the suitable points of intervention to help resolve digital divides? What are the different actors' roles and responsibilities at a) the international or European, b) the national and c) the regional/local levels in order to achieve a spatially more inclusive I.S.?

The Finnish and Hungarian national developments (programmes and strategic plans), as well as the initiatives taken by the Regional Council of North Karelia, the community intranet project launched from Nurmes, and the approach taken up by the Hungarian Telecottage Association, all indicate that *combining and harmonising investments into the different components of access* is the key to successful intervention.

In these terms, there is no single ideal point of intervention providing that the basic physical infrastructure (e.g. telephone connections suitable for Internet access in the Hungarian countryside and in North Karelia) have already been established. Securing competition and affordable prices of services (via both market liberalisation and national regulation); improving and motivating demand by developing the 'mental' factors (e.g. through general public education and particularly targeted training in ICT skills); and the creation of content by many partners, are the most productive if are co-ordinated and simultaneously attended to.

The 'pseudo-quotes' (representing general reasoning and attitudes) and the arrows connecting the different aspects are included in Figure 44 above to emphasize the fact that individual perceptions, beliefs play an important part in the decisions about whether to purchase, subscribe to, and use ICTs or not. There are many different objective and subjective factors behind the reasons for (not) doing so, and *understanding their mechanisms* is crucial for efficient intervention.

Controlling these mechanisms and underlying cycles is in no way simple, but that also means that the interactions between the several aspects of access to technologies, information and learning provide many points for intervention in disadvantaged regions. Depending on the individual context, policies and actions may aim at the following:

1 The *provision of basic infrastructure and network services* is a logical precondition to further development: making them both available and relatively affordable for the target population is a challenge in peripheral and thinly populated regions. Subsidies for service providers, tax allowances for ICT purchases, creative low-cost ICT solutions, and the establishment of public access points are suitable means.

2 Relevant education, training and a good working example can *open minds up to ICTs,* and *create interest and initiative* in society: see for example, the national Sulinet Programme and the work by individual telecottages in Hungary and the community intranet project in North Karelia.

3 From the first cycle of active users, pilot projects and their *evaluation, actual social needs come to surface*; and *technologies, solutions and content may be further developed, and disseminated* along those requirements. The Finnish examples of regular monitoring and assessment of programmes and pilot projects by governmental organisations, public R&D

institutions, in close cooperation with IT companies (see the national innovation system in Finland), as well as the attempts at the adjustment of a best practice to fit other regions (OSKU) follow this line of thinking. In Hungary, the practices of monitoring, evaluation and revision of strategic I.S. objectives have existed since about the acceptance of the national I.S. strategy (2003), yet the required institutions and procedures are not efficient, and solutions to integrate feedback from consumers are scarce (besides, there is not yet a critical mass of users in many cases, to do so). However, the monitoring and dissemination of the telecottage-practice in Hungary and beyond, too, helped by the nation-wide civil organisation of HTA, and more recently, through its institutionalisation by the state are positive examples. The European network of Eris@ and similar international forums facilitate these functions, as well.

4 A good quality and quantity of content motivates usage further. *Increased usage creates routine and confidence* in services offered via ICTs, as well as in the authorities and organisations which provide them. The mechanism that offers a positive input into social and political confidence is (or should be) an especially relevant component in recent I.S. strategic thinking in Hungary. A great routine of usage has been achieved by and large in Finland in many fields of social and economic life, and it is matched by constant technological and service innovation.

5 Then, widespread usage in fact, triggers a more *stable and substantial demand for higher quality services and boosts up ICT markets and innovation.*

189

While this has been the case in Finland (and evidently, facilitated by the existence of an advanced IT cluster in the country), it is still more-or-less missing in Hungary in general. However, in certain technologies (mobile phones), and concerning certain target groups (e.g. the higher-skilled and young; and the active users of telecottages) similar tendencies may be observed in Hungary, too.

Also as a consequence, *digital literacy and interactivity in society is promoted* in the long run, and in conjunction with technological development. The increased and more qualified demand and the feedback from users can help innovation and encourage further investment by the ICT sector (developers, infrastructure and service providers). More inclusive and better services, as well as a greater proportion (mass) of the population on-line both facilitate and necessitate more diverse content. *The amount and quality of locally produced on-line information and services can therefore increase* and content becomes more responsive to actual needs. This later brings an important benefit to the development of rural economies and local communities within a globalising world.

Intervention can occur at any point in these cycles with the condition that it is not the only focus of attention, and providing that it is accompanied with due concern with other aspects of promoting access. However, *the creation of basic facilities and the establishment of a first good working example* require particularly more attention and financial support, since market forces alone, may not initiate them or respond to the early developments sufficiently, especially in peripheral regions, rural and sparsely populated areas. Also, this crucial step calls for cooperation between many actors both within and outside the particular region. So the second part of the question comes into focus: *who* should do what? The division of labour and responsibilities between spatial and political levels is complex.

Though initiated by **local and regional actors**, the accomplishment of the OPK community intranet project in North Karelia was based on a broad spectrum of collaborating partners and stake-holders (local initiative, regional and national support, EU funding and a European network; public and private organisations; research institutions), as well as on an auspicious timing. As to the other case study, the Hungarian telecottages have been drawing on much volunteer work and local partnership-building with civil groups, local governments and businesses; while for many years were lacking sufficient support by the state (funds, as well as other assistance, public recognition). The situation was changed to some extent with the eHungary Programme within the framework of the National I.S. Strategy; however, that was some ten years after the establishment of the first telecottage. Nevertheless, already in the early years of the telecottage movement, the Telecottage Association established contacts with the ITU (UN) for the purpose of promoting their practices in the world, and to stir the interest of the national government by showing them that their work was recognised internationally. Also, different EU resources have been utilised by individual telecottages, and more recently, their presence internationally has been represented by the initiative of HTA to form the European-wide civil organisation, the EUTA.

These examples, however, can be described *from the points of view of* **international organisations**; these collaborative processes are also in their interests. For instance, the European Union strives to be competitive with the United States in the global informational economy, and an important condition for that is the promotion of the demand for, and the innovation in ICTs. Urging its member states via direct sector-oriented legislation, and non-binding guidelines, a co-ordination of objectives and funds, to liberalise their telecom markets, incorporate the subject into the national educational curricula, and to develop content – all aim at these goals.

Competition exists of course, between nation states and regions, so these objectives more or less appear there as well. Besides, budget constraints force **national governments** to look for partners in order to carry out the strategic measures and investments. In Finland, the national authorities set up good partnerships with business, and could recognise opportunities to embrace innovative regional and local initiatives. In Hungary the state realised the strategic significance of the I.S. rather late. It was also slow in comprehending the real value of the achievements of the telecottage network: a potential for re-allocating some of the central responsibilities, as well as for a unique Hungarian innovation. However, in 2003, the national stake-holders made a clear commitment here, too, and started to build up the institutional framework, with more or less success.

Another important finding from the case studies is that the specific socio-economic features of a country, a region or a locality (their centre-periphery positions, settlement patterns, economic profiles, affluence of their populations, their demographic structures, 'social qualities', etc.) determine what types of ICT infrastructure, training, and content development are required for raising an I.S. within their respective frameworks. Therefore, any intervention into the development of these many dimensions of access should take place also with *great attention to distinctiveness in terms of space and time (geography, history and culture)*.

This imperative is taken into account by Finland when consciously shaping and promoting its own model of the I.S. also as a kind of new and progressive national identity and image. Strategy designers in Hungary has been facing the problem concerning the extent and the way of incorporating national peculiarities – traditions, continuities – as constructive components of the Hungarian 'model' of the I.S., that is, a revolutionary image.

Studying the issue of spatial-cultural distinctiveness and diversity on the very local level, the example of the telecottages comes in handy. They grew out from local needs and initiatives when there was no public (educational) programme pursuing the I.S. yet, and when the construction of the national infrastructure had just gathered impetus. In a few years, the Hungarian government launched Sulinet as an appropriate response to the skills-

Table 9. Roles and competencies in I.S. development on three spatial-administrative levels.

	Physical and financial access	Mental access	Access to content	Monitoring, evaluation, dissemination	General role
Inter-national	EU guidelines (eEurope) and telecom legislation, common market regulation; international R&D and IT companies	EU guidelines (eEurope; equal opportunities, e-learning); international programmes funding projects for curriculum development, etc.	EU guidelines (eEurope: e-government; security and intellectual property issues); the on-line presence of the European Union and UN institutions	UN global forums (WSIS in Geneva and Tunis); EU Commission DG for I.S., and other related DGs; Eris@ - IANIS, LEADER networks; related ESPON projects, etc.	*Giving guidelines, open-method of co-ordination (moni-toring, evaluation) Providing financial and other assistance (through, e.g. EU pre-accession SAPARD; Structural Funds; UN: DSF)*
National	Market regulation, infrastructural investments into the backbone networks, regional development policy, state subsidies and other incentives; national innovation system for ICT research and development; encouraging PPP	National public education curricula, comprehensive access in public schools, universities (Sulinet). special promotion campaigns	e-government services, public administration on-line, e-health, intelligent transport systems, etc., legislative measures on intellectual property rights, personal data protection, digital signatures, etc.	e.Finland portal, public awards for best solutions, dissemination, transfer of best practices via the national innovation system in Finland; Interministerial Committee on I.S in Hungary, national statistics institutions, academic research	*National I.S. strategy, vision, standards and actions; monitoring and co-ordinating subnational developments; observing internat. trends and guidelines; funds from national budget for local/regional projects*
Regional-local	Creative local ICT solutions, public-private partnership in infrastructural development; local-regional enterprises, targeted financial support by local / regional government	Peer-training, raising awareness by means of local actions, mentor-network; specialised courses and assistance for different target groups (children, the retired, disabled, unemployed, local businesses)	Locally / regional relevant information services, public institutions, local enterprises and civil groups on-line; community forums, intranets, portals	Best practices exchanged via networks of local projects; portals, publications, reports etc. by the HTA; SGP Telecottage Region, Glocal Ltd. working with local & national research institutes, actively seeking idea- transfer possibilities	*Sensors & indicators of actual developments (problems and needs); initiatives promoting diversity;* *customising ICT solutions for local conditions: matching technology and people*

related problem, yet it failed to sufficiently include certain segments of the society. In peripheral regions and isolated villages, the need to bring these technologies close to the whole community, to the young and the older alike, was recognised. Civil and public telecottage activists and entrepreneurs acted on these requirements in their individual contexts while learning from each other's solutions within the expanding telecottage network. Embedded well into their particular social and cultural environments, they have an inherent sensitivity towards the actual local needs, and therefore can easier respond to them. The function of the telecottages as mentors and technology-mediators therefore has not lost its relevance despite the undoubtedly significant achievements of the national Sulinet programme.

The same can be observed in the Finnish case study. Despite the overall advanced state of the I.S. at the time in Finland, improving mental access to motivate the population for the use of the community intranet, and ICTs in general was still an obvious necessity in North Karelia in the late 1990s, and especially regarding certain groups of the society, the unemployed and the older cohorts of the population. Therefore, peer-training constituted one of the major pillars of the Learning North Karelia project.

Also, the local projects in both countries recognised that introducing ICTs necessitates the *approach of learning by doing*, facilitating the sense of achievement *bit by bit*. So however tempting it may be for the trainers and experts, a too ambitious and complicated tool must be avoided because it can easily discourage application, and can lead to the exclusion of many potential users. *The technology* (software) introduced in the community intranet project in North Karelia *suited well both the functions and the population it was to serve*. Also, the most successful telecottages have managed to develop technological service profiles most relevant to the places they operated in: besides some standard facilities, they specialise in supporting ethnic minorities, assisting elderly people, accommodating, informing, training, and networking local enterprises, and so on.

It is also notable that especially in Hungary, *local actors and civil society were rather proactive* in terms of the softer components of access development. This is understandable for at least, two reasons. First, digital literacy, openness to ICTs, as well as online content and services are issues that require relatively more 'human touch', more locally specific care than for instance, the competition in the provision of broadband services may request. Second, while authorities 'above' were preoccupied with the difficult tasks of improving the supply-side, i.e. the physical and partly, the financial access to ICTs, the demand side already called out for attention: communities and the civil society from 'below' started to show the locally specific problems and opportunities regarding I.S. development. Although, in Finland, the state pioneered in content development (helping to create a critical mass of on-line services and useful information to motivate more extensive usage), I still consider the role of local and regional initiatives there as well, important in keeping up the development of human capital and relevant digital content; i.e. sustaining the demand side, also as a basis for further infrastructural development (as indicated by the 'cycle' above).

In sum, concerning the responsibilities on the international, national and local-regional levels, there is nothing like a clear-cut division. From the case studies above, it is obvious that each and every component of access should receive some attention on all regional-political scales. Table 9 above (expanded from the basic Figure 4), in a far not all-inclusive way, summarises the roles and competencies and some of their actual examples, manifestations on the three spatial-administrative scales.

RQ 3 *Is the diffusion of ICTs or the emergence of an I.S. making horizontal interactions and flows more powerful, and thus administration and decision making more transparent and democratic?*

Based on the different case studies presented in this dissertation, there is no straightforward yes or no answering this question. Nevertheless, it has become obvious that the multi-sectoral nature of both regional socio-economic development (as a policy field, as well as the process) and the I.S. development project make them highly communication-intensive fields. They both involve much interaction between many different stakeholders operating on different (vertical) geographical and political scales, as well as ranging 'horizontally' from big and small businesses through politics, public research institutes and governments, to the (global and local) civil societies. The different parties (both the traditional ones, as for instance, the nation states in charge of controlling telecommunications and the IT

companies developing the tools; and the relative newcomers, such as the EU, the civil society, and local communities) have their own special awareness of, and therefore various approaches to, the I.S. and its territorial implications, which later in the end gradually emerge from a fusion of these many standpoints and interests. Conflicting views are not rare between the different sectors and actors; neither are the possibilities for cooperation and the occurrence of win-win situations.

ICTs, as tools are definitely utilised in this respect, as several examples from the case studies indicate: the application of e-commerce solutions by enterprises; websites, portals, interactive on-line services maintained by international agencies, national and local governments and public authorities; and the extensive use of the Internet by less and more organised civil networks and individuals seeking flexibility and freedom from traditional authoritative structures. Several examples for these can be found in both the more advanced I.S. of Finland, and the less developed Hungarian context. The difference is however, in the scale and culture of usage, and the interactivity, interoperability between the different applications. The former is related to the mental components of access, and the latter is linked more with the availability and the quality of content, and with the general construction of social-administrative systems.

Table 10. Findings from the case studies for and against the claim in RQ 3.

RQ3: *"... I.S. or the diffusion of ICTs making horizontal interactions and flows more powerful, ...?"*		Indicating "yes"	Indicating "no"
International – EU, UN (Ch. 3)		WSIS portals and several related portals; EU on-line, Eris@ network; forums drawing a greater diversity of views and interests into the international I.S. debate (human rights, censorship, digital solidarity fund, e-governance). Joint, multi-level monitoring, applying an open method of co-ordination.	The *actual presence at central debates* in the forums is still limited; major political and business interests are difficult to influence from a distance by the emerging *networks of politically and financially weaker actors* (developing countries, smaller businesses, academia, civil actors).
National (Ch. 4)	FIN (4.2)	Public administration on-line, e.Finland portal, active e-presence. On-line services offered by regional and local authorities (showing good example), educational institutions, businesses; transparent government; working interactivity in services.	This is most probably not directly due to the I.S. and the new ICTs, but *deeper social attributes* (e.g. political trust, egalitarian values.)
	HUN (4.3)	Interministerial Committee on I.S., e-government portal, experiments with interactive services (digital tax registration)	The lack of *social and political trust*: low confidence in the public sector; more focus on individual freedom and coping than on community and cooperation. ICTs are not enough to change this in the short term; the *centrally-vertically controlled mechanisms are reinforced*, with inefficiencies.
Local-regional (Ch. 5)	FIN N. Karelia and intranet project (5.2)	The essence of the intranet is to link people (public, private and civil actors) in a community, and with other communities in the region with shared forums, services and regionally relevant information.	The intranet has lost some of its attraction as Finnish content and services on the World Wide Web is increasingly accessible to the population in the region (*changing technological and social realities*)

	HUN telecottages (5.3)	Fast diffusion of innovation helped by the network of local telecottage projects, loosely co-ordinated from a centre. An on-line system of publishing good practices, and information about funding possibilities. Emerging "*teleház-regionalism*" in the SGP. *Telementor*-network.	Telecottages are very heterogeneous not only in terms of their ICTs, *skills and attitudes towards networking*.
	FIN-HUN local-local cooperation (5.4)	Partners finding and communicating with each other via ICTs (e-mail, chat); search and application for (EU and other) funds via Internet.	Effective ICTs, effective communication was inhibited by missing *language skills*, and little or no *personal acquaintance* with each other's contexts. Face-to face meetings are important.

The relative cost efficiency, adaptability and distance-bridging capacities of ICTs have made them popular means of communication between business and the public sector, among businesses, and in public-civil relations, too. However, another important point here is that ICTs are not accepted for all purposes, and especially, that they are rarely used as exclusive tools.

Firstly, much confidence on both communicating parties, sufficient positive experience from a longer routine of usage is required for a near-to-complete reliance on ICTs in, for instance e-banking, e-shopping, and electronic public services (which, has had too short time to evolve in Hungary yet; but which has been adapted in Finland in many fields of social interaction).

Secondly, face-to-face meetings, physical proximity and familiarity with both the subjects and objects of communication are still inevitable for human beings and their different organisations for a full understanding of the matter. A negative example for this is provided by the study on

the cooperation project between the Finnish and Hungarian local actors: constructive communication could not be maintained (esp. amidst the difficult objective circumstances) very long because motivation and enthusiasm, as well as confidence between the partners and in the success of the project faded fast when meetings could only take place in digital space. A deeper, personal acquaintance by the Hungarian partners with the local achievements in North Karelia would have helped much. A positive example for this same feature is the idea that both the Finnish intranet project and the Hungarian telecottage movement incorporated into their practices: the peer-training practice and the focus of the needs and the lives of actual communities were combined with the advantages of the ICTs in reasonable ways.

In Table 10 above, more positive and negative instances based on the case studies are listed, grouped according to whether they point towards approving or rejecting the thesis worded in the initial research questions.

In sum, ICTs – as any technological innovations – are social creations; the products of societies where an increasing significance has been attached to information and knowledge flows and communication processes. The diffusion and development of these technologies in turn, generate greater flows of intellectual assets and more intensive communication and interactivity. Since digital networks have been only to a very limited extent centralised and supervised, 'only' the mental capacities (and to some extent, the affluence) of the users restrict their social inclusiveness; and therefore have the potential to allow for communication and flows regardless of traditional hierarchical, administrative structures (across borders, social standing, religion, gender, professions, distance etc.) However, financial access, and cultural-mental openness to technologies discriminate across societies (hence the digital divides), and content, since it is human made, partially reproduces old barriers, too (on-line services restricted by language, fee, password, membership, etc.)

RQ 4 *What can Hungary learn from the achievements of the "Finnish model"?*

In Chapter 4, I.S. developments in Hungary and Finland are studied *from the perspectives of national authorities*: the 'official' national visions and images, central institutions, strategies and programmes. In absolute, numerical terms, the comparison between the state of the I.S. in Finland and Hungary is straightforward. Despite the fact that the degree of difference varies depending on which technological or other aspect is observed, Hungary's lag behind

Finland can be measured in several years, if not a whole decade. However, there are important qualitative conditions behind the concrete figures of ICT diffusion and the levels of usage:

1   the design of the national I.S. strategies, the degree of commitment by the government (and the connection with these to international processes and guidelines);

2   the level of national concern with regional inequalities (the disadvantaged peripheries), the degree of harmony between bottom-up and top-down actions;

3   and the institutional background for I.S. development and networking between national actors.

Concerning the first aspect, an initially more sectoral and technological orientation to developing the I.S .featured the national approach in both countries examined. It was revised and elaborated into a cross-sectoral social innovation programme in Finland sooner, in Hungary a bit later. In the latest up-dates of both national I.S. strategies and visions (in Hungary: in 2003; in Finland: in 2006) much concern is expressed with the promotion of e-literacy and positive mentality, as well as with the development of advanced on-line content.

Most probably, the experts drafting the strategy in Hungary had taken a look at many international examples after 2000 (and were aware of the guidelines and recommendations by the UN and the EU). Surely, they had examined the Finnish strategy, too (to which there are some concrete implications in the Hungarian documents). Two important features indicating this are the focus on 'service society' and the significance attributed to trust.

The dedication of the Finnish government to become a leading national model of the Information Society has been evident since the mid-nineties while in Hungary, because of the difficult social and economic conditions during the first ten years of transition, commitment came later, and more in the spirit of urgency and catching up than of becoming a leader. In both cases, however, these developments were urged both by a domestic need for modernisation and restructuring, as well as the external pressures of globalised competition, and the requirements and opportunities coming from their membership of the European Union.

Secondly, regional and social equality in I.S. development has become a clearly expressed aim in the latest Finnish approach, and is one of the two crucial horizontal objectives of the Hungarian I.S. Strategy, too. There may be, however, some difference in this regard. In Finland, equality has recently been seen as more-or-less existing (as part of the welfare model), providing a foundation for trust in I.S. services and for the whole construct of the 'Knowledge Society'. In the Hungarian case, regional disparities in opportunity are expressed more in terms of a serious problem to overcome – which originates in the generally high political and public awareness of increased socio-economic inequalities across the country since the 1990s, (and especially between urban and rural areas.)

The third important feature of national perspectives on I.S. is the institutional background to its implementation. It is almost unnecessary to say, after the lengthy description of the Finnish national innovation system, and the forming of a inter-sectoral Information Society Council in 2003, that there is a well-established and adaptable network of a diverse set of institutions and actors working together to achieve the national I.S. ambitions. Probably, it is not absolutely perfect, but it is a system that has had some time to evolve, has been tested for many years, and has the ability to adjust itself relatively flexibly to future challenges. On the other hand, the formation of the Hungarian I.S. is still in a very unstable phase, it can be more characterised in terms of an evolution and fluctuations than with a 'system'. To cut a long story short, in Hungary, establishing institutions that promote horizontal connections and networking among public, private and civil actors has started, however, I see it more of a goal yet than the means of developing the I.S.

In Chapter 5, the conditions of I.S. in these countries are looked at more *from the point of view of the people living in the rural peripheries*, looking at both the fact of spatial inequalities and examples of local and regional initiatives trying to reduce them. Taking these into consideration, the following observations can be made:

1   In both countries, regional inequalities in terms if I.S., or the spatial manifestations of the 'digital divides' generally follow the traditional disparities in

population density, urbanity, and income, as well as in the levels of education and economic growth, etc. because of the same market mechanisms and the interactions between the different dimensions of access.

2 The importance of regional I.S. strategies and local partnerships for innovative actions has been recognised in both countries, however, there is a considerable difference regarding the timing of this recognition between the Hungarian and Finnish cases.

In Finland, this happened relatively early, in the late-nineties, and more-or-less simultaneously by actors on various political levels. The top-down initiatives were clear and consistent enough for the sub-national actors to suitably adjust their development objectives and programmes, and therefore it was relatively easy to get support and recognition 'from above'.

In Hungary, the social, political and economic instabilities since the 1990s have not allowed the national level the required resources (of, time, money, constructive thinking) to formulate and communicate a coherent vision, consequently, the message to citizens and their communities about the challenges and opportunities linked with an I.S. has been very weak and unclear. Nevertheless, the structural problems and deficiencies directly hitting rural communities triggered grass-roots action already in the early 1990s, and could achieve a lot in rural areas in terms of introducing new opportunities by means of the ICTs. The local and regional activists were in this way more proactive in Hungary, and shaped their own visions and strategic goals in a much more practical and clearer way than the national government was able to. The coordination of these many local efforts however, could not be efficient without the intervention of the government. How the civil network of telecottages and the governmental eHungary programme will continue to strengthen their cooperation depends especially on the level of commitment of the future governments, i.e. whether they follow through the objectives set in the national I.S. strategy.

Understanding these qualitative (institutional and cultural) aspects is the way to find lessons for Hungary and, in general, for any country which is trying to catch up to the leading nations in I.S. development.

The Finnish example shows that *cautious reforms of the national innovation system can already mean a considerable competitive advantage* for a country. Realising this, Finland has been trying to take up a role in the European Union as an 'I.S. laboratory'. Yet it is also clear that such reorganization cannot be carried out in a matter of even a decade, for this system is reliant on intricate and sensitive conditions as trust in the government, historic identity, ethics and values are, for instance. Consequently and most importantly, *there is no concretely prescribed way how an 'enabling atmosphere' or a well-functioning 'framework for interaction' has to look like.* The Finnish model has grown out of a special context, during a longer period of time influenced by several peculiar circumstances, and will continue to develop likewise. What could be learnt from is the ways of maintaining political and other networks that in fact, do the work of I.S. development.

Copying exact practices is not plausible without any contextualisation. The institutional and social-cultural characteristics of the Hungarian society differ so much from those which have evolved in Finland and across the Nordic countries in general, that the direct insertion of best practices into the Hungarian / Central-Eastern European context is not possible. No ready model can be adopted as such. This is valid of course, on any spatial scale: to national and subnational (regional / local) actors. The example of the Finnish-Hungarian cooperation also justifies this claim: the greatest challenges in joint planning came from the major differences in the technological, social, cultural settings of the idea-host region and the place targeted by the development project.

The institutional background for I.S. development in Hungary is weak, social acceptance or even awareness of the whole issue is still low, and there is little money for the actual projects in the state budget. All these, however, are closely linked with the political developments of the past two decades. Among these circumstances, recommendations for Hungary could be centred around the following three points:

1 Before 2003, there had been neither a commitment to, nor a *positive vision* of, the Hungarian I.S. Truly, there has been recently slightly more confidence among the political and intellectual elite concerning the results from implementing the Strategy. Elitism in I.S. policies is still a problem, however: *little trusted by the wider public, or simply ignored*, as 'beyond our heads'. So, the question is whether leadership can help the broader society internalise this sense of purpose, and acknowledge the importance of the 'I.S. cause' as something that is in their own interest, and not just a political show, and a way for the rich to get richer... *Joint work with civil society and more incentives to local initiatives, more opportunities for public-private partnerships can help* eliminate this problem in the longer run.

2 The development of on-line interactive content serving administrative procedures between citizens and the public institutions has received much attention in recent years also as a way to increase trust in authorities. However, actual usage of these services is still low, restraining their upgrading and customisation through feedback, and preventing the development of an advanced on-line culture. What is not connected socially cannot be connected digitally. *The special invention Hungary needs to come up with to its own benefit and helping also other transitioning countries, is the method to break the vicious circle around distrust.*

3 Developing the I.S. involves all strategic sectors (education, telecommunications, healthcare, state administration), which are not only underfinanced in Hungary, but are highly politicised and full of conflicts, not to mention the horizontal components of the national I.S. strategy, regional development, and R&D. Among these circumstances and under the pressure of a sharpening regional competition, Hungary is still challenged to find her own way, her own model not only meaning 'form', but in the sense of 'good example'. *Implementation of the I.S. strategic objectives would be more efficient if the limited resources were invested into a specific but decisive field that could be a Hungarian 'strength', and which then could work as a catalyst for the expansion of other areas.*

6.2 Synthesis

> If we are facing in the right direction, all we have to do is keep on walking.
> (A Buddhist proverb)

In this dissertation I have attempted to show the formation of information society through one of the infinite number of existing and possible cross-sections of its total geographical and political vertical structure. This research took over 5 years, during which time I have had to deal with a much moving target not only regarding technological realities, but the changing social ones. Therefore, it was a constant process of learning and adapting, understanding, and re-defining even the most basic concepts and relations. Just as information society is.

Information, knowledge, and technologies get their meanings and importance only when they are contextualised. Their import depends on place and time and, without human agency, they have no meaning whatsoever. Since this dissertation focuses mainly on different social agents' vertical and horizontal interactions, and collective endeavours to create 'an inclusive information society', the quest for answers to the research questions involves dealing with this contextuality and temporality all the time.

Just taking one example: the same technology, e.g. the establishment of a public internet access point or a narrowband connection to Internet, is interpreted and valued in different ways by a monitoring organisation of the United Nations, by politicians working for the ministries responsible for telecommunications (of different countries), or by the R&D headquarters of an IT company; by a retired farmer, unemployed teacher, or young mayor in the Hungarian countryside; or by an entrepreneur or an international student in Eastern Finland. Adding the dimension of time to this diversity of approaches and ways of understanding makes it impossible to fix a universal significance.

Different forms and depths of the act of interactive communication involve the encounter of these dissimilar actors and their perspectives and, miraculously, even if only temporarily, resolves the gaps and tensions between their ways of understanding and knowing. Efficient communication is central to the work of the UN and the EU in negotiating and establishing visions, objectives and guidelines, in mobilising other actors, and in monitoring and reporting developments. Good communication is the key to strengthen local communities and build up social capital; and it is the essence of a national innovation system and the implementation of a national I.S. strategy, too. Without communication, there is no trust, only suspicion and isolation.

No wonder that when technology is created and employed for the purpose to enhance, or even 'revolutionise' communication between people, it is seen as a panacea to all the miseries of mankind (at least, when choosing the optimistic side of the deterministic approach). It is however, clear from the above that ICTs are social creations: born to fulfil social demand and human desires, and restricted in abilities by the human dimension, too: people's knowledge, attitudes and ethics determine their access to these tools as well as to the benefits they potentially offer. Some people with some specific knowledge and vision created the telecottage in a Hungarian village seeing its community at risk of getting isolated from information and knowledge, and the opportunities those can bring. However, only those telecentres could serve their communities that shaped their technologies to match their particular societies. Also, in their original form, they would not have been relevant in the Finnish countryside in the late 1990s. Nevertheless, a virtual telecottage, that is, the community intranet, was very popular in Eastern Finland at the same time. Technology is society.

Generally, the telecottage, in its many different manifestations, can be seen as a technology in itself, a method, technique, a piece of culture even, which helps a rural community leave its isolation and link up to the global flows of information and knowledge. The Finnish models for a national innovation system and a welfare I.S. evolved in their special context, if transferred directly to Hungary, most probably, would not work properly. However, some features of a good model can be (and has been) adopted with success, for instance, the decentralised, network configuration of participants and processes, the built-in

flexibilities and openness of the system, and the implementation of I.S. objectives as a coherent social programme.

The initial broad question in the dissertation was: *How can the benefits of information and communication technologies (ICTs) and the so-called, information society (I.S.) be extended to rural-peripheral regions and communities?* By tending to all aspects of access based on the particular needs of the rural-peripheral regions and their small communities. By mobilising all possible actors locally, regionally, and by providing a strategic vision and a reliable (institutional and financial) framework for their actions. These all require intensive flows of information, contrasting and revising knowledge, the development of know-how and learning skills and most importantly, a lot of continuous interaction horizontally and vertically, a joint learning-by-doing exercise.

When well functioning, the set of supple mechanisms between the different levels, actors, interested partners enhance both the social and technological bases for the I.S., at the heart of which there is a highly complicated and interactive network of communication. The wider and the more diverse the selection of the networked participants, the broader the scale of social benefits becomes. If these mechanisms can be maintained flexibly over a long period of time, those seemingly 'lucky coincidences' (i.e. the kind that are pointed out in relation to the development of the telecommunications sector in Finland, and the success story of local innovations) will more frequently occur, becoming sort of inherent to the system, and the advantages can be maximised.

202

Placing this argumentation into focus, the 'thing' most often referred to as Information Society, could be termed as an *Interactive Society* or *Communication Society*. Likewise, emphasizing more the networked form or the import of learning, it might as well be called a *Network Society* or a *Learning Society*. In fact, it does not really matter, since there are still those disturbing questions: Does it exist in Hungary (let us say, in 2007)? Does it exist in Finland? Is it a reality in North Karelia? (To whom?) Can it ever be an all-inclusive one? (In opportunities or in terms of benefits?) Based on the above, there is no absolute 'yes' or 'no' to any of these questions. There are several subjective ones, and those can be provided by the different actors presented above. On my part, the safest thing to say is that it depends on you, as a part of it, or as an outsider.

Appendices

Appendix 1. The structure and contents of the Bangemann Report, 1994.

Chapter I: The information society - new ways of living and working together
- A revolutionary challenge to decision makers
- Partnership for jobs
- If we seize the opportunity
- A common creation or a still fragmented Europe?
- The social challenge
- Time to press on
- An Action Plan
- New markets in Europe's information society

Chapter II: A market-driven revolution
- A break with the past Ending monopoly
- Enabling the market
- Towards a positive outcome

Chapter III: Completing the agenda
- Protection of intellectual property rights (IPR)
- Privacy
- Electronic protection (encryption), legal protection and security
- Media ownership
- The role of competition policy
- Technology

Chapter IV: The building blocks of the information society
- The opportunity for the Union - strengthening its existing networks and accelerating the creation of new ones
- New basic services are needed
- Blazing the trail - ten applications to launch the information society
    1. Teleworking
    2. Distance learning
    3. A network for universities and research centres
    4. Telematic services for SMEs
    5. Road traffic management
    6. Air traffic control
    7. Healthcare networks
    8. Electronic tendering
    9. Trans-European public administration network
    10. City information highways

Chapter V:
- Financing the information society: a task for the private sector.

Chapter VI: Follow-up

An Action Plan - summary of recommendations

Appendix 2. Categories of possible variables for a broad definition of I.S. (Following and extending the categories by Castells and Himanen; 2001.)

---

1. Technology and human skills (16 variables)

1.1 Use of old and recent telecommunication technologies; accessibility and diffusion of e-commerce applications: Internet host, telephone lines and cellular subscribers, telephone average cost, electricity consumption, PCs, Internet service provider charge, charge for telephone usage for Internet, ISP competition, high-tech. exports, secure servers, Internet speed and access, government on-line services availability, Internet effects on business, laws relating to ICT use

1.2 Knowledge, human skills: Internet users, gross tertiary science enrollment ratio

2. Economy and innovativeness (9 variables)

2.1 National: World competitiveness, GDP per capita

2.2 Business efficiency: Business efficiency (world rank)

2.3 Innovativeness: patents granted to residents, R&D intensity, receipts of royalties and license fees, scientists and engineers in R&D

2.4 Labor force – job market: high-skilled IT job market, share of part-time employment

3. Welfare (6 variables)

3.1 Education: combined primary, secondary and tertiary gross enrollment ratio (%), public expenditure on education

3.2 Health: life expectancy at birth, public expenditure on health

3.3 Welfare: disparities in income or consumption: Gini coefficient; disparities in income or consumption: the richest 20% to the poorest 20%

4. Openness (9 variables)

4.1 Politics, freedom: circulation of daily newspapers, freedom of press, Gender-related Development Index (GDI), women in parliament, incarceration rate (imprisoned per 100,000 pop.)

4.2 "Globality": recognized refugees, environment: CO_2 emissions,

4.3 Environment: "greenness" of politics and population (based on election information), GDP per unit of energy-use.

Appendix 3A. Method of survey and analysis: limitations and solutions

TNS trends (Telecommunications Networks and Services, ESPON 1.2.2, 2003)

1. Distribution of questionnaires: April and May 2003, in printed copies, as attachments to e- mails, and were also published electronically, i.e. in the form of web questionnaires to be filled in using the Internet.

2. Response rate: 15 responses from ministries/regulators from 13 countries, and 12 from companies from 7 countries: 40% and 10-15%, respectively, of the answers minimum expected from the 29 countries. While the answers given by companies were judged as less country-relevant, and therefore a higher response rate was not that crucially important, having no ministry/regulator responses from over half of the 'ESPON countries' posed a real problem, and a serious limitation to the possible ways of analysis and interpretation.

3. The quality of the responses: most of the answers were accurate enough to be accepted. Some respondents (see e.g. Denmark and Malta, in the tables in Appendix 2 and 3) ignored several points completely, arguing that no considerable territorial inequalities exist in their countries in the provision of telecommunications infrastructure and services – in such cases, reaction to other questions, and additional comments were instructive enough.

4. The questions
a) Two groups of questions according to two main themes on the basis of what they investigated:
• Features of (perceived) territorial inequalities, and the assumed reasons behind
• Awareness of territorial inequalities in TN&S trends, and policy intention/measures to overcome them

b) Types of questions:
Open questions: The answers to most of them (esp. those which can be translated, simplified into yes/no questions) were "scored". However, it is important to note that these responses were rather difficult and less reliable to compare across countries, so they were taken as additional information, for more accuracy.

Simple-choice, closed questions: The choices represent a measure on a relative scale (e.g. very even, generally even, generally uneven, very uneven were given scores 4, 3, 2, 1 respectively).

Multiple-choice, closed questions: If each choice had a ranking dimension (e.g.: which tools of intervention, and how important they are...), the answers were weighted according to their importance (place in order) attributed to them. Without a ranking task, (e.g.: the number of territorial obligations imposed on operators), the number was taken as a measure (none: 0, one: 1, more than one: 2).

5. Analysis of information
a) Descriptive textual
b) Quantified ('scored', as described above) and represented in a scatter plot figure along the axes of the two main themes of investigation:
• The choice of questions was based on the reliability, clarity and the validity of the responses.
• The scores given to evaluate answers were averaged and then transformed to a more convenient 0-100 scale. This method has however, some weaknesses to be noted (i.e. the arbitrary and debatable "quantification" of responses of a rather subjective and qualitative nature; attributing scores to and averaging scalar data), so the numbers should not be considered exact, or mappable as such (given the low response rate and small sample, the latter was impossible, anyway).
• Nevertheless, categories of countries can be identified according to relative distances from "average" values, and the correspondence between the two measured themes.

Appendix 3B. The list of survey questions sent to the ministries and regulators responsible for the telecommunications sector in the ESPON countries (*ESPON 1.2.2 project*)

1. What are the territorial aspects of Universal Service Obligation (USO) in your country?

2. Do you monitor the trends in territorial differences in levels of telecommunications infrastructure and service provision, uptake, etc? If not, why not?

3. What are the features of territorial evolution of telecommunications in general, and esp. of broadband in particular (over the last decade, or since deregulation came in; e.g. even spread vs. uneven spread)? What are the specificities (i.e. compared to other countries, or Europe in general) of your country in terms of telecoms territoriality? (E.g. peripherality, 'extreme' rural, mountainous areas, islands, patterns of rich and poor, etc.)

4. According to your understanding, what are the drivers of this territoriality – for example, scale of markets (which markets?), costs of providing services, etc? Which one of these seems to be the most significant?

5. What patterns of competition between territories concerning telecommunications can be observed?

6. Will the deployment of advanced telecommunications services reduce or exacerbate territorial disparities in economic development, well-being, quality of life…?

7. What could be done to reduce territorial disparities in telecoms provision?

8. Are there any regulations imposed on telecommunications companies about territorial obligations? Do you see "territory" as significant in terms of market regulation? (E.g. concerning spatial coverage targets, covering rural area in return for urban licence.)

9. Is competition 'working' across territories? Are there any areas in the country which do not benefit from competition? Are companies colluding, i.e. making separate agreements on service provision in specific regions?

10. What features characterise the territoriality of local loop unbundling?

11. How much do SMEs in rural or remote areas benefit from Universal Service Obligations? Are they benefiting from competition? (Or do large firms capture most of these benefits, rather?)

12. On your opinion, should EU Structural Funds be used to support telecommunications investments in regions? If not, why not? If yes, what would be priorities for structural fund-supported telecoms / ICT investment in your country?

13. How are telecommunications policy and spatial planning / regional policy connected? Are these in the same ministry? Are they integrated in any way? (I.e. through 'joined up' policy.)

Appendix 4. Comparative I.S. statistics for the Nordic countries

1A-C: information tools at home; 2A-B: telephone subscriptions by households; 3A-B: Internet connection at home. (mainly physical and financial access components)	FI	NO	SE	IS	DK	International
4A-C: usage of Internet (adding mental access and content availability); 5A-E: access and usage by enterprises	*Norden, 2005 (if otherwise not indicated)*					*Eurostat, 2004 (if otherwise not indicated)*
1A	PC at home, % of households (and in 2002)	54	60	72	78	75	
1B	Portable computer (notebook) at home, % of hhs.	19	35	27	50	34	
1C	Handheld computer at home, % of hhs	n. a.	2	2	0	4	
2A	Telephone subscription lines per 100 inhabitants, 2004 (peak year)	45.6 (1997:55.4)	67.1 (2002:74.2)	70.7 (2000:75.7)	51.1 (1997:57)	64.5 (2001:72)	
2B	Mobile subscriptions per 100 inhabs., 2004	95.5	103.0	108.5	99.2	95.5	
3A	Internet connection at home, % of hhs.	54	64	73	84	75	
3B	BB at home, % of hhs (*in thinly populated areas*)	36 (*30*)	41 (*32*)	40 (*36*)	63 (*54*)	51 (*42*)	NL:31, EE:20, GE:18, **EU15:17**, EU25: 15, HU:6
3C	Internet at home on portable computer, % of hhs. (*in thinly populated areas*)	15 (*6*)	25 (*23*)	20 (*15*)	37 (*31*)	28 (*20*)	
3D	Internet at home via mobile phone, % of hhs.	n. a.	14	7	1	12	
4A	Regular users of Internet - min. once a week, % of population (*in thinly populated areas*)	63 (*51*)	74 (*70*)	76 (*73*)	81 (*76*)	73 (*66*)	LU:59, GE:50, EE:45, **EU15:41**, EU25:38, HU:21, GR:17
4B	Daily users of Internet in last 3 months, % of pop. (*in thinly populated areas*)	46 (*34*)	50 (*45*)	57 (*52*)	65 (*58*)	57 (*48*)	
4C	Internet usage for e-commerce in last 3 months, % of pop. (and in 2004)	<u>84 (72)</u>	83 (73)	73 (49)	77 (65)	70 (59)	EE:69, LU:53, GE:43, **EU15:40**, EU25:36, HU:10, GR:7
5A	Internet access in enterprises (of all sizes), % (and in 2002)	<u>98</u> (94)	91	95	97	97	BE:96, GE:94, **EU15:90**, EU25:89, CZ:90, SK:71
5B	Fixed BB access in enterprises, % of all eps.	<u>81</u>	76	81	78	82	

Continuation of Appendix 4. Comparative I.S. statistics for the Nordic countries

6A-B: Public-private sector on-line interaction (content-related); 7: online security ('mental' component and content related)	FI	NO	SE	IS	DK	International
8A-B: IT sector in the labour market (all elements of access involved); 9A-B: e-learning (mental and content-related access)	*Norden. 2005 (if otherwise not indicated)*					*Eurostat, 2004 (if otherwise not indicated)*
5C	Websites in enterprises, % of eps. with 10-19 employees / 100+ / of all sizes	65 / 93 / 76	59 / 89 / 66	80 / 95 / 84	54 / 98 / 69[1]	74 / 95 / 82	(% of all enterprises:) UK,NL: 66, **EU15:60**, EU25:58, EE:52, GR:49
5D	Customized webpage in enterprises for their repeat clients, % of all eps.	11	9	11	13	12	
5E	Extended ICT usage[2] in enterprises, % of all eps.	75	65	82	68	81	
6A	Enterprises interacting with the public sector, % of all eps. (two-way interaction)	91 (71)	69 (57)	92 (47)	97[3] (62)	85 (56)	EE:84, GR:77, CZ:75, EU25:52, **EU15:50**, HU:35, UK:33
6B	Individuals interacting online with public authorities in the last three months, % of pop. (two-way interaction)	47 (11)	52 (21)	52 (21)	55 (20)	n. a	LU:45, GE:33, UK:22, HU:16, GR:8, CZ:7
7	Online security at home: firewall and antivirus software updated in the last 3 months, % of households with Internet	65	83	71	74	75	CY: 77, SK:50, SI:48, GE,HU:46, UK:42, EE:1
8A	The share of ICT-related occupations in the economy, 2003, % of all employed	23	n. a.	24	n. a.	27	UK:28, GE:22, **EU15:22**, GR:14[4]
8B	The share of ICT-related occupations in the private sector, 2001-02, % of the employed	10.3	7.1	9.4	n. a.	8.1	EU145:6.3, HU:7.1, GE:4.7, GR:3
9A	Students using Internet for education, training, % of all students (between age 16-74)	87	18	23	21	56	
9B	Employees using Internet, % of all employed (between age 16-74)	22	3	6	13	15	

[1] data from 2003 for Iceland, [2] more then basic ICT use = access to Internet + website + interaction with public sector online and/or banking & financial transactions and/or orders via Internet, [3] data from 2002 for Iceland, [4] OECD: IT Outlook 2004.

Appendix 5. The I.S. index defined by ESPON 1.2.3, 2006.

5A. I.S. Performance and the evolutionary stages of I.S. in 29 European counties.

The ESPON 1.2.3 project took a life-cycle approach to reveal differences between the development levels of I.S. in 29 countries in Europe. They used eEurope and World Economic Forum statistics, and to be able to calculate their average, applied linear transformation to rescale the two indices to the same range (0-1). The stages in the cycle, and the relevant variables:

1. Readiness: enabling factors (basic infrastructure, affordability and skills);
2. Intensity: availability and use ICTs.
3. Impact: economic indicators of operational restructuring. ICT-use for social inclusion & participation.

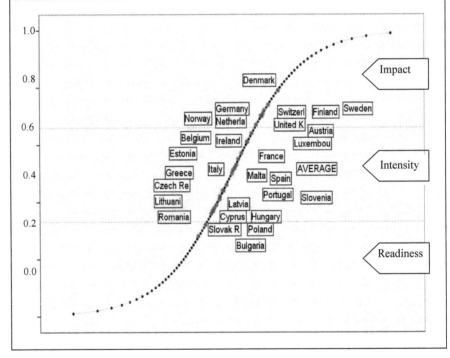

5B. The composition of the ESPON 1.2.3 I.S. index.

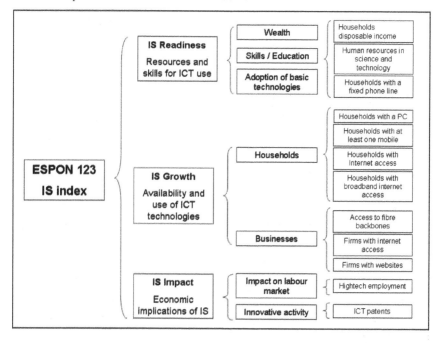

Appendix 6. The RISI initiative and NOKIS. (*Based on information: EC / European Commission*)

The Regional Information Society Initiative (RISI)

RISI had 2 phases:

- **RISI 1** (including NOKIS) to form regional information society strategies, through the realisation of which the development would get a positive direction.
- **RISI 2**: support for I.S.-applications, and their experience to be transferred to other areas.

It was coordination by the Directorate Generals for Employment (DG V), Telecommunications (DG XIII), and Regional Policy and Cohesion (DG XVI) of the European Commission.

RISI 1 covered 22 regions from 11 Member States were selected by the European Commission. 14 regions were funded under Article 10 of the European Regional Development Fund (*), and an additional eight regions received funding under Article 6 of the European Social Fund (**).

Region	Country	Project Acronym
Steiermark (Styria)*	Austria	Telekis
Liege*	Belgium	Fasil
North Karelia**	Finland	Nokis
W. Finland Alliance*	Finland	Paraddis
Midi-Pyrenees**	France	Teleparc
Limousin*	France	Acti Limousin
Poitou-Charentes*	France	Serise
Schleswig-Holstein*	Germany	Infosh
Bremen**	Germany	Brise
Brandenburg*	Germany	Bis2006
Athens**	Greece	Athina
Epirus*	Greece	Rise
South West**	Ireland	Stand
Shannon*	Ireland	Shipp
Calabria*	Italy	Arianna
Murcia**	Spain	Essimur
Extremadura*	Spain	Infodex
Blekinge**	Sweden	It-Blekinge
Vasterbotten*	Sweden	Ac-Direkt
Yorkshire & Humberside*	UK	Compris
Wales**	UK	Wis
North of England*	UK	Nistrat

NOKIS of the province of North Karelia was launched within RISI 1 in 1997.

It had a total budget of FIM 2.9 million (approx. € 0.5 M); made up of a 50% contribution by the Finnish State and 50% from Structural Funds, from Objective 6.

The partners in NOKIS were:

- the Regional Council;
- the University of Joensuu and the North Karelian Polytechnic;
- the Joensuu Science Park;
- the cities of Joensuu, Lieksa & Nurmes, and the Municipalities of Ilomantsi and Juuka;
- the Employment and Economic Development Centre of N.K.;
- Lieksa Development Agency Ltd (industrial park of Lieksa);
- and the Regional Government of eastern Finland (Joensuu Unit of the Health and Security Department).

RISI 2 had 9 pilot projects of I.S. application: 7 were "pluri-regional pilot projects" funded under Article 10 of the ERDF, and 2 pilots were funded under Article 6 of the ESF.

Lead Region	Acronym	Inter-Regional Partners
Midi-Pyrénnées (France)	Enterskillsnet	(6) FR,FR,UK,IE,FI
North West Ireland (Ireland)	CRISM	(7) IE, BE, DK, NL, UK
Madeira (Portugal)	TOURIST	(6) PT,FI,SE,IT,AU,UK
Eje Atlantico (Spain and Port.)	OUEA	(2) ES, PT
Northrhine-Westphalia (Germany)	IDAN	(9) DE,DE,UK,ES,BE,BE,NL,FI,SE

Appendix 7A

District (seutu-kunta)	Municipality (kunta)	Area	Water cover of total area	Distance from Joensuu (km)*	Population change, 1991-2004 (% of pop. '91)	Population, 2004	Population density (inh./km²), 2004	Population density on land area, 2004	Dependency Ratio (DR**), 2004	DR change by % points, 1991-2004
Pielinen Karelia	Juuka	1846	343	90	-15.7	6177	3.3	4.1	61	7
	Lieksa	4068	643	101	-19.1	14080	3.5	4.1	59	5
	Nurmes	1855	250	138	-16.0	9193	5.0	5.7	61	7
	Valtimo	838	37	163	-22.2	2769	3.3	3.5	56	-5
Joensuu district	Eno	1088	149	35	-10.7	6879	6.3	7.3	58	8
	Ilomantsi	3173	402	73	-18.3	6538	2.1	2.4	64	8
	Joensuu	1312	139	0	7.4	57587	43.9	49.1	45	-2
	***Kiihtelysv.	530	44	36	n.a.	2635	5.0	5.4	n.a.	n.a.
	Tuupovaara	661	57	55	n.a.	2217	3.4	3.7	n.a.	n.a.
	Kontiolahti	1030	248	21	15.9	12339	12.0	15.8	52	2
	Liperi	1161	421	27	1.1	11641	10.0	15.7	56	0
	Outokumpu	584	139	49	-15.7	7803	13.4	17.5	55	2
	Polvijärvi	958	157	83	-16.0	5048	5.3	6.3	59	0
	Pyhäselkä	352	71	16	9.8	7554	21.5	27.0	56	0
Central Karelian district	Kesälahti	583	195	110	-14.8	2712	4.7	7.0	64	3
	Kitee	1142	277	79	-12.6	9877	8.7	11.4	54	0
	Rääkkylä	700	274	117	-16.3	2936	4.2	6.9	64	3
	Tohmajärvi	751	50	55	-16.7	5511	7.3	7.9	64	0
	Vartsilä	144	8	79	n.a.	663	4.6	4.9	n.a.	n.a

*Distances are on road between the municipality centres and Joensuu city centre,. In case of Pyhäselkä, the average is given calculated from the distances of the two municipal centres, Reijola (8) and Hammaslahti (24). ** DR: (cohorts 0-14 + 65+) / cohort 15-64 x 100; *** Kiihtelysvaara and Tuupovaara administrations merged with the town of Joensuu, and Värtsilä was included within Tohmajärvi in Jan. 2005.
(Based on data from: North Karelia – Regional Council and http://www.matkahuolto.info/.)

Appendix 7B.

District (seutu-kunta)	Municipality (kunta)	Unemployment rate, 2004	Unemployment rate change, 1991-1997 (% points)	Unemployment rate change (% points), 1997-2004	Employment in agriculture (%), 2004	Employment in industry %	Employment in services %	Empl. sector unknown %
Pielinen Karelia	**Juuka**	19.9	14.2	-6.2	16.8	30.6	48.9	3.7
	Lieksa	23.4	15.5	-5.4	10.1	28.1	58.5	3.3
	Nurmes	19.5	19	-11.3	14.4	19.3	63.4	3.0
	Valtimo	22.7	20.4	-9	30.1	14.4	50.1	5.5
Joensuu district	**Eno**	24.1	17.1	-5.7	9.3	39.0	49.9	1.8
	Ilomantsi	24.3	15.8	-4	13.0	19.7	64.1	3.2
	Joensuu	17.2	15.5	-7.2	1.7	23.7	73.0	1.6
	Kiihtelysv.	15.5	12.8	-9.3	n.a.	n.a.	n.a.	n.a.
	Tuupovaara	20.1	13.8	-5.3	n.a.	n.a.	n.a.	n.a.
	Kontiolahti	13	12.8	-8	4.4	27.1	66.9	1.7
	Liperi	14	13.7	-5.5	13.1	23.8	61.0	2.0
	Outokumpu	18.4	14.6	-7.4	6.0	33.3	57.2	3.5
	Polvijärvi	19.4	16.7	-5.2	24.2	22.3	49.1	4.4
	Pyhäselkä	14.7	11.7	-6.9	6.8	26.4	64.2	2.6
Central Karelian district**	**Kesälahti**	20.3	13.8	-3.8	19.0	29.5	48.0	3.5
	Kitee	16.9	12.4	-5.4	13.5	29.4	54.0	3.1
	Rääkkylä	19.3	15.4	-6.1	27.5	19.8	48.1	4.7
	Tohmajärvi	21.9	14.7	-3.4	19.3	16.8	59.5	4.4
	Vartsilä	18.4	17.9	-9.6	n.a.	n.a.	n.a.	n.a.

* Kiihtelysvaara and Tuupovaara administrations merged with the town of Joensuu, and Värtsilä was included within Tohmajärvi in Jan. 2005. (Based on data from: North Karelia – Regional Council.)

214

Appendix 8. Background information about the survey of telecottages in the Southern Great Plain Region, 09-10.2005

---

1 Finding the targets: The list of 74 telecottages (TCs) in the region (including: respondent's name, e-mail address, telephone number, TC's address, and sometimes, the location of their websites) was obtained from the portal of the SGP Telecottage Association (http://www.telehaz-del-alfold.hu/). The on-line public database of the Hungarian Telecottage Association (http://www.telehaz.hu/) provided further information concerning the age of the telecottages and the identity of their managing-operating organisations. There was some inconsistency between the two catalogues (10 TCs were mentioned only in either the SGP or the HTA list); and in a few cases, the e-mail addresses were not valid. Eventually, 72 telecottages were included in the analysis.

2 Sending out the questionnaire: I asked the TC managers to fill in the form, who I assumed to have worked there for longer and more permanently than the more changeable staff. I did this directly and personally in e-mail, *and* via the head of the SGP Telecottage Association. Since a significant time of their work is supposed to be on-line, I not only sent my request in e-mail, but also, prepared the questionnaire on-line (i.e. a form located at an URL address). This latter tool was practical for several other reasons: During the survey, I could not expect to be able to visit the target region. The answers came immediately and automatically to my e-mail account in an easy-to-interpret form. In case of incomplete or inaccurate answers, I had the opportunity to promptly ask the respondents to revise the problematic sections (and in fact, many did so). Also, this was a way to save time and trouble for the respondents, since they did not have to deal with attached files or printing and posting the form.

3 The content of the questionnaire: most of the questions were closed, multiple-choice questions, or required a few words from the respondents.

Part I: contact information of the respondent and the telecottage (address, organisation)

Part II: basic information on the telecottage: year of opening, type of building, year(s) of moving and reasons for that, year(s) of changing management and reasons for that, technological equipment, main services, the number of full- and part-time staff, specialities important regionally or nationally.

Part III: questions concerning connections with other telecottages, the regional and national Associations, and their local contexts: TCs they had received / given advice, technical assistance, and other kind of support from / to, TCs they had engaged in common projects with, and TCs with whom they would work together in the future; how well they know other telecottagers in the region (by name, as friends, as a frequent business relation, etc.); their contacts with TCs outside the region, international connections (TCs or other actors with similar goals); their relationships with their local authorities and organisations, and the regional and national Associations.

Part IV: vision of their future sustainability; complementary comments and questions by the TCs.

The purpose of the research was briefly described in the e-mails I sent. I promised the respondents to share the results of the research with them, 5 TC managers even asked me to do so at the end of the form.   *(Continued.)*

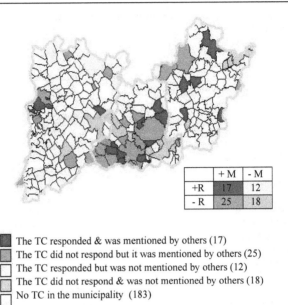

	+ M	- M
+R	17	12
- R	25	18

■ The TC responded & was mentioned by others (17)
▨ The TC did not respond but it was mentioned by others (25)
□ The TC responded but was not mentioned by others (12)
▨ The TC did not respond & was not mentioned by others (18)
□ No TC in the municipality (183)

The distribution of the 72 telecottages according to being mentioned (+M: 48) and having responded (+R: 29) in the SGP.

4 Response rate: After two rounds of e-mails directly to the TCs, and a request via the SGP Association, by lucky coincidence, I could visit the SGP region and some of the TCs from which I was still waiting for an answer. Despite these efforts, by the end of the 5th week, only 29 TCs had completed the form (10 before my visit, 9 right after my visit, and 10 more following another, 3rd round of e-mails), which means a 40% response rate. Since the information gained with Part III of the questionnaire 'brought in' 25 further TCs as contacts of the respondents, I got some understanding of the relationships between 54 TCs in the SGP region.

5 Follow-up: I published the results of the survey on-line with the help of HTA and opened a forum on their portal to receive comments and criticism. In the following months, hundreds of visits were paid to the forum; however, I received there no comments. I received an e-mail from someone who had had much positive experience in working with the TCs in the region, and defended them against my critical (and provocatively 'scientific') conclusion that there were not much evidence for TC-networking in the SGP.

References

Aarsæther, N. & Bærenholdt, J. O. (eds.), 2001. The Reflexive North. Copenhagen: MOST and Nordic Council of Ministers, NORD 2001:10.

Abler, R. F., 2001. Geography among the sciences. *Fennia* 179:2 Helsinki., pp. 175-179.

Academy of Finland (Suomen Akatemia) http://www.aka.fi, last accessed: 01.2007

Adair, B. L., 2002. Democratisation and Regime Transformation in Hungary. *Problems of Post-Communism*, Vol. 49, No. 2, March/April 2002, pp. 52-61.

Ahonen, P., 2001. Soft Governance, Agile Union? Analysis of the Extension of Open Coordination in 2000. *In: UNPAN: United Nations Online Network in Public Administration and Finance.* http://unpan1.un.org/intradoc/groups/public/documents/NISPAcee/UNPAN007710.pdf

Ahonen, S., 2000. NOKIS – Information Society in North Karelia. Summary at http://ec.europa.eu/ regional_policy/innovation/innovating/pdf/nokis_en.pdf.

Ahonen, V.-V. & Ala-Harja, M., 2004. Widespread Interest in the Information Society - Finland's Prime Minister's Best Practices Award Attracts Plenty of Entries. *The e.Finland Weblog*, 15.09.2004. http://e.finland.fi/netcomm/news/showarticle.asp?intNWSAID=27808, last retrieved: 10.2007.

Åkermarck, M., 2004. Number of Internet Connections Reached 1.23 Million in Finland. *Telecom & Mobility Statistics, e.Finland*, 07.12.2004. http://www.e.finland.fi/netcomm/news/showarticle.asp?intNWSAID=30666, last accessed: 01.2007.

Ali-Yrkkö, J. & Hermans, R., 2001. Nokia in the Finnish Innovation System. Helsinki: ETLA.

Ali-Yrkkö, J., 2001. Nokia's networks – gaining competitiveness from cooperation. Helsinki : ETLA / Taloustieto.

Allen, J. & Hamnett, C. (eds.), 1995. A Shrinking World? Global Unevenness and Inequality. Oxford: The Open University.

Altorjai, Sz. & Bukodi, E. 2005. Social Quality in Hungary: In the Framework of ENIQ. *European Journal of Social Quality*, Vol. 5, 1/2, pp. 138-150.

Åke E. Andersson, 1989 (ed.) Advances in spatial theory and dynamics. Amsterdam: North Holland.

Associazione Oikos, http://www.oikos.org/ baten.htm (on Gregory Bateson), last retrieved: 01.2007.

Axelero - www.axelero.hu, website of major Internet service provider in Hungary.

Bærenholdt, J. O. & Aarsæther, N., 2002. Coping strategies, social capital and space. *European Urban and Regional Studies* 9(2), pp. 151-165.

Bærenholdt, J. O., 2002. Coping Strategies and Regional Policies – Social Capital in the Nordic Peripheries. Future Challenges and Institutional Preconditions for Regional Development Policy, Vol. 2. Stockholm: Nordregio.

Bangemann, M., 2004. Report on Europe and the Global Information Society: Recommendations of the High-level Group on the Information Society to the Corfu European Council. Bulletin of the European Union. Supplement No. 2/94 [follow-up paper for White Paper] (commonly called the *Bangemann Report*)

Bateson, G., 1972. Steps to an Ecology of Mind. New York: Ballentine Books / Canada: Chandler Publishing Company.

Bauman, Z., 2001. The Individualised Society. Cambridge: Polity Press.

Beaton, M., 2002. Hungarian Telecottages: Tailoring ICT to Rural Business Needs. Presentation in the Workshop of ICT Solutions for Rural Areas; Brussels 1 Dec. 2002 http://www.ruralwins.org/images/MaryBeaton.pdf.

Beck, U., 1992. Risk Society: Toward a New Modernity. London: Sage.

Bekenstein, J. D., 2003. Information in the Holographic Universe. *Scientific American*, 08.2003, pp. 58-65.

Bell Labs Computing and Mathematical Sciences Research Division: The Significance Shannon's Work. http://cm.bell-labs.com/cm/ms/what/ shannonday/work.html, last retrieved: 01.2007.

Bell, D., 1974. The coming of post-industrial society: a venture in social forecasting. London: Heinemann 1974.

BellResearch: published results of surveys; www.bellresearch.hu , last accessed: 10.2007.

Beluszky, P. & Sikos T., T., 2007. Változó falvaink. Budapest, MTA Társadalomkutató Központ..

Beniger, J. R., 1991. Information Society and Global Science. In: Dunlop, Ch. & Kling, R. (eds.): Computerisation and Controversy: Value, Conflicts and Social Choices. San Diego: Economic Press.

Bihari, G. (ed.), 1999. Teleházak és távmunka Magyarországon. (Telecottages and telework in Hungary. – S.N.) Teleház Kht. Budapest.

BISER: Benchmarking the Information Society: e-Europe Indicators for European Regions; project portal at http://www.biser-eu.com/, last accessed: 01.2007.

BME-ITTK & TÁRKI, 2001. World Internet Project 2000-2001 – "A digitalis jövő térképe" (The map of the digital future") Report on the population of Hungary and the Internet.

BME-ITTK, GKIeNET, BellResearch, TÁRKI & ITHAKA, 2007. Magyar Információs Társadalom Éves Jelentés 2006 (Hungarian I. S. Annual Report 2006). Budapest.

Bourdieu, P. 1983/86. The Forms of Capital. In Richardson, J. G. (ed.): *Handbook of Theory and Research in the Sociology of Education*. Westport, CT: Greenwood Press. Pp. 241-258.

Csákó, Mihály, 1998. Általános iskolai pedagógusok és az iskolai számítógépek használata (Primary school teachers and the use of computers in schools – S.N.) *Új Pedagógiai Szemle*, 1998/2, pp. 97-108.

Borgmann, A., 2006. Technology as a Cultural Force: For Alena and Griffin. *The Canadian Journal of Sociology*, Vol. 31, No. 3, pp. 351-360

Breivik, P. S., 1997. Student Learning in the Information Age. Phoenix: American Council of Education / Oryx Press Series on Higher Education. http://www.ntlf.com/ html/lib/ilul_pref.htm, last accessed: 01.2007.

Brown-Syed, C., 1993. The New World Order and the Geopolitics of Information. *In:* Hernon – Schwartz (eds.) *LIBRES: Library and Information Science Research.* Elsevier.

Bruijn, P. de & Lagendijk, A., 2005. Regional Innovation Systems in the Lisbon Strategy. *European Planning Studies.* Vol. 13, No. 8, December 2005, pp. 1153-1172.

BT Group -- British Telecommunications plc, 2007. Universal service obligation in the EU. http://www.btplc.com/Thegroup/Publicaffairs/EuropeanAffairs/Briefings/UniversalserviceobligationintheEU/UniversalserviceobligationintheEU.htm Accessed in 04.2007.

Cairncross, F., 1995. The Death of Distance: A Survey of Telecommunications. *The Economist.* 30 September 1995.

Camagni, R., 2002. *Territorial competitiveness, globalisation and local milieux.* In: European Spatial Research and Policy Vol. 9 No. 2/2002

Cantwell, J.A., Iiammarino, S. & Noonan, C.A., 2000. Sticky places in slippery space – the location of innovation by MNCs in the European regions. *In:* N. Pain (ed.), *Inward Investment, Technological Change and Growth: The Impact of Multinational Corporations on the UK Economy.* London: Macmillan.

CAPGEMINI, 2006. On-line Availability of Public Services: How is Europe Progressing? Web Based Survey on Electronic Public Services, June 2006.
http://ec.europa.eu/information_society/eeurope/i2010/docs/benchmarking/online_availability_2006.pdf

Castells, M. & Himanen, P., 2002. The Information Society and the Welfare State. The Finnish Model. Oxford University Press.

Castells, M., 1996, 1997, 1998. The Information Age: Economy, Society and Culture. Vol. I: The Rise of the Network Society (1996/2000). Vol. II: The Power of Identity (1997). Vol. III: End of Millennium (1998). Oxford: Blackwell Publishers Ltd.

Centre for Regional Studies of the Hungarian Academy of Sciences – organisation website: www.rkk.hu.

Charter, S. The Earth Dwellers' Guide to Sustainability – The BIG Picture. http://freespace. virgin.net/steve.charter/ bigpicture/index.html , last retrieved: 09.2004.

Clark, N., 2000. Plenty of mobile phones, but where's the good life? *New Statesman,* 24 January 2000, pp. 32-33. Also on-line: http://www.newstatesman.com /200001240026, last accessed: 10.2007.

C.A.P. - College Administration Publications, Thinking about the Web. http://www.collegepubs. com/ref/SFX960715.shtml, last accessed: 10.2007.

Corning Inc., 2005. Broadband Technology Overview. White Paper WP6321. http://www.corning.com/docs/ opticalfiber/wp6321.pdf.

CRIS, portal: Campaign for Communication Rights in the Information Society. www.chrisinfo.org Last retrieved: 10.2006.

Cronberg, T., 1992. Technology in Social Sciences: the Seamless Theory. Technical University of Denmark, Lyngby.

Csaba, L., 2000. Between Transition and EU Accession: Hungary at the Millennium. *Europe- Asia Studies*, Vol. 52, Issues 5, pp. 805-828.

Delhey, J. & Newton, K., 2003. Who trusts? The origins of social trust in seven societies. *European Societies*, 5:2, pp. 93-137.

Dénes, T. 2000. Biztonságos információ(s) társadalom? *Info-Társadalomtudomány* 2001/53, pp. 33-44.

Denzin, N. K. & Lincoln, Y. S. (eds.), 1994. Handbook of qualitative research. Thousand Oaks (CA): Sage.

Dessewffy, T., 2002. Az információs társadalom lehetőségei Magyarországon. *Médiakutató*, 1/2002. http://www.mediakutato.hu/cikk/2002_01_tavasz/08_informacios_tarsadalom, last accessed: 10.2007.

Dessewffy, T., 2004. Bevezetés a Jelenbe. Budapest, Tankönyvkiadó.

Dessewffy, T., 2006. A legdélibb skandináv. *Élet és Irodalom*, 26; 30 June 2006.

Dijk, J. A G. M. van, 1996. The One-dimensional Network Society of Manuel Castells. *The Chronicle*. http://www.thechronicle.demon.co.uk/archive/castells.htm, last retrieved: 10.2007.

DiPiro, J. T., 2002. Balancing Technology with Personal Interaction in Pharmacy Education. *American Journal of Pharmaceutical Education*. Vol. 66., pp. 440-442.

Dodge, M. & Kitchin, R., 2001. Mapping cyberspace. London: Routledge.

Dombi, G., 2001. Információs társadalom és politika. Introduction in: Dombi, G. & Lafferton, E. (eds.): *Az Információos Társadalom felé*. Budapest: Replika Kör, pp. 7-13.

DTE (Dél-alföldi Teleház Egyesület): Southern Great Plain Telecottage Association, Hungary. Website of the organisation: http://www.telehaz-del-alfold.hu, last accessed: 10.2007.

Dunning, J. H. (ed.), 2002. Regions, Globalization, and the Knowledge-Based Economy. Oxford: Oxford University Press.

Dutta, S., Lanvin, B., Paua, F. (eds.) & the World Economic Forum, 2003. Global Information Technology Report 2002-2003. Oxford University Press, USA.

EBRD (European Bank for Reconstruction and Development), 1999. Transition Report. Abstract. http://www.ebrd.com/pubs/econo/4050.htm, last accessed: 10.2007.

eFinland & Statistics Finland, 2004. IT Use Among Finns Increasing Rapidly. In: eBusiness Statistics, 20.08.2004. http://e.finland.fi/netcomm/news/showarticle.asp?intNWSAID=26947, last accessed: 10.2007.

eFinland, 2004a. Background for Finnish PISA Success. *The eFinland Weblog*, 08.12.2004. http://www.e.finland.fi/netcomm/news/showarticle.asp?intNWSAID=30773, last accessed: 10.2007.

eFinland, 2004b. Finland's Minister Tuula Haatainen on the Findings of the International OECD PISA Review Concerning Finnish Students. *The eFinland Weblog*, 08.12.2004. http://www.e.finland.fi/netcomm/news/showarticle.asp?intNWSAID=30772, last accessed: 10.2007.

eFinland, 2004c. China Takes the Finnish Upper Secondary School System for a Model. *The eFinland Weblog*, 08.10.2004. http://e.finland.fi/netcomm/ news/showarticle.asp?intNWSAID=28730, last accessed: 10.2007.

eFinland, portal, introduction http://e.finland.fi - A Window to Finnish Information Society. http://www.e.finland.fi, last accessed: 10.2007.

Ehrlich, É., 1999. The Communications Infrastructure of the Central and Eastern European Countries. http://userpage.fuberlin.de/~jmueller/its/conf/torino99/papers/ehrlich.doc. Institute for World Economics of the Hungarian Academy of Sciences. Last accessed: 01.2003.

Enyedi, Gy., 1996. Regionális folyamatok Magyarországon az átmenet időszakában. Budapest.. Ember – település – régió. Budapest: Hilschler R. Szociálpolitikai Egyesület.

Erdőháti N., M. (2003). Tarifakörkép: az internetezés ára. *E-kereskedelem on-line*, 15.05.2003. http://e-ker.hu/news.php?id=1691 &type, last accessed: 10.2007.

Eskelinen, H., Hirvonen, T. & Frank, L. (2003) Fine-grained patterns of the digital divide: Differences in broadband access within Finland. Paper for the 43rd ERSA Congress, Jyväskylä, 27-30 Aug. 2003. http://www.ersa.org/ersaconfs/ersa03/ cdrom/papers/231.pdf.

ESPON – European Spatial Planning Observation Network: www.espon.eu, last accessed: 10.2007.

ESPON 1.2.2: European Spatial Observatory Network programme, project 1.2.2 "Telecommunication Services and Networks: Territorial Trends and Basic Supply of Infrastructure for Territorial Cohesion" – Information and 1.2.2 Final Report; www.espon.lu.

ESPON, 2004. ESPON Project 1.2.2: Telecommunication services and networks: Territorial trends. Interim Reports and Final Report. (Finnish national case study, working papers, and discussions; prepared by the Finnish research team; http://www.espon.eu/mmp/online/website/content/projects/259/653/index_EN.html, last accessed: 10.2007.

ESPON, 2006. ESPON Project 1.2.3: Identification of Spatially Relevant Aspects of the Information Society. Final Report: http://www.espon.eu/mmp/online/ website/content/projects/259/649/index_EN.html, last accessed: 10.2007.

Eurobarometer, 2005. Europeans and languages (Wave 63.4 survey results); European Commission. http://ec.europa.eu/public_opinion/archives/ebs/ebs_237.en.pdf

European Commission, 1999. eEurope: An Information Society for All. Communication on a Commission Initiative for the Special European Council of Lisbon, 23-24 March 2000. http://europa.eu.int/information_society/eeurope/2002/news_library/pdf_files/initiative_en.pdf.

European Commission, 1999-2000. eEurope: An Information Society for All – Initiative (1999); eEurope 2002 Action Plan (2000) http://europe.eu.int/information_society/eeurope, last accessed: 10.2007.

European Communities / CORDIS: Community Research & Development Information Service, http://cordis.europa.eu/en/home.html, last accessed: 10.2007.

European Communities / European Commission, DG for Research, http://ec.europa.eu/research/, last accessed: 10.2007.

European Communities / European Commission: Summaries of the Union's legislation – Information Society http://europa.eu/scadplus/leg/en/s21012.htm, last accessed: 10.2007.

European Communities / European Commission: e-Ten project portal http://europa.eu.int/information _society/activities/eten/index_en.htm, last accessed: 05.2007.

European Communities / European Commission: *Europe's I.S. - Thematic Portal.* http://europa.eu.int/ information_society/index_en.htm, last accessed: 01.2007.

European Communities / European Commission: Regional Policy; RISI 1 and 2. http://ec.europa.eu/regional_policy/innovation/innovating/infosoc.htm, last accessed: 10.2007.

European Communities DG XI, 1999. The European Spatial Development Perspective (E.S.D.P.) – Comments and recommendations from the European Consultative Forum on the Environment and Sustainable Development. Brussels.

EUTA (European Union of Telecottage Associations): www.hu.euta.hu, last accessed: 10.2007.

Faludi, A. & Waterhout, B., 2002. The making of the European Spatial Development Perspective – No masterplan. London and New York: Routledge.

Faludi, A., 2004. The Open Method of Co-ordination and 'Post-regulatory' Territorial Cohesion Policy. *European Planning Studies.* Vol. 12, No. 7, pp. 1019-1033.

Faludi, A., 2006. The European Spatial Development Perspective – Shaping the Agenda. *European Journal of Spatial Development,* November 2006.

Faluvégi, A., 2004. A társadalmi-gazdasági jellemzők területi átalakulása és várható hatásai az átmenet időszakában. In: *Discussion papers MT-DP 2004/5.* Institute of Economics, Hungarian Academy of Sciences, Budapest.

Farkas, J., 2002. Információs- vagy tudástársadalom? Budapest: Infonia-Aula.

Figyelőnet, 2002. Megszűnik a Mindenkiek csomag – a Freestart ingyenes marad. 29 April 2002. http://www.fn.hu/index.php?id=16&cid= 37506, last accessed: 10.2007.

Finnfacts: Independent Media Service Unit of Finnish Industry and Business. *The Story of Finland; 5.4: ICT in Finland.* http://www.finnfacts.com/english/ country/story/worldeconomy/ict.html, last accessed: 10.2007.

Fischer, G., 2005. Monopolviselkedés monopólium nélkül. *eVilág,* Oct. 2005 (on-line journal). http://www.pointernet.pds.hu/ujsagok/evilag/ 2005-ev/10/20070222164100588000000162.html, last accessed 10.2007.

Frank, L. D., Hirvonen, T. & Inkinen, T., 2006. A Territorial Perspective on the Information Society. In: Eskelinen, H. & Hirvonen, T. (eds.): *Positioning Finland in the European Space.* Helsinki: Ministry of the Environment, Ministry of the Interior, Finland. Edita Prima Ltd., pp. 110-120.

Freedom House: Reports. http://www.freedomhouse. org/, last accessed: 10.2007.

Friedland, L., 1996. Electronic Democracy and New Citizenship. *Media, Culture and Society.* Vol. 18. no. 2. pp. 185-215.

Fritsch, M. 2006. The ESDP process: basic information for non-insiders. Box 1 in: Eskelinen, H. & Hirvonen, T. (eds.): *Positioning Finland in the European Space – Introduction.* Helsinki: Ministry of the Environment, Ministry of the Interior, Finland. Edita Prima Ltd., p. 9.

G8 – Summit Meeting at Kyushu-Okinawa on 22nd July, 2000. Okinawa Charter on Global Information Society. http://www.g8.utoronto.ca/summit/2000 kinawa/gis.htm, last retrieved: 01.2007.

Gáspár, M., 2000. Átjáró -- Nemzeti Teleház Stratégia és Program 2000-2006. Budapest: Teleház Kht.

Gáspár, M., 2003. Kisközösségek hálózati szolgálata – partnerségben - A Magyar Teleház Szövetség 2002-2006 évekre szóló stratégiáját megalapozó tervezet. Vitaanyag. (Transl.: Networks serving small communities – in partnership. Draft plan for the 2002-2006 strategy of the Hungarian Telecottage Association. – S.N.). www.telefalu.hu/test/service. php?spec=&act=myed_download&did=8&spec=dl&imgid=438, last downloaded: 10.2007.

Gáspár, M., 2004. Teleházország (Telecottage-land). Budapest: Gondolat Kiadó.

Gáspár, M. & Takács, M., 1997. Építsünk teleházat! (*Let's build telehouses!* -- with contents in English) Erdei Iskola, Magyar Teleház Szöv. (Hungarian Telecottage Assoc.), Budapest.

Giddens, A., 1990. *The Consequences of Modernity.* Cambridge: Polity Press.

Glatz, F. (ed.), 2002. Információs társadalom és jogrendszer. (Magyarország az ezredfordulón – Stratégiai Kutatások a Magyar Tudományos Akadémián). Budapest: MTA (Hungarian Academy of Sciences).

Global Knowledge Partnership (GKP) Internet portal: http://www.globalknowledge.org/, last accessed: 10.2007.

Gløersen, E., Dubois, A., Copus, A. & Scürmann, C., 2005. Northern Peripheral, Sparsely Populated Regions in the European Union. Nordregio Report 2005:4. Stockholm: Nordregio.

Gonzales, C., 2004. The Role of Blended Learning in the World of Technology. *In: Benchmarks Online.* University of North Texas, Sept. 2004. http://www.unt.edu/benchmarks/archives/2004/september04/eis.htm, last retrieved: 10.2007.

Government Policy Programmes, Finland, 2006. An Information Society for All: Building the Finnish Information Society. Presentation for *The Club of Rome Symposium,* 20th Nov. 2006. http://www.roomanklubi.fi/download.php?id=389282,58,1, last accessed: 10.2007.

Graham, S. & Marvin, S., 2001. Splintering Urbanism: Networked Infrastructures, Technological Mobilities and the Urban Condition. London: Routledge.

Groot, R. & Sharifi, M. A., 1994. Spatial Data Infrastructure, Essential Element in the Successful Exploitation of GIS Technology. EGIS. http://libraries.maine.edu/Spatial/gisweb/spatdb/egis/eg94142.html, last retrieved: 10.2007.

Győrffy, D., 2006. Governance in a Low-Trust Environment: The Difficulties of Fiscal Adjustment in Hungary. *Europe-Asia Studies* Vol 58, No. 2, March 2006, pp. 239-259.

Halloran, J. & Calderón Vera, K., 2005. Basic Social Service sin Rural Settlements – Village and remote homestead community care-giving. Synthesis Report, Hungary 2005. *Peer Review in the Field of Social Inclusion Policies,* European Commission.

Hanhike, T. & Nupponen, T., 2000. The Spearhead project of telework in Finland. *Euro-Telework project reports on-line*. http://www.telework-mirti.org/fin.htm, last accessed: 01.2007.

Harjuhahto-Madetoja, K. (I.S. Programme Director), 2007. Tietoyhteiskuntastrategian toimeen-pano. Presentation at *Suomi-Ilmiö - eilen, tänään ja huomenna, ICT Forum. M/s* Silja Symphony, 10th Jan. http://mentorit.fcg.fi/CMS/content/liitteet/ICT-Forum-esitykset-binder-20070115.pdf

Harmaakorpi, V. & Melkas, H. 2005. Knowledge Management in Regional Innovation Networks: The Case of Lahti, Finland. *European Planning Studies*, Vol. 13, No. 5, July 2005, pp.641-659.

Harvey, D., 1989. The Condition of Postmodernity. Oxford: Blackwell.

Heikkilä, J., Kallio, J., Saarinen, T & Tuunainen, V.K., 1998. Grocery Shopping For the Elderly and Disabled: Finnish EC Experiments. Electronic Markets, Vol. 8, No.2., pp. 17-19.

Heinonen, J., 2004. Finland Deepens Cooperation with China. *The eFinland Weblog*, 08.10.2004. http://e.finland.fi/netcomm/news/showarticle.asp?intNWSAID=28714, last retrieved: 10.2007.

Henten, A. & Kristensen, Th. M., 2000. Information society visions in the Nordic countries. *Telematics and Informatics* (ed. Thompson, J.B.), Vol. 17, Issues 1-2, Feb.-May pp. 77-103.

Herrschel, T., 2007. Global Geographies of Post-Socialist Transition – Geographies, societies, policies. In the series: *Routledge Studies in Human Geography*. London: Routledge.

HÍF, 2001. (Hírközlési Felügyelet -- Communications Authority of Hungary; http://www.hif.hu) Yearbook 2000, Monitoring reports Overview of the Communications Market 2000-2001. Budapest.

HIF, 2000-2007. (Nemzeti Hírközlési Hatóság - Communications Authority of Hungary). Mobil gyorsjelentés. http://www.hif.hu/?id=dokumentumtar &mid=1054&lang=hu, last accessed: 06.2007.

Himanen, P., 2001. The Hacker Ethic and the Spirit of the Information Age. (Prologue by L. Torvalds and Epilogue by M. Castells.) Random House Inc.: New York, NY, USA.

Hodson, D. & Maher, I., 2001. The open method as a new mode of Governance: The case of soft economic policy co-ordination. In: Journal of Common Market Studies, 39(4), pp. 719-746.

Hollander, P. 2002. Hungary ten years later. *Society*, September/October 2002, pp. 66-72.

Hollander, P., 2006. Letter from Hungary - Truth & lies. *The New Criterion*, December 2006.

Horváth, Gy., 2000. Hungary (National review) In: *Transition, Cohesion and Regional Policy in Central and Eastern Europe*. Eds.Bachtler, J., Downes, R. & Gorzelak, G. Aldershot: Ashgate Publishing Ltd.

Hungarian Telecottages Association (HTA) www.telehaz.hu, portal, last accessed: 10.2007.

Husso, K., 2001. Universities and scientific research in the context of the national innovation system of Finland *Fennia* 179:1, pp. 27-54. Helsinki.

HVG (Heti Világ Gazdaság), 2005. Sulinet Express: Összesen 150 ezer új számítógép. *HVG, 01st Dec. 2005*, http://hvg.hu/itthon/20051201sulinet.aspx, last accessed: 10.2007.

HVG (Heti Világ Gazdaság), 2007. Sulinet Express: bukás vagy siker? *HVG, 31st Jan. 2007*, http://hvg.hu/itthon/20070131_sulinet.aspx, last accessed: 10.2007.

IANIS - eRegion Hub portal http://www.ianis.net, last accessed 10.2007.

IDC, 2003. Information Society Index (ISI). Interactive Information Society map, http://www.idc. com/groups/isi/main.html, last accessed: 10.2007.

Info Highway (ed. P. Lavin; 1994). *The Bangemann Report -- Common IT sense in spades: but will anyone listen?* In: Info Highway 1994/Vol. 1 ('E-mail Volume') http://www.infohighway.co.uk/info highway/9bang.html , last accessed: 10.2007

Information Society Council, Finland (Tietoyhteiskuntaneuvosto; 2003-): the English language website of the organisation: http://www.valtioneuvosto.fi/hallitus/tietoyhteis kuntaneuvosto/en.jsp, last accessed: 01.2007.

Inglehart, R., 1999. Trust, Well-being and Democracy. In Warren, M.E. (ed.): *Democracy and Trust.* Cambridge, Cambridge University Press. pp. 88-120

ITU (International Telecommunication Union). http://www.itu.int/osg/spu/statistics/DOI/index.phtml on the DOI, last accessed: 10.2007.

Interviews, Finland: *Joensuu, 05.10.2003*: (carried out jointly with Th. R. Hasvold, Univ. of Tromsö), with **Satu Ahonen**, programme coordinator at the North Karelian Regional Council.; *Nurmes, 08.10.2003*: (jointly with Th. R. Hasvold, Univ. of Tromsö) with **Ilpo Koskikallio**, Glocal Ltd.; his colleagues T. Tervo (project leader), **V.-M. Hurskainen** (Nurmes NetCenter), and **S. Laaninen** (principal of Nurmes Vocational School), Nurmes.; *Koli, 11.10.2003*: with **Tarja Cronberg**, the founder of the first telecottage in Ruvaslahti, Polvijärvi, N. Karelia (1986), and Dir. of the Regional Council in North Karelia (1993-2001). (Currently, Dir. of COPRI, Copenhagen Peace Research Inst.; Assoc. Prof. at the Technical University of Denmark; Member of Parliament in Finland, leader of the Green Party).

Interviews, Hungary: *Budapest, 03.12.2003*: with **Mátyás Gáspár**, founder of the Csákberény Telecottage, and the President of the Hungarian Telecottage Association (1994-2004); currently Honorary Pres. of HTA and the Pres. of the European Union of Telecottage Associations (2004 -); *Mártély, 06.2004*: with **Árpád Csernai** and **Anita Hegedűs**, the founders and managers of Mártélyi Teleház (1998).

ITHAKA, ITTK & TÁRKI, 2004. World Internet Project 2001-2004: "A digitalis jövő térképe": A magyar társadalom és az internet. (The map of the digital future – Hungarian society and the Internet -- S.N.) Budapest: Infónia Alapítvány.

ITU (International Telecommunication Union), 2001. Telecentres in Hungary. http://www.itu.int/ITU-D/univ_access/casestudies/hun_mct.html, last accessed: 10.2007.

ITU (with KADO), 2005. Measuring Digital Opportunity. *WSIS Thematic Meeting on Multi-Stakeholder Partnerships for Bridging the Digital Divide* (Seoul, R. of Korea, 23-24 June 2005) Doc.: BDB-WSIS/06, 23 Nov. 2005. http://www.itu.int/ osg/spu/statistics/DOI/linkeddocs/Measuring_Digital_Opp_Revised_23_Nov_2005(2).pdf

ITU, 2006. World Telecommunications Indicators - Technical Notes. Last accessed in 01.2007 at http://www.itu.int/ITU-D/icteye/Indicators/WTI_ Technotes.pdf.

Jeffs, T. & Smith, M. K., 1999. Informal Education. Conversation, Democracy and Learning. Ticknall: Education Now Books.

Johnston, R. J., Gregory, D., Pratt, G. & Watts, M. (eds.), 2000. The Dictionary of Human Geography. Blackwell Publishing Ltd.

Juma, C. & Yee-Cheong, L. (eds.), 2005. Innovation: Applying knowledge in development – Achieving the Millennium Development Goals. UNDP / United Nations Millennium Project, Task Force on Science, Technology and Innovation. London (UK) / Sterling, Va.: Earthscan.

Kane, P., 2001. Second sight. *The Guardian* 29th March 2001. Also online: http://technology. guardian.co.uk/online/story/0,3605,464604,00.html, last accessed: 10.2007.

Kasvio, A., 2000. Information society as a national project – Analysing the case of Finland (date of on-line publication: 22.05.2000), last accessed: http://www.uta.fi/~ttanka/Finland220500.html Last accessed: 12.2003.

Kasvio, A., 2001. Information society as a theoretical research programme - Methodological starting points for concrete analysis. University of Tampere, Information Society Research Centre, http://www.info.uta.fi/winsoc/engl/lect/THEORY.htm, last accessed: 05.09.2004.

Käyhkö, J., 2001. *Where lies the horizontal scientist? Fennia* 179:2, Helsinki. Pp. 181-184.

Keay, J., 1996. Welfare Reform Doomed Finance Minister: Hungarian Fell Off Tightrope. *International Herald Tribune*, 20 February 1996.

Kellerman, A., 1989. Time, space and society: Geographical-societal perspectives. Boston: Kluwer Academic Publishers.

Kiander, J. (ed.), 2000. 1990s economic crisis: the research programme of the Academy of Finland, conference 1999. Helsinki: Government Institute for Economic Research (VATT).

Kiander, J., 2004a. Growth and employment in Nordic welfare states in the 1990s: a tale of crisis and revival. *VATT Discussion Papers*, no. 336, Helsinki: Government Institute for Economic Research (VATT).

Kiander, J., 2004b. The evolution of the Finnish model in the 1990s: from depression to high-tech boom. *VATT Discussion Papers*, no. 344, Helsinki: Government Institute for Economic Research (VATT).

Kiss János, P. 2003. Az alföldi városok fejlődésének adottságai az 1990-es évek új feltételrendszerében. In: Tímár, J. & Velkei, G. (eds.): Várossiker alföldi nézőpontból. MTA RKK Alföldi Tudományos Int. & MTA Társadalomkutató Kp., Békéscsaba - Budapest, pp. 39-54.

Korkut, U., 2005. The Relationship Between Democratisation and Invigoration of Civil Society: The Case of Hungary and Poland. East European Quarterly, XXXIX, No. 2, June 2005, pp. 149-177.

Kornai, J. 1994. Transformational Recession: The Main Causes. *The Journal of Comparative Economics.*19/1, pp. 39-65.

Kornai, J., 2006. The great transformation of Central Eastern Europe Success and disappointment. *Economic of Transition* Vol. 14 (2).

Koskikallio, I. (project manager), 2003. The description of "The Learning Upper North Karelia" project. Text received during interviews in Nurmes 8th Oct. 2003.

226

Kosztolányi, G., 2000. Hungarian Identity, Globalisation and EU Accession. *Central Europe Review*, Vol. 2, No. 6 (14.02.2000). Online: http://www.ce-review.org/00/6/essay6.html, last accessed: 10.2007

Kovács, E. (ed.), 1992. "Telekunyhók" a vidék fejlesztéséért. Hogyan építsünk tájékoztató állomást? (Transl.: "Tele-huts" for the development of the countryside. How shall we build an information station? – S.N.) Szakirodami szemle – Országos Széchenyi Könyvtár Könyvtártudomanyi és Módszertani Központ, Budapest.

Kozma T., 2005. Moral education in Hungary fifteen years after transition. *Journal of Moral Education*. Vol. 34, no. 4, December 2005, pp. 491-504.

KSH (Central Statistical Office, Hungary) downloadable data tables; last accessed: 10.2007.

Kupiainen, H. & Lehikoinen, A., 1990. Tietotuvat Mikkein Läänissä. Esitutkimusrapportti. (Transl.: Information cottages in the Mikkeli region. Preliminary report on research. – S.N.) University of Helsinki, Regional Research and Educational Cenntre, Mikkeli.

Laki, M. & Szalai, J., 2006. The Puzzle of Success: Hungarian Entrepreneurs at the Turn of the Millennium. *Europe-Asia Studies*, Vol. 58, No. 3, May 2006, pp. 317-345.

Lambooy, J., 2005. Innovation and Knowledge: Theory and Regional Policy. *European Planning Studies*. Vol. 13, No. 8, pp. 1137-52.

Lash, S. & Urry, J., 1994. Economies of Signs and Space. London: Sage Publications.

Latour, B., 1987. Science in Action: How to Follow Scientists and Engineers Through Society. Milton Keynes: Open University Press.

Leadbeater, Ch., 1999. The Weightless Society – Living in the New Economy Bubble. New York: Texere.

Leadbeater, Ch., 2000. Living On Thin Air – The New Economy. London: Penguin Group.

Lin, N., 2001. Social Capital. A Theory of Social Structure and Action. In series: Structural Analysis in the Social Sciences, 19. Cambridge, UK: Cambridge University Press.

Lumio, M., 2006. Telecommunications in Europe. In: Statistics in Focus – Industry, trade and services, 2006/9. Luxembourg: European Communities / Eurostat.

Lyon, D., 1988. The information society: Issues and illusions. Cambridge: Polity Press.

Lyotard, J.-F., 1984. The Postmodern Condition: A Report on Knowledge. Minneapolis: University of Minnesota Press.

MacBride Commission, 1980. Many Voices, One World. Towards a New, More Just and More Efficient World Information and Communication Order. Paris: UNESCO (Reprinted in 2003 by Rowman & Littlefiled).

Machlup, F., 1962. Knowledge Production and Distribution in the United States. Princeton, NJ: Princeton University Press.

Machlup, F., 1980. Knowledge: Its Creation, Distribution and Economic Significance. Vol. 1: Knowledge and Knowledge Production Princeton, NJ: Princeton University Press.

MacKenzie, D. & Wajcman, J. (eds.), 1985. The Social Shaping of Technology: How the refrigerator got its hum. Milton Keynes and Philadelphia: Open University Press.

Maclay, K., 2003. Amount of new information doubled in the last three years, UC Berkley study finds. UC Berkley News, Press Release 28.10.2003 http://sanjose.bizjournals.com/sanjose/stories/2003/10/27/daily27.html, last retrieved: 05.2007.

Magyar, B., 2001. Információs társadalom: az eddigi lépések. In: Dombi, G. & Lafferton, E. (eds.): *Az Információós Társadalom felé*. Budapest: Replika Kör, pp. 223-230.

Magyar, B. & Z. Karvalics, L., 2000. "Information Society" in Eastern Europe? Chances, possibilities, tasks and programs. *East European Quarterly*, 34:4, Winter 2000, pp. 509-522.

Magyar Tanya- és Falugondnoki Szövetség (Hungarian village-caretaker association).Website of the organisation: http://www.falugondnokok.hu/, last accessed: 10.2007.

Mäkinen, M. 1995. Nokia Saga: A Story of the Company and the People who Transformed It. Gummerus: Jäyvskylä.

Markkula, M., 2003. The Finnish Road to Success. *E-government articles, eFinland*. http://e.finland.fi/ netcomm/news/showarticle.asp?intNWSAID=13642, last retrieved: 10.2007.

Marková, I. (ed.), 2004. Trust and Democratic Transition in Post-Communist Europe. Oxford: Oxford University Press, The British Academy.

Masuda, Y., 1980. The Information Society as Post-Industrial Society. Tokyo: Institute for Information Society and New York: The World Future Society.

McQuaid, R. W., Lindsay, C. & McCracken, Martin, 2003. Alternative job search strategies in remote rural labour markets: the role of ICT.. Gateway 4 Rural Development and the new rural economy. Paper for *Regional Studies Association Conference* on 'Reinventing Regions in the Global Economy' Pisa, Italy, 12-15 April 2003. http://www.regional-studies-assoc.ac.uk/ events/pisa03/gateway4.pdf.

Medinfo - www.medinfo.hu, website of Medinfo, Hungary.

MEH – eK (Prime Minister's Office, eGovernment Centre, Hungary), 2003. e-Kormányzat Stratégia és Programterv. (e-Government Strategy and Programme Plan) http://misc.meh.hu/binary/6392_letoltheto_ strategia_rovat_ekormaynzat_strategia.pdf

Miettinen, R., 2002. National Innovation System - Scientific Concept or Political Rhetoric. Helsinki: Edita.

Minges, M. / ITU, 2000. Counting the Net: Internet Access Indicators. http://www.isoc.org/inet2000/ cdproceedings/8e/8e_1.htm, last accessed: 10.2007.

Ministry of Industry, Employment and Communications, Sweden: An Information Society for All. The Government Bill 1999/2000:86. http://www.sweden.gov.se/sb/d/2156/a/20015;jsessionid=ara4-Uzvsx3c, last accessed: 10.2007.

Ministry of Informatics and Communications (IHM), Hungary, 2003. The Hungarian Information Society on the Eve of the Accession to the European Union: snapshot on strategic objectives.

http://www.wiphungary.hu/resources/pdf/info_soc_eng.pdf (archived by WIP: World Internet Project Hungary; not available any more on the Ministry's website).

Ministry of Informatics and Communication (IHM), 2003. Hungarian Information Society Strategy (HISS / MITS) http://www.itktb.hu/engine.aspx?page= MITSkezdo_hun, last accessed: 10.2007.

Ministry of Informatics and Communication (IHM), 2006. Az információs társadalom 2002-2006. évi magyarországi fejlődéséről a Magyar Információs Társadalom Stratégia Tükrében. (Report on the development of I.S. in Hungary, 2002-2006). Budapest, 7 June 2006. http://www.epractice.eu/document/2925, last accessed: 10.2007.

Ministry of the Interior, Finland, website on EU Regional Development: http://www.poliisi.fi/intermin/home.nsf/pages/14B5AA3C04DFDE07C2256FB300447C60?opendocument, last accessed: 10.2007.

Molnár, Sz., 2000. A "megtartó" teleház – Variációk közösségre és technológiára. (Transl.: The "bonding" telecottage – variations on community and technology - S.N.). http://www.ittk.hu/infinit/2000/0706/, last accessed: 05.2007.

Molnár, Sz., 2001. Információs Magyarország 1.0. *Infinit* (weekly online journal of ITTK, Budapest), 24th May, 2001. http://www.ittk.hu/infinit/2001/0524/ index.html, last accessed: 05.2007.

Molnár, Sz., 2002. Az utolsó szó jogán. *Infinit* (weekly online journal of ITTK, Budapest), 30th May, 2002. http://www.ittk.hu/infinit/2002/0530/index. html, last accessed: 05.2007.

MONEP, 2005. (Modern Networked Periphery) Regional Programme of Innovative Actions in Eastern Finland, 2002-2004 within ERDF Innovative Actions 2000-2006. Programme website, downloadable Final Report., Experiences and Brochure at: http://www.innovatiivi settoimet.fi/en/isit/index.htm, last accessed: 02.2007.

Montagnini, L., 2003. Innovation and Responsibility in the context of the Information Society. The Giannino Bassetti Foundation Web Site: http://www.fondazionebassetti.org/06/docs/montagnini-bibliografia.htm, last accessed: 01.2007.

Montealegre, R., 1997. *The interplay of information technology and the social milieu* In: Information Technology and People, 10 (2) 106-131 MCB University press ISSN 0959-3845

Morgan, M. R. Information competencies: the case study of AUS Economic students in Mexico. http://www.ifla.org/IV/ifla66/papers/120-171e.htm, last retrieved: 01.2007.

Munnich, L. W. Jr., Schrock, G. & Cook, K., 2002. Rural Knowledge Clusters: The Challenge of Rural Economic Prosperity. (Report for the U.S. Economic Development Administration.) Hubert H. Humphrey Institute of Public Affairs, University of Minnesota / State and Local Policy Program. http://www.eda.gov/ImageCache/EDAPublic/documents/pdfdocs/u_2eminn_2elit_2erev3_2epdf/v1/u.minn.lit.rev3.pdf

Murray, B., 2001. The Hungarian Telecottage Movement. Chapter 5 in: Latchem, C. & Walker, D. (eds.): Perspectives on Distance Education. Telecentres: Case studies and key issues. The Commonwealth of Learning, Vancouver.

Nagy, G. & Kanalas, I, 2003. Régiók az Információs Társadalomban. (Regions in the Information Society). Centre for Regional Studies of the Hungarian Academy of Sciences, Kecskemét.

Naisbitt, J., 1984. Megatrends. Megatrends: Ten New Directions Transforming Our Lives. London : Futura.

Negroponte, N. 1998. Beyond Digital. In: Wired 6.12, December 1998. http://www.media.mit.edu/people/ nicholas/Wired/WIRED6-12.html, last retrieved: 10.2007

Negroponte, N., 1996. Being Digital. Vintage.

Nemes-Nagy, J., 1995. A piacgazdasági átmenet terei. (The spatial aspects of transition). *Falu-Város-Régió*, 5-7-8, pp. 6-11.

Nemes-Nagy, J. 1998a. Vesztesek – nyertesek – stagnálók. *Társadalmi Szemle*, 8-9. pp. 5-18.

Nemes-Nagy, J., 1998b. *A tér a társadalomkutatásban – bevezetés a regionális tudományba* (Space in research on society -- an introduction to regional science). Szó-Kép Kft. Budapest.

Németh, E., 1997. *Teleházak Magyarországon -- Kultúrák találkozása* (Telecottages in Hungary – Meeting of cultures). In: Ön-Kor-Kép 7/12.

Németh, S., 2002. Információs társadalom: egy geográfus finnországi tapasztalatai (Information Society: Experiences of a Geographer in Finland). Paper presented at the Seventh National Conference for Geographers on 25th Oct. 2002, Eötvös Loránd University, Budapest, Hungary (published on CD).

Németh, S., 2005. Information society and regional development: The cases of Finland and Hungary. Licentiate Thesis, Papers no. 2 and 3/B. Faculty of Social Sciences, University of Joensuu. Copies available in the libraries of the Geography Dept. and the University.

Németh, S., 2006. Social Capital and ICTs in Local Development: The Case of the Hungarian Telecottage Movement. Forthcoming in: Marginality in the 21st Century: Theory, Methodology and Contemporary Challenges, eds. Gareth Jones, Walter Leimgruber and Etienne Nel. Aldershot: Ashgate.

NIIF, National Information Infrastructure Development Institute (Nemzeti Információs Infrastruktúra Fejlesztési Intézet). www.niif.hu, last accessed: 10.2007.

NOKIA company website in English: www.nokia.com

Norden / Nordic Council of Ministers & Statistics Denm§ark / Finland / Iceland / Norway / Sweden, 2002. Nordic Information Society Statistics 2002. Helsinki: University Press. http://www.norden.org/pub/uddannelse/forskning_ hojereudd/sk/Julkaisu_final.pdf

Norden / Nordic Council of Ministers & Statistics Denmark / Finland / Iceland / Norway / Sweden, 2005. Nordic Information Society Statistics 2005. In: *TemaNord 2005:562,* Copenhagen. Also online: http://www.stat.fi/tup/julkaisut/isbn_92-893-1200-9_en.pdf.

North Karelia - Regional Council (Pohjois Karjalan Maakuntaliitto), 2006. Statistics of North Karelia, 2005. http://www.pohjois-karjala.fi/Resource.phx/ maakunta/maakuntaeng.htx, last accessed: 10.2007.

North Karelian municipalities websites (www.municipalityname.fi)

Nurminen, T., 2004. Linux has arrived at the University. University of Helsinki website news archives, http://www.helsinki.fi/news/archive/10-2004/6-17-05-25, last accessed: 10.2007.

Ó Siochrú, S., 2004. Will the Real WSIS Please Stand-up? In: International Communication Gazette, Vol. 66, no. 3-4, pp. 203-224. SAGE Publications.

O'Brien, R., 1991. Global Financial Integration: The End of Geography. London: Pinter.

OECD, 1991. Hungary 1991, OECD Economic Surveys. Paris: OECD.

OECD, 2001. Understanding the Digital Divide. Paris: OECD. Also on-line: http://www.oecd.org/dataoecd/38/57/1888451.pdf

OECD, 2004. Information Technology Outlook 2004. Paris: Organisation for Economic Cooperation and Development.

Oinas, P. 2005, Finland: A Success Story? *European Planning Studies*, Vol. 13, No. 8, Dec. 2005, pp.1227-1244.

Oksa, J., 1992. Regional and Local Responses to Restructuring in Peripheral Rural Areas in Finland. *Urban Studies*, Vol. 29, No. 6, pp-991-1002.

Oksa, J., 1995. Are Leaping Frogs Freezing? Rural Peripheries in Competition. In: Competitive European Peripheries (eds. Eskelinen, H. & Snickars, F.) Heidelberg: Springer-Verlag.

Oksa, J., 2001. How to be rural in information age; Case of Rural Community Network in Finnish Periphery. XIX Congress of the European Society for Rural Sociology, 3-7 September 2001, Dijon, France.

Oksa, J., 2004. Difficult job of transferring a success-story. Paper presented at: IRSA XI *World Congress of Rural Sociology* Trondheim, Norway, 25-30.07.2004.; and at 4S and *EASST Conference*, Paris, France, 25-28.08.2004.

Oksa, J. & Turunen, J., 2000a. Local Community Net – Evaluation Study of the Learning Upper Karelia Project - English Summary and Conclusions. http://www.joensuu.fi/ktl/projsoc/infosoc/upperka2.htm, last accessed:.09.2003.

Oksa, J. & Turunen, J., 2000b. Local Community Net as a New Model of regional Policy: Case of the Learning Upper Karelia Project. Paper for *MOST CCPP workshop*: whether, how and why regional policies are working in concert with coping strategies locally? Joensuu, Finland 15-19.2000.

Oppiva Pohjois Karjala kansalaisverkko (community intranet) http://www.oyk.fi/

OPPK - Oppiva kanslaisverkko (North Karelia), project website, Internet portal for entering the community network. http://www.oyk.fi/, last accessed: 10.2007.

Oxford English Dictionary. http://dictionary.oed. com/, last accessed: 10.2007.

Padovani, C. & Nordenstreng, K., 2005. From NWICO to WSIS: another world information and communication order? In: Global Media and Communication, Vol. 1 (3), pp. 264-272. London, Thousand Oaks, New Delhi: SAGE.

Paija, L., 2001. What is Behind the Finnish 'ICT Miracle'? *Finnish Economy and Society*. Journal, no. 3 / 2001. Helsinki: ETLA – The Research Institute of the Finnish Economy.

Paija, L. & Rouvinen, P., 2004. The evolution of the Finnish ICT cluster. In: G. Schienstock (ed.) Embracing the Knowledge Economy. The Dynamic Transformation of the Finnish Innovation System, Cheltenham: Edward Elgar, pp. 47–64

Parliament of Finland, website: on The Committee for the Future http://www. eduskunta.fi/efakta/vk/tuv/ tuvesite.htm, last accessed: 10.2007.

Pascual, P. J., 2003. e-Government. E-ASEAN Task Force, UNDP-APDIP. An "e-primer" available on-line: http://www.apdip.net/publications/iespprimers/ eprimer-egov.pdf.

Patomäki, H. (2003). An Optical Illusion: The Finnish Model for the Information Age. *Theory, Culture & Society*, 2003 (SAGE); Vol. 20(3): 139-145.

Pearson, I. (ed.), 1998. The Macmillan Atlas of the Future. MacMillan Publishing Company.

Pearson, I., 2005. The Pearson's Guide to the Future. a collection of papers; http://www.btinternet.com/ ~ian.pearson/docindex.htm, last retrieved: 10.2007.

Pelkonen, A. 2005. State Restructuring, Urban Competitiveness Policies and Technopole Building in Finland: A Critical View on the Glocal State Thesis. European Planning Studies, Vol. 13, No. 5, July 2005, pp. 685-705.

Perczel, Gy., 2003 (ed.) Magyarország társadalmi-gazdasági földrajza, (Social-economic geography of Hungary). ELTE Eötvös Kiadó, Budapest.

Rédei, M. 2007a. Az innováció európai térbeli képe, (The European spatial pattern of innovation). In: Modern Geográfia. 4.
http://www.moderngeografia.hu/tanulmanyok/regionalis_tanulmanyok/redei_maria_2007_4_a.pdf

Rédei, M. 2007b. The Hungarian migration regime: from talent loss to talent attraction, Geographical Phorum. Vol. 5/ 6. Craiova. pp.134-145.

Pintér, R., 2000a. A kezdet végén. *Infinit* (weekly online journal of ITTK, Budapest), *Infinit Műhelymunka*, 11th May, 2000. http://www.ittk.hu/ infinit/2000/0511/muhely2.html, last accessed: 05.2007.

Pintér, R., 2000b. Magyarország információs társadalmi fejlettsége – előtanulmány. *Infinit* (weekly online journal of ITTK, Budapest), *Infinit Műhelymunka*, 20th April, 2000. http://www.ittk. hu/infinit/2000/0420, last accessed: 05.2007.

Pintér, R., 2004. A magyar információs társadalom fejlődése és fejlettsége a fejlesztők szempontjából. Szociológiai doktori értekezés. (PhD dissertation in Sociology). Budapest, ELTE – Társadalomtudományi Kar.

Polanyi, M., 1958/1998. Personal Knowledge. Towards a Post Critical Philosophy. London: Routledge

Porat, M. U., 1977. The information economy: Definition and measurement. Washington, DC: U.S. Department of Commerce, Office of Telecommunications.

Porter, M., 1990. The Competitive Advantage of Nations. New York: The Free Press.

Poster, M., 1995. CyberDemocracy: Internet and the Public Sphere. University of California, Irvine. http://www.humanities.uci.edu/mposter/writings/democ.html, last retrieved: 10.2007.

Putnam, R. D., 1993. Making democracy work. Princeton, NJ: Princeton University Press.

Putnam, R. D., Leonardi, R. & Nanetti, R. Y., 1993. Making democracy work: civic traditions in modern Italy. Princeton (N.J.): Princeton University Press.

Pyati, A. K., 2005. WSIS: Whose vision of an information society? In: *First Monday*, Vol. 10, no. 5, http://firstmonday.org/issues/issue10_5/pyati/index.html (peer-reviewed journal on the Internet) Last accessed: 10.2007.

Rantala, O., 2001. Regional Economic Developments in Finland in the 1990s and the Outlook to 2005. *Finnish Economy and Society*. Journal, no. 2 / 2001. Helsinki: ETLA – The Research Institute of the Finnish Economy.

Rédei, M. 2007a. Az innováció európai térbeli képe, (The European spatial pattern of innovation). In: Modern Geográfia. 4.
http://www.moderngeografia.hu/tanulmanyok/regionalis_tanulmanyok/redei_maria_2007_4_a.pdf

Rédei, M. 2007b. The Hungarian migration regime: from talent loss to talent attraction, Geographical Phorum. Vol. 5/ 6. Craiova. pp.134-145.

Regional Council of North Karelia & NOKIS (North Karelia Towards Information Society), 1999. By Joint Work Party to the Information Society – Information Society Strategy and Action of North Karelia 1999-2006. Joensuu.

Regional Council of North Karelia (RCNK), 1999. NOKIS programme (N.K. Towards Information Society). By Joint Work Party to the Information Society -- Information Society Strategy and Action of North Karelia 1999-2006. Joensuu.

Regional Council of North Karelia (RCNK), 2006. The European Strategy of North Karelia – English Summary. Joensuu.

Reich, R., 1991. The Work of Nations: Preparing Ourselves for 21st Century Capitalism. New York: Knopf.

Richta, R., 1963. Člověk a technika v revoluci našich dnů / Man and Technology in the Revolution of Our Day, Vydal závod Mír v Praze, 1963.

Robertson, R., 1992. Globalisation: social theory and global culture. London: Sage.

Rogán, A., 2001. A digitalis Magyarország. In: Dombi, G. & Lafferton, E. (eds.): *Az Információós Társadalom felé*. Budapest: Replika Kör, 231-240.

Rogers, E. M., 1995 (1962). Diffusion of innovations. New York: Free Press.

Ryder, M., 2004. Articles on the Theory of Technology. Ryder's homepage at http://carbon.cudenver.edu/~mryder/;

on ANT: http://carbon.cudenver.edu/~mryder/itc_ data/ant_dff.html University of Colorado at Denver, School of Education Last retrieved: 10.2007.

Schienstock, G. & Hämäläinen, T., 2001. Transformation of the Finnish innovation system. A network approach. *Sitra Report Series 7.* Helsinki.

Science and Technology Policy Council of Finland (Valtion Tiede- ja Teknologianeuvosto), at Min. of Education website. http://www.minedu.fi/OPM/Tiede/ tiede-_ja_teknologianeuvosto/?lang=en, last retrieved: 10.2007.

Scott, A. J. & Storper, M., 2003. Regions, globalisation, development. In: Regional Studies, vol. 37: 6&7, pp. 579-593. Also on-line: www.sppsr.ucla.edu/up/webfiles/storperpaper5.pdf, last accessed: 05.07.2006.

SGP Regional Development Agency, 2003. South Great Plain Region: The south-eastern gate of the enlarging European Union. SGP Regional Dev. Council.

SIBIS: project portal at http://www.sibis-eu.org/ Last accessed: 10.2007.

Sirkkunen, Esa, 2004. Towards civic-oriented information networks. In: Sirkkunen, Esa – Kotileinen, Sirkku (eds., 2004) *Towards Active Citizenship on the Net -- Possibilities of citizen oriented communication: case studies from Finland.* Tampere: Journalism Research and Development Centre, University of Tampere, Dept. of Journalism and Mass Communication; pp. 9-25.

Sitra - Finnish National Fund for Research and Development (Suomen Itsenäisyyden Juhlarahasto), organistaion website. http://www.sitra.fi; last accessed: 10.2007.

Sitra, 1997. Revising of the national information society strategy in Finland will focus on people and everyday life. http://194.100.30.11/tietoyhteiskunta/ english/st5/eng001.htm, last accessed: 01.2007.

Sitra, 1998. Quality of life, Knowledge and Competitiveness – Premises and objectives for strategic development of the Finnish Information Society. Helsinki.

Sitra, 2002. OSKU – a way for citizens to access the information society. In: *Annual Report 2002* (pp. 6-7).

Skidén, U., 2003. Finland tops Global Network Readiness Report. *Government technology,* May 2003. eRepublic Inc. Also online: http://www.centerdigitalgov.com/international/story.php?docid=51819, last retrieved: 10.2007.

Slevin, J., 2000. The Internet and society. Cambridge: Polity Press

Sölvell, Ö. & Porter, M. E., 2002. Finland and Nokia. *Harvard Business Online.* 25 Jan. 2002.

SSH Communications Security Corp., org. website: http://www.ssh.com, last accessed: 05.2007.

Statistics Finland, 2000. Science and Technology in Finland 2000. http://www.stat.fi/tk/yr/st2000.html, last accessed: 08.2002.

Statistics Finland, 2001. On the Road to the Finnish Information Society III – Summary http://www.tilastokeskus.fi/tk/yr/tietoyhteiskunta/ttyk_en.html, last accessed: 05.2007.

Stein, J., 2001. Reflections on time, time-space compression and technology in the nineteenth century. In: May, Jon and Thrift, Nigel: Timespace: Geographies of temporality; pp. 106-119. London and New York: Routledge.

Storper, M., 1997. The Regional World – Territorial Development in a Global Economy. The Guilford Press New York, London.

Storper, M. & Venables, A. J., 2004. Buzz: face-to-face contact and the urban economy. In: *Journal of Economic Geography*, Vol. 4, No. 4, Oxford University Press.

Sulinet - www.sulinet.hu, website of Sulinet, Hungary, last accessed: 10.2007.

Sveiby, K.-E., 1994 (1998). What is Information?
http://www.sveiby.com/Portals/0/articles/Information.html, last retrieved: 05.2007

Sveiby, K.-E., 1997. Tacit knowledge. http://www.sveiby.com/Portals/0/articles/Polanyi.html last retrieved: 10.2007.

Szakadát, I., 2001. Tartalom mindenek felett, infrastruktúra mindenek alatt. In: Dombi, G. & Lafferton, E. (eds.): *Az Információós Társadalom felé.* Budapest: Replika Kör, pp. 15-41.

Szekeres, Zs., 1998. Pillanatkép a Sulinetről. *Telecomputer – Magyar Nemzet*, 3/3, 23rd Feb. 1998.

Tamás, P., 2001. Az elkésettek stratégiái, avagy a posztszocialista információs társadalom jövőképeiről. In: Dombi, G. & Lafferton, E. (eds.): *Az Információós Társadalom felé.* Budapest: Replika Kör, pp. 43-73.

TÁRKI Rt. & IHM, 2001. Lakossági részvétel az információs társadalomban: jelentés az alapozó lakossági felvételről. (Transl.: Public survey on participation in the information society – Report on basic take-up – S.N.) http://www.ihm.gov.hu/ data/26534/No05-TARKI.doc, last accessed: 06.2006.

Technopolis Ltd., IRISI, Eris@ & Lena Tsipouri, 2002. Final Report for the Thematic Evaluation of the Information Society. Prepared for the European Commission DG Regional Development. http://ec.europa.eu/regional_policy/sources/docgener/evaluation/doc/information_society.pdf

TEKES – National Technology Agency of Finland (Teknologian kehittämiskeskus), org. website: http://www.tekes.fi/; on FinnWell: http://www.tekes.fi/ohjelmat/finnwell/, last accessed: 10.2007.

Teleház Magazin, 2004. *The land of virtual telecottages.* Anita Hegedűs interviewing the author in Jan. 2004, http://telehazmagazin.hu/rovat.php?rid=3, last accessed: 10.2007.

TEKES and Statistics Finland: R&D investments in Finland http://ircfinland.fi/eng/innovation/policy/ investmentpros.htm, last accessed: 05.2007.

TEP -- Technológiai Előretekintési Program, Informatika, Távközlés Média – Munkacsoport jelentés, Vice Secretary of State, Ministry of Education, Budapest, 2000

Thompson, G. F., 2003. Between Hierarchies and Markets: The Logic and Limits of Network Forms of Organization (Chapter 3: Social Network Analysis) Oxford: Oxford University Press, March.

Thrift, N., 1996. Spatial formations. London: Sage.

Thrift, N., 2002. *The future of geography.* In: Geoforum 33. pp. 291-298.

TIEKE - Finnish Information Society Development Centre (Tietoyhteiskunnan kehittämiskeskus ry.), http://www.tieke.fi, last accessed: 05.2007.

Toffler, A., 1980. The Third Way New York: Bantam Books.

235

Toffler, A., 1972. Future Shock. New York: Bantam Books.

Tukiainen, J., 2003. ICT Cluster Study – Helsinki Region. Helsinki City Urban Facts Offiice Web Publications, 2003/2. http://www.hel2.fi/Tietokeskus/ julkaisut/pdf/03_12_30_tukiainen_vj2.pdf

Tuomi, I., 2004. Broadband Status in Finland – Draft, 04.03.2004. http://www.meaningprocessing.com/personalPages/tuomi/articles/FinlandBB.pdf

Tuorila, H., 2004. People Over Fifty in Finland as Users of Internet. *eFinland, Article of the Month*, 01.10.2004. http://www.e.finland.fi/netcomm/news/ showarticle.asp?intNWSAID=28452, last accessed: 10.2007.

Tykkyläinen, M., 2006. Dynamics of job creation, restructuring and industrialisation in rural Finland. *Fennia* 184:2, pp. 151-167, Helsinki.

UNCTAD, 2005. ICT Benchmarking Tool - user manual. http://www.e-stdev.org/benchmarking/ help.htm#stats, last accessed: 10.2007.

United Nations Development Programme (UNDP). http://www.undp.org/, last accessed: 10.2007.

United Nations Statistic Division. United Nations Common Database http://unstats.un.org/unsd/cdb/cdb_help/cdb_quick_start.asp, last accessed: 10.2007.

United Nations, 2001. Today's technological transformations – creating the network age. Ch.2 in: *Human Development Report 2001*. United Nations Development Programme, 2002.

Urry, J., 2002. The Tourist Gaze. London: Sage Publications.

Välijärvi, J., Linnakylä, P., Kupari, P., Reinikainen, P. & Arffman, I. (Institute for Educational Research, Univ. of Jyväskylä), 2002. The Finnish success in PISA - and some reasons behind it: PISA 2000. Jyväskylä: Kirjapaino Oma Oy.

Varga, R., 2001. *Támogatásra várnak a teleházak* (Telecottages are waiting for support). *Népszabadság* 01.12.2001, Budapest. P. 5

Viherä, M.-L., 1999. Ihminen tietoyhteiskunnassa. Kansalaisten viestintävalmiudet ansalaisyhteiskunnan mahdollistajana. *Summary: People and Information Society. The Citizens' Communication Skills and the Opening of New Prospects for the Civil Society*. Dissertation. Publications of the Turku School of Economics and Business Administration. Series A-1:1999

Virilio, P., 1986 (1977). Speed and Politics: An Essay on Dromology. New York: Semiotext(e)

Virilio, P., 2005. Negative Horizon: An Essay in Dromoscopy. London: Continuum New York

Virta, K. & TEKES, 2004. FinnWell Builds a Bridge Between Healthcare Companies and Organizations. http://www.irc-finland.fi/eng/news/uutis_tiedot.asp?id =3565&paluu=, last accessed: 10.2007.

Virtual Finland: http://virtual.finland.fi/, last accessed: 10.2007.

Wadsworth, Y., 1998. What is Participatory Action Research. Resource paper no. 2, Action Research International ('an on-line international refereed journal with an open and non-adversarial refereeing system'). http://www.scu.edu.au/schools/gcm/ar/ari/p-ywads worth98.html, last accessed: 05.2007.

Webster Merriam On-line English Dictionary (for definitions of access, information, etc.)

Webster, F., 2002. Theories of the information society. Second edition. London and New York: Routledge.

WEF - World Economic Forum, 2002-2004. Global Competitiveness Reports 2001-2002, 2003-2004, and 2004-2005. Center for International Development (CID) at Harvard University.

Wellman, B., Haase A.Q., Witte, J. & Hampton, K., 2001. Does the Internet Increase, Decrease, or Supplement Social Capital? Social networks , Participation, and Community Commitment. In: *The Internet in Everyday Life*, special issue of the *American Behavioral Scientist*, Vol. 45. Nov. 2001.

Wellman, B., Quan-Haase, A., Boase, J. & Chen, W., 2002. Examining the Internet in Everyday Life. (Wellman's keynote address, *Euricom Conference on e-Democracy*, Nijmegen, NL, 10.2002). Centre for Urban and Community Studies, University of Toronto. http://www.chass.utoronto.ca/~wellman/publications/euricom/Examinig-Euricom.htm, last accessed: 10.2007.

Wellman, B., Quan-Haase, A., Witte, J., & Hampton, K.N., 2001. Does the Internet increase, decrease, or supplement social capital? Social networks, participation, and community commitment. American Behavioural Scientist, 45(3), 437-456.

Wetmore, D. E. (as a speaker at 'Productivity Institute, Time Management Seminars' CT USA) on 'Speed reading' http://www.balancetime.com/ speed_reading.php, last retrieved: 10.2007.

Wiberg, M. (ed.), 2005. The Interaction Society: Practice, Theories, and Supportive Technologies. Information Science Publishing, IDEA-Group Inc.

Wikipedia – The Free Encyclopaedia. http://en. wikipedia.org/ used for the entries: technology, diffusion of innovation.

Williams, R. & Edge, D., 1996. The social shaping of technology. In *Research Policy* Vol. 25, pp. 856-899.

Wilson, M. I. & Corey, K. E. (eds.), 2000. Information tectonics: space, place and technology in an electronic age. Chichester: Wiley.

Word IQ. On-line: http://wordiq.com (for the definition of 'information'), last accessed: 10.2007.

World Bank. Development Data and Statistics, http://www.worldbank.org/data/, last accessed: 10.2007

World Bank, 2002. Social Capital and Information Technology / Potential Development Benefits of Information Technology and Social Capital. http://www1.worldbank.org/prem/poverty/scapital/topic/info1.htm, last accessed: 10.2007

World Economic Forum (WEF). http://www. weforum.org/ Accessed: 10.2007.

World Summit of the Information Society, Geneva (WSIS/D.) (2003). Declaration of Principles – *Building the Information Society: a global challenge in the new Millennium*. 12 December 2003. ITU, UN. http://www.itu.int/wsis/index.html, last accessed: 10.2007.

World Summit of the Information Society, Geneva (WSIS/P.A.; 2003). Plan of Action. 12 December 2003. ITU, United Nations. http://www.itu.int/wsis /index.html, last accessed: 10.2007.

World Summit of the Information Society, Tunis (WSIS/T.; 2005). Tunis Commitment and Agenda for the Information Society. 18 November 2005. ITU, United Nations. http://www.itu.int/wsis/index.html, http://www.itu.int/wsis/tunis/newsroom/index.html. Last accessed: 10.2007.

Wurman, Richard Saul (1989) Information Anxiety. New York: Doubleday.

Wyatt, S., Henwood, F. & Miller, N. & Senker, P. (eds.), 2000. Technology and in/equality – questioning the information society. Routledge, London.Wyatt et al.

WWP-info, on the definition of technology. http://www.wwp-info.com/, last accessed: 10.2007.

Z. Karvalics, L. 1998. Information society development in Hungary. ITTK publication: http://www.ittk.hu/english/docs/is_development_hungary_zkl.pdf, last accessed: 05.2007.

Z. Karvalics, L. 2002. Az információs társadalom keresése. Budapest: Infonia-Aula.